An Idea, Its Genesis, and

MICROCHIP

the Revolution It Created

JEFFREY ZYGMONT

PERSEUS
PUBLISHING

A Member of the Perseus Books Group

Library of Congress Control Number: 2002112395

ISBN 0–7382–0561–3

Perseus Publishing is a member of the Perseus Books Group.

Find us on the World Wide Web at http://www.perseuspublishing.com

Perseus Publishing books are available at special discounts for bulk purchases in the U.S. by corporations, institutions, and other organizations. For more information, please contact the Special Markets Department at the Perseus Books Group, 11 Cambridge Center, Cambridge, MA 02142, or call (800) 255–1514 or (617) 252–5298, or e-mail j.mccrary@perseusbooks.com.

Text design by Jeff Williams
Set in 11-point New Aster by the Perseus Books Group

First printing, January 2003

1 2 3 4 5 6 7 8 9 10—06 05 04 03

Bob Noyce said that "optimism is an essential ingredient for innovation. How else can the individual welcome change over security, adventure over staying in safe places?"

To Bob Noyce,
and every other optimist.

CONTENTS

ACKNOWLEDGMENTS

SOON AFTER I STARTED RESEARCHING this book, I recognized that the story could not be accurately told unless it showed how free enterprise encouraged so much exuberant invention. Scouring for an economist to help me understand how willful human actions could bring us microchips, I found David Henderson, a research fellow at the Hoover Institution. David also gave me personal encouragement, which is just as essential as any kind of professional help.

Book work is discovery. It sets its own course, introducing you to people who complete the story you only dimly perceive at the outset.

Most of the contributors I encountered during this journey are represented in the narrative. A few are not, but I value the insight and information they provided no less. Turner Hasty, a colleague and friend to both Jack Kilby and Robert Noyce, helped me understand the character of those two men, while he conveyed some of the spirit of semiconductor discovery. Similarly, Floyd Kvamme, who worked for Noyce at Fairchild, and Charles Phipps, an early associate of Kilby's at Texas Instruments, shared their recollections of the technology's formative era.

Ronald Curry, Intel's director of marketing, and Dennis Monticelli, a Fellow at National Semiconductor, patiently reviewed milestones in the technological progression of microchips. James Beniger, a faculty member at the University of Southern California, and Tim Lenoir, of Stanford University, spoke with me more generally about the role that technology plays shaping culture.

Pocket calculators—revolutionary little machines not too long ago—turned out to be more essential to the story than I had foreseen. For help untangling their early history, I first found Nigel Tout, a British calculator collector and enthusiast. He sent me to Guy Ball, who is an amateur historian in the best sense of the term: his commitment to the topic comes from inveterate personal interest.

The Special Collections and University Archives of Stanford University provided a trove of material. But more than the historic documents and invaluable recordings, Archivist Margaret Kimball and staff offered me a somewhat sanctified study place that was simultaneously congenial.

Early in the project, I planned to include additional chapters to illustrate the ways that microchips created the new abilities that have changed our behavior and perceptions. To that end, I spent an afternoon at Fonar Corporation on Long Island, talking to its founder, Dr. Raymond Damadian, about his invention of magnetic resonance imaging. At NASA's Goddard Space Flight Center, near Baltimore, I met with three of the scientists responsible for the Hubble Space Telescope: Astrophysicist Edward Cheng, Hubble's program manager, Ed Cheung, who designs new hardware for the craft, and Brian Falfel, who directs instrument development. In Dallas, Charles Hanson and Stuart Klapper briefed me on Raytheon's infrared video camera, which makes spectral vision available at affordable prices. Hanson is the program's technical director. Klapper manages the effort that places night vision on cars.

Although I did not use the explicit information those people provided, their experiences and their insight deepened my appreciation for the accomplishment that microchips represent.

This book received the committed professional support that a literary endeavor demands. When she was a senior editor at

Perseus Publishing, Jacqueline Murphy conceived the idea of a kind of biographical narrative that illustrates the astounding technological progress we've witnessed during the last four decades. Jacqueline closed the deal with my agent, Kristen Wainwright, a capable representative who directs The Boston Literary Group. Then Amanda Cook took over as the Perseus senior editor who directed the project through its completion.

But Amanda's assistant, Lolly Axley, ambitiously stepped in for a spell, serving as acting editor when Amanda took maternity leave for the birth of her son, Aidan. Lolly recognized that the story's dense technical content and its well populated plot required straight-ahead narration with a lot of guideposts to link its episodes. Graciously, but relentlessly, she pushed me to fashion an effective tale from a tangle of fascinating details.

I'm only half joking when I tell friends that my wife is my day job. In fact, I am very grateful for Donna's unfailing support when I forego income in order to hunker down with a manuscript that's giving me fits. I hope that my efforts prove worth the sacrifice. Writing is no different than any other occupation: you work first for your family's approval. Thus my greatest literary asset is my striving to satisfy the scrutiny of Donna and our children, Erik and Greta, and eventually, when she grows old enough to read, of granddaughter Madeleine too.

PROLOGUE

Changing Minds

JOHN AND SUE LIVE ON GRAND ISLAND just a few miles upriver from where Niagara Falls carves a gorge with ancient indifference to human clamor. Maybe the region's geology imparts a kind of epochal insight. The couple fashions their home as a placid safe haven. They don't reject new technology. But they select it judiciously.

John and Sue like baseball, and therefore they let cable television enter their safe haven. They don't take any of the so-called premium channels that would bring them too many tiresome movies, vulgar comics, and mawkish singers-cum-circus acts. Instead they set up their cable subscription for maximum baseball. When the Yankees play, Sue wants to watch the game clear through, from opening pitch to final out, without any between-inning cuts to catch up on the contests shown on other channels. So John retreats to a separate TV, where he is free to surf around all of Major League Baseball.

Now, in an era that is mislabeled the Computer Age, cable television may not appear to occupy the technical vanguard. But consider that the ball games that entertain Sue and John on so many summer evenings first arrive at the couple's cable company as dense streams of digitally encoded signals beamed earthward by a satellite. Forget the fact that so much of the inner workings of the satellite itself consist of unimaginably compressed and compact electronic circuits that contain millions and millions of parts. Forget that variations of the same microscale circuits made it possible even to design and construct the satellite, and that they were instrumental in launching it into orbit and keeping it there. Forget too that the cameras that film each game contain such circuits and that the untended devices that originally translate the action into digital signals and then beam them skyward to the satellite also rely on them. Set all of that aside and consider only the baseball seen by Sue and John.

To deliver just the Yankees—never mind John's surfing selections—the cable operator must accomplish a tremendous amount of work. And it must accomplish it faster than an eye-blink. Digital encoding means that all of the fluidly changing images that comprise each panoptic ball game have been fractured into infinitesimally tiny sections, like the dots that make up a pointillist's painting. Each little section is represented by long, long strings of binary numbers—ones and zeros arranged in sequences that look arbitrary and ridiculous to the human eye. To electronic equipment, those ridiculous-seeming binary numbers constitute words, and such words tell gangs of those same miniature circuits inside the cable company's equipment how to translate the endless stream of digitally encoded signals sent down by satellite. The instructions pass so quickly that the equipment reconstructs and reassembles—in proper order—all the tiny fragments at just about the same instant that the actions that the fragments represent occur at Yankee Stadium.

Then much more occurs, such as all the follow-up work done instantly as the cable company feeds the signals through racks stacked with multiplexers and amplifiers and other such gear that prepare the signals for distribution. Next, the company releases the signals over its webbed concatenation of lines and through its spoked hubs and nodes until almost instantly they appear as reconstructed video images at the home of John and Sue, as well as at the homes of the uncounted others who also choose to watch the Yanks play the Sox, or maybe the Royals take on the Dodgers. Or who instead want to see a tiresome movie, or maybe a cursing comedian, programs that arrive at the cable company in the same manner as all the sports shows.

None of the equipment that performs all of that work—accomplishing it instantly, automatically, and reliably—is a computer in the way that we commonly think of computers: the machines on our desks reserved for e-mail and word processing. But our deskbound computers are powered by variations of the same tiny circuits that enable the cable equipment to deliver all of the baseball that Sue and John care to see.

Thus a fundamental technology enters their home. It's not computing, and it's certainly not cable television. It is the essential component that accounts for each: those miniature electronic circuits. They are microchips. Sometimes they're called *computer chips*. They're also labeled *integrated circuits* because although they're so small, they integrate and consolidate millions of parts into one. The territory they occupy is known as *microelectronics* because the chips perform electronic activities, like computing, inside microminiature dimensions. One chip would scarcely cover this word.

Microchips account for the biggest change that has occurred in our culture during the past four decades. They amount to a new human capability that is so advantageous it has reordered our lifestyles. Already the change is so complete that it has burrowed down to the roots of our culture. It's gone subterranean. It's one of our foundations now, one of the unnoticed abilities that is bound so tightly into human experience that it shapes our ideas, determines our actions, and expands our expectations. Like the furnace in the basement, the clothes that fill the closet, the automobile waiting in the garage, it is so dependably present that it stays hidden inside our thoughts. We don't need to call it to mind when we wake up every morning and ask, *Now what should I do today?* and *How should I do it?* It's already built into the answers we give those questions because this new capability is already a part of every activity.

It has become so penetrating that it serves people even as they attempt to escape from its intrusions. Sue doesn't want a computer in the house. It would become an idle extravagance. Why complicate her life? Yet she uses more computing power than early spaceships contained every time she drives a car.

The technology serves her transparently. When Sue runs out to the store, she doesn't need to first think, *I can use my car to get there.* The idea of driving her car is built into her decision to visit the store. In fact, without her car, the idea of just running to a shop or anyplace else would never pop into her head. Even short trips would amount to ordeals.

Similarly, when she starts her car, Sue doesn't need to first think, *Now I'll use the marvelous little microelectronic controller that makes this engine run.* Using the controller comes with using the auto. So in a way, deciding to use the controller is built into the decision to go to the store. It's hidden. It doesn't need to be considered. Still, her car wouldn't be waiting in the garage without the device.

Without microchips to govern engines, far fewer of us could own cars today. Pollution and fuel avarice would have cut their numbers. Automobiles would have reverted to mere playthings for millionaires and for scheming politicos around 1990 or 1995 if it weren't for those capable little controllers managing tasks it is impossible to manage by any other method. When Sue's Pontiac Grand Am arches over the Grand Island bridge, with its V–6 running at a very ordinary 3,000 rpm, the controller makes 150 decisions every second about when to fire a spark plug, while it makes 150 other decisions during the same second about when to open a fuel injector and how long to hold it open. That's all in one second alone, accomplished amid a succession of similar decisions occurring every second that the engine runs. Like all microelectronics, it works beyond human comprehension.

Yet it is a human creation. Microchips are tiny flakes of silicon, the same mineral that makes up rocks. But of course, these silicon chips are manufactured. The people who make them—they've been called alchemists—equip each itsy fleck with so many millions of built-in microscopic structures that the best way to think of one is like a brain with its uncountable neurons. Microchips are also made to think. They are machines that produce decisions. Because they're small enough to hide just about anywhere, clever inventors have embedded them in all sorts of devices, bringing synthetic judgment to the brainless, yawping machines that are the products of the prior big change, which was the Industrial Revolution. Today's Microelectronic Revolution is the distribution of synthetic thought to the edifices inherited from the Industrial Revolution.

The current age is often called the Computer Revolution, but that's just because computers are the most obvious representation of the change. The boxes with keyboards and screens that sit on every desk didn't exist until the new capability called microchips made them possible. But our revolution is bigger than just computers, and it is even bigger than computing's most revolutionary aspects, such as e-mail and the whole sprawling Internet. In fact, the revolutionary capability that makes computers also makes the Internet by making the Internet's elaborate switching gear and its seek-and-find routing gear that manages to intermesh intelligently all those millions of commands and replies coming from all those millions of computers traveling over millions and millions of miles of communication cable strung over every continent.

Microelectronics makes a lot more than just that. It makes cell phones and the networks of radio wave relays that they rely upon, including those obtrusive towers. It makes deep-probing medical scanners. It makes modern automobiles. It makes cable TV. It makes videocassette recorders and CD players, DVDs, Gameboys, PlayStations, and the whole related gaggle of entertaining distractions. It makes annoying musical greeting cards. It makes microwave ovens. It makes space craft. It made *Jurassic Park*, the movie. It makes the high-speed injection molding machines that squeeze out Lego blocks. It makes Talking Barbie. It makes the military's Patriot defensive missile and its Tomahawk offensive missile. It makes the global positioning system, GPS, which keeps you from getting lost in the woods, any woods, anyplace on Earth. It makes scanning electron microscopes and atomic particle accelerators. It makes your airline seat assignment. It makes Wal-Mart's price-chopping inventory methods happen. It makes Doppler radar for weatherman Al Kaprielian and all of his yapping colleagues in every burg and metropolis you care to mention. It makes your watch. It even makes your morning toast, if you happen to own a KitchenAid Accu-Sense Toaster.

Its effects are pervasive and ubiquitous. Since about 1960, microelectronics has advanced, improved, spread out, and grown to influence every human activity, from our business practices to our domestic lives; our leisure, recreation, and entertainment; our medicine, military affairs, education, industry, and travel; and any other field you care to name. In all of those endeavors, microchips have extended our abilities significantly. We think and we act the ways that we do in part because we rely on the abilities extended to us by this invention.

It's like steel. When was the last time you thought about steel? Still, its contributions to our culture are essential and immediate. We wouldn't live the same way if we didn't have it. But once even steel was a revolutionary technology. It changed things. It made life irrefutably easier. The benefits of steel were so apparent that no one questioned them. People embraced it. Culture reshaped around it. Then it faded into the background.

Today no one ponders, *Now how can I cut up this carrot to eat for my dinner?* But at one time that question would have been an issue of survival, and you can bet that the first person to use a knife didn't take it for granted.

Microelectronics is like that: It changed things. But its benefits began accumulating only about forty years ago. Already it has become our defining craft, the most sophisticated invention that people have put to work so far. This is *our* revolution.

This book tells how it arrived. Specifically, it tells how the revolution arrived by telling about the people who created the new capability and about the circumstances that motivated them. It is not a comprehensive account of everything that happened. Rather, it is representative: It illustrates how it all happened, and why. It is a collection of stories about motivated people engaged in the struggle of invention. Their stories are very important because they demonstrate that all of us, collectively, created the conditions that permitted and encouraged the inventions. If we recognize our role, we can choose to sustain those favorable conditions.

The revolution would not have happened under other circumstances. Scientific and technical progress only appears inevitable because discoveries accumulate sequentially, the way a child learns words before he or she strings sentences together. In this case, scientists and researchers needed to understand and to control fundamental electrical properties before later scientists and researchers could adapt those properties, shrinking their scale incomprehensibly to create microchips. But that adaptation was never preordained. It was not a mere product of patience, arriving after humankind simply waited a few millennia for microchips to evolve with inevitable destiny as heirs to the scientific and technical knowledge that preceded them. After all, fundamentals can remain unexplored. Resources can sit unutilized. Existing practices can simply persist, unchallenged and even protected by prevailing beliefs and by the power elites enriched by those beliefs. Innovators can rot in idle dormancy.

Innovators, the quick and daring people who create adaptations from the resources they receive, come out only when they're encouraged by circumstances. Therefore circumstances matter a lot. They matter at least as much as the innovators themselves. After all, ambitious and creative people live everywhere. Inside any chunk of humanity, sampled from any spot on Earth, you'll find the same distribution of talent—the same percentage of dullards, of brilliants, and the same large, mediocre middle—as you'll find in any other chunk. Sure, you won't find any physicists in primitive cultures. But they only lack training. You'll find as many people who could be physicists if they lived in a culture that produced them. What distinguishes peoples isn't so much their abilities as it is their circumstances. Particular circumstances bring actions out of some that could have come from some others had the others encountered the same situations.

In the brief, recent history of the chip, the specific discoveries and innovations occurred spontaneously because intelligent, inquisitive, and ambitious people intersected with a culture that encouraged and rewarded them. First, attitudes helped create the right circumstances. They are our collective attitudes, producing a culture that welcomes material progress. They include optimism enough to embrace change and curiosity enough to encourage inquiry. They include generosity. That's generosity sufficient to reward a person's enterprise and to exercise the fair play that discourages mighty institutions from quashing tenuous upstarts. It is also the noble generosity that trusts in democratic outcomes, letting people make their own choices, individually and unimpeded.

But those attitudes only permitted the innovations. The work also required motivation and encouragement. That came from commerce. That came from familiar capitalism, with

Adam Smith's invisible hand moving faster than it's ever moved, competitively selecting the most beneficial discoveries and developments.

The story of the microchip is a story about incentives available and choices made in intensely competitive businesses. It is about discoveries pursued for the promise of rewards—rewards that included wealth, personal independence, public recognition, and the intensely private satisfaction of unscrambling puzzles and revealing mysteries. The story encompasses countless independent decisions made by hordes of independent scientists, engineers, and the businesspeople at their elbows. The separate participants learned from each other. They struggled to outdo each other. They raced. They grasped ardently at every good idea, and they burned through many bad ideas. The only rule that directed the entire chaotic undertaking was that the best ideas would win.

Outside of that environment, certainly some sort of microchip would have emerged by now. But the revolution didn't occur only from the fundamental idea of a microchip. That was just the earliest prerequisite. The revolution occurred because of the astonishing sophistication chips attained. It's the sophistication that makes them so useful. That sophistication came only through trial-and-error on a grand scale.

There can be no map to guide technical experimentation over so much terrain because no mapmaker can possibly foresee all the possibilities that must be proposed, tried, discarded, or refined for sophistication to reach such astounding heights. The process, spontaneous, undirected, comprehensive, must assess more possibilities than one source could ever supply. They have to come from many different sources, the more sources the better, because the greater the available choices, the greater the chance that some will be superb choices, which can be selected above the mere it'll-do choices. To find the superb ones, all the possibilities have to be discovered, explored, mixed and remixed, and placed side by side in an open marketplace where people can look at them all and say, *Yeah, I like what this one does. I'll take this one.*

That adaptive mechanism built into capitalist commerce may seem very ordinary to a people whose coming-of-age rituals include stints behind the counter at McDonald's. Still, it occurs only in extraordinary circumstances because only extraordinary circumstances can account for the extraordinary pace of profound development that has improved our lives so substantially just forty-three years after a stubbornly inquisitive man worked a quiet innovation alone in a laboratory in Dallas. That was Jack Kilby, in 1958, which is where this story begins.

Sure, other factors contributed as well. Silicon chips could not have emerged out of the first Stone Age. They emerged from a modern era that already possessed such advantages as communication and transportation to spread useful ideas rapidly. But those resources can spread mediocre ideas just as well. Superb ideas have to emerge before they can proliferate. They require a culture that creates a free-for-all competitive incubator.

Of course, the culture wasn't created by the chip-makers. They were lucky enough to inherit it, but the culture was created by us, and it is sustained by us. Therefore as much as our ideas, our actions, and our expectations are products of microchips, microchips are also a product of us. As much as this book tells their story, it also tells ours.

PART ONE

Laying the Foundation

☰ 1 ☰

Thinking Small

ANY STORY THAT BEGINS with human initiative also tells the story of the culture that engendered that initiative. But if you expect explicitly to laud and celebrate the culture, you need to look carefully to find it because its role in the story is hidden. The contributions culture makes are invisible. They are especially invisible to the people inside the culture, who accept the preconditions it creates as simply the way life works.

Therefore, today, in this culture, we see nothing extraordinary in Jack Kilby's private ambition or in his aim to find personal fulfillment through professional achievement. In that regard he was the same as the rest of us: We all pick professions with a mind to fulfilling ourselves. And we find nothing special about the professional mobility that gave him liberty to seek more hospitable employment or in the critical fact that other job options even existed. We all chart private routes through professions made varied by commercial dynamics. If you don't like the situation here, you can seek other employers who give a different flavor to the particular profession you chose to find personal fulfillment. That's simply the way life works.

But even if he didn't fully appreciate the mechanisms that placed them in view, the opportunities he saw made Jack Kilby feel particularly dissatisfied in Milwaukee in the 1950s while he worked for a company called Centralab. Kilby was an electrical engineer. At Centralab he conducted research into the new sorts of gadgets and gizmos that were just then energizing his favored profession. But in his eyes he seemed to be merely watching events, the same way the whole, pregnant electrocosm around him was watching, anxious for some seminal invention to burst past the barrier that had suddenly stalled electronic progress.

Certainly someone would discover it soon. The field itself seemed ready to burst with swaggering scientists, each one eager to devise a way to miniaturize electronic gear, to pack more whirring, ticking, humming, blinking circuits aboard rockets and jets. Rockets and jets, the purest distillations of striving modernity, desperately needed circuits that processed their flight data as adroitly as the skycrafts themselves performed superterranean leaps, dives, arcs, and spirals. All the big-name outfits like Westinghouse, RCA, General Electric, and the fabled Bell Labs had assigned researchers to find ways to compress electronics small enough to fit aboard aircraft and spacecraft.

Kilby had ideas too. He felt prodding impulses, and he glimpsed tantalizing insights that suggested not so much a solution as an untried capacity to discover a solution. Yet in Milwaukee that capacity remained untried. Centralab operated on the rim, but not inside the whorling vortex of miniature electronics.

So in May 1958, after he had silently whiled away so many efforts and so much simmering ambition for one long decade at Centralab, Kilby moved to Dallas to start a more promising job at bold, bounding Texas Instruments. He and his wife caravanned down from Milwaukee with their two young daughters inside a five-year-old Ford and a three-year-old Chevy. A job switch was one thing, but long-range relocations weren't so commonplace then. Jack's wife was uncomfortable about the move. Kilby's labmates up in Wisconsin wondered why Jack was leaving. Even Kilby considered the relocation quite drastic. The summer's heat arrived early that year, oppressing the travelers. In Tulsa, stopping at Jack's parents', the Kilbys had air-conditioning installed in the good car, the Chevy. When Kilby at last took possession of his gray steel desk in Dallas on May 19, the unfinished Semiconductor Building wasn't yet centrally cooled. A new home, a new town, a new job, a new boss. New coworkers. New routines. An unfamiliar lab. The debilitating Texas heat. Yet two months after his arrival at Texas Instruments, Kilby would invent a miniaturization method that would change the whole world.

The speed of that discovery notwithstanding, Jack Kilby acts with careful deliberation, and that attribute may explain why it took him ten years to overcome the inertia that held him at Centralab. Born November 8, 1923, in Jefferson City, Missouri, Kilby had passed all his adult life around Milwaukee and nearby Chicago. He started his career at Centralab in Milwaukee in 1947, at age 23, fresh from the University of Illinois with a bachelor's in electrical engineering. He later completed a master's in electrical engineering at the University of Wisconsin in 1950 while still working at Centralab. Patient, careful, and deliberate, tall and lank with long-running limbs, Jack Kilby had bided his time as a research engineer in near exile.

Centralab operated more on the periphery of electronics inquiry. Its research bounced around according to the changing enthusiasms of its owner, an energetic entrepreneur named Chester O. Wanig. Mostly his enthusiasms followed his opportunities. Once, after scooting the 90 miles southward to Chicago, he returned from the headquarters of Sears Roebuck & Co. with an order to supply the retailer with 10,000 tabletop radios. Centralab didn't make radios. But the products were common enough. Centralab already made some of the electronic parts they used. And, after all, its research and development lab could work out a way to put the parts together.

The company had capabilities, and it had even seen a bit of glory. In 1942, while making electronic gear for weapons in the war against Hitler, Centralab devised a way to build certain electronic parts directly onto the circuit boards that would bind the parts together. The method worked like the silk screens used in printmaking, except Centralab's ink conducted electricity. By building up a pattern in multiple passes over a ceramic plate, the screening deposited capacitors and resistors, two of the components that performed vital functions inside blinking, whirring electronic circuits. It also laid down pathways to connect the components, eliminating the frail wires that would otherwise loop from one to another. The method made manufacturing much easier because you could make a number of circuit parts at once, using one process. Therefore you could make circuits more quickly, and you could make them less expensively. Most important, the approach suggested a principle that Jack Kilby later resurrected in his seminal invention: Multiple circuit parts could be made on one piece of material, built-in and integrated.

But by the 1950s, Centralab's chief aim was simply to manufacture electrical and electronic products cheaply so that it could sell them cheaply and make up for the low profit it made per item by selling an awful lot of items. Mostly it made storage batteries, the big, rechargeable batteries that are still used in cars today but scarcely anyplace else. At one time, before electric utility lines reached everywhere, a lot of households used storage batteries to power appliances like radios. Centralab sold its storage batteries to Sears, which was a very good customer to have in the middle of the twentieth century. Sears was America's largest retailer by a long shot. It sold to urban shoppers in its stores, and it reached rural folk with its hefty, has-it-all catalog. Sears could sell more storage batteries than anyone. Of course, to supply those batteries to Sears, you had to let them go cheaply. Therefore Centralab had to operate on the cheap. It couldn't spend profligately on expensive, speculative research. Its lab stuck closer to practical ideas that were more certain to pay off. Still, while at Centralab, Kilby managed to make some investigations into miniaturization. For example, he designed a small hearing aid, using a very small vacuum tube for amplification.

Before transistors, the vacuum tube was the basic building block of electronics. A light bulb is a vacuum tube that's specially constructed to glow, although the tubes used in early electronic products like radios, radar, and thirty-ton computers looked more like chemistry lab test tubes turned upside down and filled with small, metal, Tinkertoy parts. Run electricity through a vacuum tube and you can make it deliberately manipulate and control electrons, which is the essence of electronics.

While Kilby abided at Centralab, transistors appeared and began to take over the same vital functions that, until the 1950s, could only be performed by tubes. They amplified an electrical current, creating a strong current out of a weak one. They blocked current selectively, turning it off like a switch and then turning it back on when you wanted it turned on. Therefore transistors could be used instead of ubiquitous tubes to construct electronic circuits. Because they were made from a solid material, transistors didn't burn out like tubes, which burned out all the time. The first electronic computer—a sprawling, thirty-ton assemblage called the Electronic Numerical Integrator and Computer, built at the University of Pennsylvania in 1945—burned through 2,000 tubes every month. Like light bulbs, tubes went dead when their fragile, wire filaments eventually disintegrated from heat and electrical pressure. Transistors also didn't consume as much electricity, so that a circuit constructed of transistors instead of tubes ran on a lot less power. And best of all, transistors were much smaller than tubes. Therefore, with transistors, electronic wares could grow smaller.

Transistors were first announced on June 30, 1948, following their invention by the celebrated Bell Labs scientists John Bardeen, Walter Brattain, and William Shockley. (Stubborn, flamboyant, and brilliantly original, Bill Shockley was the founder and patron of the transistor business, and he's still the most interesting character who ever inhabited the place.) The new devices were fashioned out of semiconducting materials. Called simply semiconductors, the materials seemed magical. They were able to conduct electricity when they were in certain states and to block electricity when in certain other states. By controlling the states of the semiconductor devices—the transistors—circuit designers used them to direct and manipulate current in ways that transmitted or received radio signals, for instance, or that mimicked logical decision making. Yet each transistor was one piece, in effect a small fleck of stone-like material stuck with wires to get current into it and to take current out of it. They were therefore called solid-state, and as solid pieces, semiconductor transistors contained no parts that could burn out.

By contrast, tubes were chock full of delicate parts just waiting to burn out or maybe even jiggle loose. Tubes weren't going anywhere. They were retrograde. They cost less than transistors because by now their manufacture was well practiced. But that was the most you could say about them. People used tubes only for nondemanding jobs that could tolerate their stingy deficiencies. Kilby's exercise making a tube-amplified hearing aid only warmed his simmering frustration. Why was he fussing around with tubes? Transistors had already taken over all the rocket-age products that were now screaming out for minicircuits.

Kilby recognized that fact just as every diligent electrical engineer recognized it. He stayed current with the speeding pace of electronic development. He followed the breakthroughs occurring outside of Milwaukee. He read the technical literature. He sat through the dense presentations at engineering

conferences, hearing firsthand reports about ideas and innovations. He listened to disquisitions from biggies in the electronics industry, from researchers at such high places as Bell Labs
itself, where the secrets of semiconductors first yielded to
Bardeen, Brattain, and Shockley. Like every good engineer,
Kilby grew seduced by the allure of miniaturization.

As the 1950s rolled toward the 1960s, just about everyone
involved in electronics was caught in the competitive frenzy to
make circuits smaller. That's because the rewards would be so
large. Not from computers. No one yet anticipated that the big,
expensive, specialized thinking machines could ever become
commonplace products. After engineer J. Presber Eckert and
physicist John Mauchly built their pioneering Electronic
Numerical Integrator and Computer (called the ENIAC) in 1945,
they left the University of Pennsylvania to begin making the
machines as a business. They sold their first UNIVAC, the Universal Automatic Computer, to the U.S. Census Bureau in 1951.
Any organization that purchased one of these million-dollar
Delphic oracles very happily sequestered the fulminating
prophet in its own, secluded sanctuary, where white-coated
priests and priestesses could minister to it undisturbed. They
were special-purpose, outside-the-mainstream machines used
only to solve exceedingly difficult problems by people with a
whole lot of special training.

Only about 50 UNIVACs were installed here and there by the
time the miniaturization movement called Kilby out of Centralab. No one expected to miniaturize computers. Sure, semiconductor companies like Texas Instruments would happily sell
transistors to the small handful of electronics outfits that made
the small handful of computers produced at the time. But they
expected to sell a lot more semiconductors elsewhere—especially to places that needed circuits far smaller than any you
could make using tubes. The miniaturization movement that
created microelectronics arose out of needs that were unrelated
to computing, and for a while, the field of microelectronics and

computers grew as separate undertakings—one striving, the other aloof.

The late 1950s overflowed with places to put shrunk-down circuits. Consumer goods had acquired some ambitions toward miniaturization, with transistors first replacing tubes in radios in 1954. Commercial and military aviation had revved up after World War II, roaring into the jet age. Planes needed navigation equipment, communication gear, pilot controls, and instruments. Fast-flying military craft needed weapons that were more adroit than a mechanical trigger on a gun carriage.

All of these needs were vitally urgent because Nikita Khrushchev's Soviet Union was rattling sabers at the United States. Suddenly the Soviets possessed a more menacing means to deliver their explosives: The U.S.S.R. launched the first intercontinental ballistic missile aboard a mule-kicking Vostok rocket on August 26, 1957. Then, on October 4, it hurled humankind's first satellite into orbit. The Sputnik I was followed by Sputnik II just one month later. Forget about piloted bombers. The damn destruction now could strike from outer space. In America citizens no longer felt insulated by the span of oceans.

Meanwhile, TV viewers watched live as a U.S. Vanguard rocket blew up upon launch at Cape Canaveral, Florida, on November 26, 1957. Talk of a "missile gap" separating the Soviets from the Yanks grew louder. Politicians responded by creating NASA on July 16, 1958. The National Aeronautic and Space Administration's first big mission, Project Mercury, proposed to shoot guys into space atop Atlas rockets. An Atlas might have looked serenely powerful and singularly impressive standing isolated beside its launch gantry. But the American rocket was still a far sight smaller than Soviet space vehicles.

"The Russians had big missiles that could carry a few tons of stuff. We had much less capability so that our military needed more compact, lighter, more capable electronic equipment," explains Kilby. They needed equipment for guidance, navigation, control, and communication. They needed equipment that could make calculations that were somewhat less involved than full-bore, thirty-ton-computer calculations but that were vital nonetheless. Reading conditions like pressure or altitude, time, distance, or direction, the instruments had to flash electrons rapidly through circuits that could determine appropriate actions. Point a little this way. Nudge a little that way. It would also be nice if the equipment held together better. Electronic equipment made from so many different parts, with so many wires tacked by shiny solder to hold all the parts together, was chronically unreliable. The stuff broke down whenever a wire jiggled loose. And with so many wires, sooner or later one always worked loose.

Most of all, the circuits needed to be made miniature. They needed to be shrunk down to fit in any crevice or nook an engineer could locate. And they had to be light, so their weight wouldn't drag against struggling thrusters. Only semiconductors could achieve those objectives. By 1957 and 1958 everybody in electronics understood that fact, and the understanding animated semiconductor research, transforming it from dusty esoteria to a high-stakes, high-energy undertaking. Jack Kilby recognized it, but Kilby worked at Centralab, a battery maker with aspirations but no budget.

"It was pretty clear that semiconductors were gonna require much bigger investments than Centralab was prepared to make," he says. "That was my basic reason for leaving."

In 1958, at age thirty-four, Kilby wrote to some of the top-flight employers in solid-state electronics. He inquired about research into miniaturization specifically. Motorola was willing to let him split his lab time between circuit shrinking and some other, unspecified assignments it would mete out to him. IBM wanted to put him to work on its homegrown solution to the circuit dilemma, involving a variation of the screening method first employed at Centralab. Kilby didn't think the approach held much promise. (IBM eventually abandoned it, confirming his assessment.)

He also sent an inquiry to Texas Instruments, a relative new-comer that was making a name on the strength of ambition alone. TI had been established in 1930 to explore for oil. It became an electronic equipment company when it began sell-ing versions of the instruments it made for its own geophysical research. It became a semiconductor company when its elec-tronic interests led it into early transistors.

Coincidentally, Kilby's letter to TI crossed the desk of Willis Adcock just when Adcock was shopping for an engineer to begin a research program in miniaturization. The order had come down from above, from TI's tech-savvy executives who wanted to catch some of the dollars that the U.S. government was tossing toward microcircuits. Adcock was head of research for the company's recently created Semiconductor Products Division. He considered Kilby for the job, but on paper the gan-gly, laconic researcher from Centralab was unqualified. Kilby held only a master's degree. Company policy gave research jobs to Ph.D.s. But Adcock knew Kilby from the tech-fest circuit. The two men had met at conferences, where they had talked about transistors and other such semicon topics du jour. Adcock liked Jack Kilby. He had a hunch about the man's quiet abilities. So he violated corporate policy and gave him the research job anyway. Kilby started as a senior project engineer at job grade thirty.

"The best thing I ever did was hire Jack," Adcock reflects. But Willis Adcock was already a semiconductor celebrity in his own right. He had joined Texas Instruments as a young chemist in 1953. Shortly afterward, he devised a method for making sil-icon transistors. Before that, all transistors were made of the semiconductor material germanium, and the grand ambitions of the entire eagerly expanding semiconductor industry depended on germanium transistors alone. But germanium didn't do well in a lot of demanding, high-stress conditions. The transistors broke down and quit working after they broke a sweat, after they grew too hot. But heat could get awfully hard

to avoid. Circuits themselves shed degrees, and more complicated circuits contained more heat-producing parts. Some
super circuits could conceivably bake themselves. Besides, high
external temperatures prevailed in a lot of places where people
wanted to employ electronic circuits, especially in places like
rockets and jets.

The semiconductor silicon could withstand high temperatures, but silicon was only a theoretical semiconductor in the
early 1950s. Except for a few experimental bits made here and
there, it was unused because no one had yet figured out how to
process the stuff reliably. In fact, many people insisted it would
never be processed adequately enough to challenge germanium
as the primo material for making transistors. Willis Adcock
proved them wrong. TI announced his innovation on May 10,
1954, instantly acquiring semiconductor stardom and grabbing
an unchallenged, two-year lead in supplying silicon transistors
to companies that made electronic gear.

In the half-decade after Adcock arrived in Dallas, TI's semiconductor activities had grown into a productive enterprise.
The Semiconductor Products Division made germanium transistors at a new plant up in Sherman, Texas, fifty miles north of
Dallas. In 1958, germanium was still the everyday semiconductor, and the Sherman facility supplied the transistors that filled
IBM's ample computers. (Kilby remembers the high achievement of the art, displayed at IBM's corporate offices in New
York: "They had a big machine in a glass room on the first floor
that had forty-thousand transistors in it. It was considered a
minor miracle.")

But in addition to germanium products, TI also made silicon
transistors according to the crystal-growing technique Adcock
had pioneered in 1954. Silicon was still exotic, still uncommon
compared to germanium, and therefore silicon transistors com-
manded princely prices. They sold mostly to the military,
mostly because the military needed transistors that stood up to
searing heat. Adcock himself had moved up to direct semicon

development for the ascendant manufacturer. In the lab, his researchers looked for better ways to make semiconductors and for better ways to use them so that TI could sell more of the high-profit products. The company was accomplished, ambitious, confident, dynamic, and growing. Its culture encouraged innovation. It rewarded achievement. It demanded boldness and determination. It gave its technical investigators liberty to follow their noses.

That was the Dallas organization that Jack Kilby found on May 19, 1958. The place had passion, and it embraced a business approach exactly the opposite of Centralab's. Texas Instruments spent lavishly on research. The entire company was staked on technical advancement. TI aimed to come up with new ideas before other companies came up with something similar. It could set higher prices for cutting-edge products that offered capabilities people couldn't get by any other means. The higher profits would compensate it for the funds it spent on research. What's more, its discoveries would help the company grow larger by expanding into new markets that its new products created.

The approach also required TI to aim its investigations accurately at the innovations it expected to be most profitable. It wasn't enough to be merely interesting. Advanced technologies also had to be useful before many people would buy them, especially at the high prices that made all the development worthwhile. Therefore TI's research in the late 1950s focused on semiconductors, those quirky, new materials that were opening all the unforeseen vistas in electronics. The field was still in its first decade. Its newness alone assured opportunities. Much remained to be discovered.

Thus Jack Kilby's starting assignment at TI was wide open: circuit miniaturization, whatever that might mean. "I was allowed to define it," he states. "Nobody really told me what to do or how to go about it."

He had brought some ideas, but Kilby also realized that he couldn't dither around with vague notions for very long. He recognized two big constraints on his research. One was the allure of government money. After all, military needs at the moment drove the frenzied inquiries into circuit reduction. But military contracts would come with strings. Government research aimed at specific targets that the government defined. The work might be lavishly funded, but it was confined, conducted without much latitude for open inquiries and serendipitous discoveries. Kilby wanted to avoid such restrictions. The second limit was the unspoken necessity to use semiconductors, which probably meant using them in unconventional ways that no one else had yet conceived. TI had simply invested too much money in semiconductor technology to accept any alternative approach to miniaturization.

Through its various agencies, the U.S. government was looking at a few alternate approaches, flinging lucrative research contracts at electronics companies as the separate military services each competitively pushed their own pet approaches. The Army was sold on an idea called micro-modules. The plan was to build all electronic circuit parts in the same shape and size, whether they were transistors, resistors, capacitors, or any other device someone might dream up. Each little micro-module would incorporate uniform little connectors, built into the blocks so that the separate components would snap together like Lego toys to create whole circuits. The approach would require no wires. It would certainly make circuits easier to assemble. But Kilby didn't believe it would make them appreciably smaller.

The Air Force backed an idea called molecular electronics. It suggested a sort of alchemy. Molecular electronics would do away with the separate devices inside a circuit altogether, relying instead on solid elements that could perform the same functions, the way naturally occurring crystals receive radio waves. Engineers would no longer have to skillfully devise current paths among transistors, resistors, capacitors, and such. The molecular structures of the new elements would more elegantly perform the same functions. Circuits wouldn't need to be miniaturized. Circuits would become obsolete. Thus the Air Force paid researchers generously to create or to discover such magical elements.

At the moment of Kilby's arrival, TI wasn't taking miniaturization research money from any agency because it hadn't yet committed itself to any of the voguish approaches. But the temptation loomed. Says Kilby, "I thought if the kinds of things I was interested in didn't work out, I might be asked to do one of those. But I didn't want to do that, and wasn't enthused about it."

TI already made semiconductor transistors successfully. And transistors, which were generally much smaller than the tubes they supplanted, pushed in the right direction. But Kilby was looking at more than just transistors. The problem bedeviling electronic circuits was that they contained too many pieces, and transistors accounted for just some of the pieces. They were typically the workhorse circuit elements: Because of their ability to block or to permit a current to pass—often called *gating*—transistors could be strung together to create *go, no-go* logic chains that triggered appropriate actions. But they still required support from other circuit parts, combined with transistors in ways that precisely manipulated current flow. Resistors, one of the primary support elements, slowed down a current. Capacitors, another common part, temporarily stored small electrical charges. All those circuit parts—transistors, resistors, capacitors, and any others—needed to be somehow combined into a very small package, a package that fit inside cramped places and at the same time left room to accommodate even more circuit components so that the circuits, although smaller, could become more complex and therefore more capable.

To erase the congestion—consolidating all the separate pieces with their dense tangle of wires and brittle blobs of hardened solder—Kilby considered Centralab's 1942 innovation, the screened-together, printed-on circuits that were by then widely used. The method let you build a bunch of parts at once, already adhered to a little ceramic board so that the circuit came out as a single piece.

But the technique used conventional materials. It didn't touch semiconductors. If you wanted to include semiconductors—transistors—in such a circuit, you had to add them after the other consolidated components were built. Kilby needed to do more than just add semiconductors to a conventional circuit. He somehow had to use semiconductors as the foundation for his miniature circuits. Resistors and capacitors had never been made out of semiconducting substances. You could build better performing resistors and capacitors, and build them much more cheaply, using conventional materials. Germanium and silicon simply didn't possess the right properties to make good capacitors and resistors.

Still, pondered Kilby, if he *could* make all the pieces out of one material, out of semiconductor, then he might try an approach similar to Centralab's screen printing. As a matter of fact, if he could make all the parts out of semiconductor, he could one-up the printing method because he wouldn't have to use a base. He wouldn't have to adhere the parts to anything. They'd come out as one solid chunk of material, the way a transistor was one chunk, with wires merely tacked onto different regions of the chunk. One piece of material could contain all the separate parts, the transistors, resistors, and capacitors, all integrated, inseparable, yet still configured as a circuit.

Patiently, persistently, inwardly absorbed, Kilby stacked and tumbled ideas, insights, concepts, combinations, and variations. His mind plodded, unperturbed by the unaccountably hot Dallas summer. Thoughts coalesced. He turned them over some more.

At this time, Texas Instruments used to almost shutter down in July by encouraging its workers to take simultaneous vacations. But Kilby, a new hire, hadn't accumulated any vacation time by July 1958. Therefore much fuss gets made about circumstances in Dallas when Kilby's innovation first flashed into his mind. The lab where he worked was close to abandoned on July 24.

But, says Kilby, "the thought that I was alone in a deserted building has been exaggerated." Some workers always stuck around. Besides, TI was a bursting company on the grow. In 1958 it was just starting to move staff into its new Dallas Expressway site off the undeveloped, northern rim of the city. Kilby was among the first occupants of the Semiconductor Building. The company employed a lot of other newcomers too, all Bob Cratchets like Kilby who hadn't yet earned vacation time. Kilby shared the month's calm with about fifty other workers. "I don't think that has anything to do with the story," he says, "but it makes a good one."

Far more remarkable is the fact that Jack Kilby conjured up the idea so quickly. He had been at work at TI for only two months. But of course, he'd spent ten years just hearing about other people's innovations. He had spent a decade watching; wondering; storing up ideas; making silent inquiries into dense, unsettled mysteries. At last the big, quiet Midwesterner had been freed to inquire in daylight. Texas Instruments encouraged his bold ponderings.

Thus every morning after he scuffed to the gray Steelcase desk where his knees scraped to fit underneath, Kilby thought with plodding detachment and singular focus. He thought about silicon, he thought about circuits, and he thought about shrinking circuits. His thoughts worked aloof of the evaporative heat and the unsettled home. His mind replayed all of its experiences. It cast back through all of its dim ponderings spanning a decade while it also applied new stimuli into the mix. Kilby had semiconductors here in the flesh. He could grab a whole handful in his Great-Plainsman's paw and experiment over at a workbench, bending his neck to bring his head closer to his relentless inquiries. He built up the idea to integrate silicon circuits in a series of reverberant investigations that lasted two weeks, arriving as a kind of intensified culmination of his first two months at TI.

The entry Jack Kilby penned into his lab notebook on July 24, 1958, summarized his insight: "The following circuit elements could be made on a single slice: resistors, capacitor, distributed capacitor, transistor." (Some forty years later he accepted a Nobel Prize for that inventive jolt.)

Reaching that conclusion required Kilby to abandon prevailing assumptions. The essence of his idea—that if you make all circuit elements out of the same type of semiconductor material, you can make them all on a single piece of that material—required him to accept that other circuit components, not just the transistors, could also be made out of semiconductor. According to the conventional wisdom, the idea was ludicrous. In the late 1950s, resistors sold for about a penny apiece. Capacitors cost just a few cents more. Crank-'em-out specialists like Centralab made them, companies that kept their manufacturing costs so low that they could eke out a few fractions of a penny on each part they sold, selling millions and millions of them to make their profits. On the other hand, semiconductor houses like TI made only high-priced components, transistors and the occasional diode, because their manufacturing processes were so expensive to operate that you'd never justify turning out penny-apiece products. "At that time," explains Kilby, "the amount of silicon required to make a resistor would have made a silicon transistor that you could sell for ten dollars. So making resistors was not an obvious thing to do."

But Kilby reasoned that the advantages of building a circuit from a single piece of semiconductor would offset the cost penalties. Integration would reduce wiring and assembly costs while it assured reliable operation of the finished circuit. And the separate devices that made up the circuit could be squeezed very close together, essentially within one chunk of stone. That is, the circuit could be miniaturized.

What's more, Kilby's concept retained accumulated knowledge. Engineers wouldn't have to scrap decades of experience and start over because the design and operation of circuits wouldn't change. Electronic product designers would still have to lay out transistors, resistors, capacitors, and such in arrangements that deliberately marshaled electric currents. But because the circuits would be monolithic, with all those deliberately arranged devices cast into the same piece of semiconductor, the vexing problems of circuit size and circuit complexity could be vanquished.

Kilby figured that such shrunk-down, integrated circuits should be made from silicon rather than germanium. After all, the military wanted minicircuits most urgently, and military circuits had to be made of silicon so they would withstand the debilitating heat inside, say, a rocket ship. But to test the idea, he used blanks of germanium. Silicon was still exotic and expensive. Germanium bars were laying around the lab like wrappers from yesterday's Hershey bars. Kilby knew that if his idea worked with germanium, it would also work with silicon.

The most immediate challenge was simply to show that separate devices could be grouped on a single scrap of semiconductor. Kilby collared two technicians who floated from task to task among the engineers in the semicon lab. Together they subdivided the surface of germanium bars that were about half the size of a stick of Dentyne. They scratched out and shaped regions of the material to function as capacitors, as resistors. They hand-fashioned a half-dozen of these world's first integrated circuits, figuring they would need that many as insurance against the occasional bum bar of material. "Semiconductor manufacturing in those days was a somewhat hit and miss proposition," explains Kilby. "Even transistors, which had been produced for years, had less than perfect yields. Sometimes as few as twenty percent of them worked."

Only a handful of Kilby's coworkers even knew what he was up to. Most were skeptical. Kilby remained unshakably confident: "I was quite sure it would work. I didn't know whether any particular one would work, but I knew that the idea would work."

On September 12, 1958, Kilby prepared to test the sample circuits. Laid out on a laboratory workbench, each bar was crudely blobbed onto a block to hold it steady. A few gold threads bound each small semiconductor block, connecting its carved-out regions. Larger wires attached each block to a power supply, whereas another set of wires at the back end of the solid circuit ran to an oscilloscope. Kilby's invention was fashioned to operate as a phase-shift oscillator, a common and simple subcircuit that was usually built into a larger, more complicated one. A phase-shift oscillator changed the direction of flowing electrons. If Kilby's idea worked, the solid-state semiconductor oscillator would convert the direct current from the power supply into an alternating current. If it worked, the oscilloscope screen would light with evenly undulating, gracefully arcing lines curving upward and downward and upward and downward in the pattern of universal probity called a sine wave.

Kilby applied power with an effortless gesture. His gaze moved with insouciant ease to the oscilloscope. The screen's green phosphor animated: a bright, unbroken squig moved in comfortable symmetry, upward and downward and upward and downward in rhythm with cosmic electrical shift. Circuits would forevermore be integrated.

☰ 2 ☰

The Wild West

JACK KILBY'S INVENTION logically solved the problem of circuit congestion. Logically, the idea of grouping together a capacitor and a resistor or two, adding a few transistors, and presenting them as one component provided a means to make circuits smaller. Smaller circuits made more capable equipment because they made room for enough electronic components to, say, effectively guide a missile, or maybe detect and jam radar. Logically, Kilby's solution also advanced semiconductors by integrating those few parts that would otherwise be separate inside a single, button-sized piece of the stuff. But in practical terms, such devices stood well beyond the manufacturing abilities of Texas Instruments or, for that matter, any other semiconductor hopeful of the late 1950s.

At the time, Kilby himself couldn't quite devise an effective way to tie together the separate parts he would integrate inside a stone chip. Even though they shared the same bit of material, each individual capacitor, resistor, or transistor still occupied a separate region inside the material. Those regions still needed to be interconnected by wires or by the equivalent of wires. The biggest shortcoming of Kilby's earliest design was its failure to provide practical, easily producible interconnections. Good interconnections were simply impossible because the early inadequately structured semiconductors at Kilby's disposal could not accommodate any integrated pathways.

Kilby's idea might have remained a practical impossibility. But the semiconductors of 1958 were still so raw and emergent that improvements were arriving rapidly from other quarters. Texas Instruments was far from the only organization of semiconductor savants. The field's enticing novelty, its promise, its intrigue, and its opportunities encouraged expansion and attracted other oddball inventors. Independently, animated by their own ambitions and their own inquisitive impulses, they filled in with startling innovations that made Kilby's concept of integrated silicon circuits a workable reality.

Compared to Kilby, Jean Hoerni seemed an unlikely contributor. At least in their demeanors, the two men were opposites. Hoerni was urbane and overeducated, garrulous, headstrong, and aloof. He worked for a tenuous, unestablished rival to TI, a company called Fairchild Semiconductor. At the time of Kilby's invention, Fairchild was so small that it scarcely registered as a competitive challenge to the Texan. Fairchild was still brand new. Its biggest concern was simply staying alive.

But Fairchild made silicon transistors, and that alone was an achievement. The company had skipped any excursion into germanium. Instead it had set out from its founding in 1957 to make the most difficult variety of silicon transistors, a type called *diffused junction*.

But the same shoddy quality that afflicted everyone else in semiconductors bedeviled Fairchild too. It was costly enough to discard most of the products you made because they just didn't work. The problem grew worse when the few that you thought had survived—and which you had therefore pushed through final assembly and packaging—failed later. Fairchild, a company so delicately small and new that it could not afford flub-ups, recognized that transistors that failed after they were installed in equipment could wreck its reputation. The problem could grow expensive enough to wreck its balance sheet. The threat was so urgent that Jean Hoerni started looking for a solution as a first assignment when Fairchild was newly formed, before it even began shipping transistors out its door.

He began by improvising on the fundamental structure of transistors, looking for some new shape or configuration that might make them more reliable. Transistors at the time were sealed up inside small metal cans, with three little wires splaying out from the bottom, used to attach each transistor to a circuit. The dot of silicon, which was the actual transistor, was hidden inside the can. But that didn't protect the frail little thing from contaminants already inside. Hoerni wanted to find a way to coat a transistor so that errant specks of dust orbiting around in its can wouldn't destroy the device when they fell on it. Other researchers outside of Fairchild were trying to do the same thing. But no one had succeeded in making a protective coating that could stick to the silicon.

Hoerni brought his own creative view to the problem, trying to rearrange a transistor's structure to make it more dependable. But his overall interest in the problem grew out of the larger milieu that was growing up rapidly around semiconductors. All sorts of people were joining the race to make better products, and each one was striving to beat the others. They weren't working cooperatively—unless researchers happened to work for the same company. They worked coincidentally. Thus, Hoerni's ponderings over the form and structure of transistors had nothing to do with the fact that, far off at Texas Instruments, form and structure hung up Jack Kilby's concept of an integrated silicon circuit. Hoerni was wholly unaware of Kilby's work. In fact, the two men bent to their separate tasks more or less simultaneously, with Hoerni's first flash of insight occurring just before Kilby had left Centralab.

The same expanding, ebullient milieu that encouraged Kilby's uncharacteristic escape to Dallas had also summoned Jean Hoerni into semiconductors. But the experiences that brought Hoerni to Fairchild enmeshed him somewhat more intimately with the tumult, with the commercial and technical maneuverings that characterized semiconductor development. Hoerni helped found Fairchild, arriving at the role by way of fast-burning Shockley Semiconductor Laboratory, which was established by transistor-inventor William Shockley. Shockley was the archetype of semiconductor entrepreneurs: brilliant, daring, brash, tireless, and egotistical. In fact, Shockley possessed those qualities in such abundance that they wrecked him, sabotaging his company by driving away Hoerni along with the other brainy insurrectionists who became Hoerni's business partners at Fairchild.

Shockley's vocation as physicist began way back in August 1932, with a two-week road trip that better befitted a bull rider or maybe a stunt flier. He drove with young Frederick Seitz, who would become Dr. Frederick Seitz, a distinguished physicist himself. Shockley was twenty-two, a new grad from Stanford leaving Palo Alto, California, for Boston, to earn a Ph.D. from MIT, the Massachusetts Institute of Technology. Seitz needed to reach New Jersey to begin his own doctoral studies at Princeton. Shockley's mother telephoned Seitz from her home in Hollywood to arrange the car pool. They would share expenses and travel in Shockley's snappy DeSoto convertible. "Thus began one of the most carefree two-week periods I have enjoyed in the intervening decades," Seitz later recalled.

"Shockley, I soon realized, was then strongly influenced by the Hollywood culture of the time, fancying himself to be a cross between Douglas Fairbanks Sr. and Bulldog Drummond." Captain Hugh "Bulldog" Drummond was a suave, gentlemanly spy series hero of novels and films, the era's James Bond. "Moreover," said Seitz, "he accepted pronouncements of the Hollywood stars on political, social and economic issues with the same degree of seriousness that I would have taken of those of . . . President Hoover. Moreover, he had a loaded pistol in the glove compartment."

From Palo Alto they looped south, cutting through Arizona, New Mexico, Texas, Arkansas, Kentucky, Ohio, and onward into the urban east. While en route, they went spelunking through Carlsbad Caverns. When a rainstorm in west Texas washed out the road ahead of them, they abandoned the DeSoto for an overnight hike into the desert. "Bulldog" carried his pistol into the black dome, cracking off rounds to warn away howling coyotes. The next morning the pair escaped just ahead of local cops who had come out to track the two desperadoes who, the cops said, had been shooting it up the night before.

Shockley was the Jack Kerouac of twentieth-century science, composed of very large contradictions, excitable to the threshold of singing dementia. Like Kerouac in his field, Shockley made some material contributions that were significant, but they were probably less important than the spirit and energy he spilled into the undertaking. His singular achievement that no ordinary physicist could have matched was to attract the band of gifted disciples that included Hoerni. Shockley's main feat was simply to bring them together because the group's interplay, as much as the standout achievement of any one member, led to key innovations that Kilby's first stab at circuit integration still lacked.

They came just to work for Bill Shockley. He had conceived theoretically of transistors almost by brain work alone when employed by Bell Labs, the former Murray Hill, New Jersey, haunt of Alexander Graham Bell himself. Then, with Bardeen and Brattain, he had made the first ones. (The trio took their Nobels about ten years after the invention.) In 1956, Shockley left Bell Labs to turn his ideas into personal fortune and fame. He set up Shockley Semiconductor Laboratory in a shed in his old hometown, Palo Alto, on the peninsula that spreads south from San Francisco, a region that would later be called Silicon

Valley. The company was a raw and ambitious research organization. It aimed to sell silicon transistors, as soon as its researchers figured out how to make them.

At the time, most transistors were still made of germanium. Texas Instruments alone made some from silicon, using the method developed by Willis Adcock a couple of years earlier. But Adcock's were *grown-junction* transistors. The label referred to the process by which silicon was impregnated with essential impurities. Pure silicon possessed no electronic value. It became a semiconductor only after it was carefully doped with particular impurities—which had to infuse through the silicon in precise concentrations. To make grown-junction transistors, the impurities were added early to a vat of molten silicon so they could mix with the material while it was still a singeing sludge. As solidifying crystals grew into hardened silicon, they contained the right mix of impurities at the outset.

The *diffused-junction* transistors that Shockley set out to make relied on an entirely different process. The method promised to yield more transistors from a given amount of silicon. It started by cutting wafers of uncorrupted silicon—slicing a cylindrical slab of the material the way a deli takes slices from a salami. The round, thin wafers were pure silicon, no impurities allowed. Next the corrupting substances seeped into the wafers in diffusion furnaces, where relentless heat opened the silicon for the invading impurities to infuse it, sweating in through the surface the way hickory flavor permeates slabs of ribs in a smoker. Then, after they were doped in the furnaces, each flat wafer was sawed into many small squares—as if a salami slice was diced into little pieces. Each flat, little piece of diffused silicon equaled a separate transistor.

By contrast, grown-junction varieties consumed much more of the starting cylindrical boule to make a single transistor. The cylinder started out already impregnated, with the impurities stratified through it so that separate transistors had to be split off top to bottom, like kindling split from a log. Not only did that yield fewer transistors, but the final transistors were also long and narrow, and therefore more difficult to package and more awkward to incorporate into equipment.

Thus diffused-junction transistors were more economical to make—created in big, smoke-house batches—and they were also more compact and economical to assemble.

Shockley had first conceived diffused silicon transistors when he worked at Bell Labs. But by the middle '50s no one had yet managed to make commercial versions of the things. In Palo Alto, as proprietor of the Semiconductor Lab, Shockley aimed to develop the process so that he could produce and sell high-frequency transistors, ones that worked fast enough for elite operations like high-speed computing. Therefore he gathered a luminous research staff that could grapple past the concept to find a way actually to manufacture the devices.

Shockley drew an astounding collection of semiconductor enthusiasts to Palo Alto. He was irresistibly appealing. When Shockley wasn't theorizing or inventing, he performed legerdemain. He pulled practical gags. He climbed mountains. He raised ants, constructing elaborate obstacle courses equipped with fulcrumed teeter-totters. To youthful and aspiring chemists, physicists, engineers, and other science-guild members, going to work for Bill Shockley was like taking a bit part alongside James Dean. For a while, before the same Shockley ego that attracted the gang eventually drove them away, he used to boast that the lab was his "Ph.D. production line."

Jean Hoerni was thirty-two years old when he joined. Swiss born, he was a double physicist with doctoral degrees from the University of Geneva and the University of Cambridge. Pre-Shockley, Hoerni was still at his studies, doing postdoctoral research at Cal Tech—the California Institute of Technology in Pasadena, California. But he noticed the early roils of semiconductor commerce. He'd been a student his whole life, yet Hoerni recognized that more interesting discoveries were occurring outside of academe. He approached Bell Labs for a job, just in time to bump into Shockley as Shockley was moving out. Hoerni joined the new Palo Alto venture in 1956.

Other laborers on the Ph.D. production line would eventually earn greater distinction than Hoerni. Robert Noyce was a physics doctor out of MIT when he first went to work for the new transistor division of Philco, an outfit once known as the Philadelphia Storage Battery Company. Ambitious and eager, Noyce had turned down offers from Bell Labs, IBM, and RCA because he thought he would advance faster as a research engineer in an organization like Philco that was cutting its first teeth in semiconductors. But he soon grew disillusioned. Noyce wanted to pioneer. Philco wanted only to keep pace. Therefore he left Philly for the new West that Shockley was starting, joining the Semiconductor Lab as employee number seventeen. Shockley made Noyce director of research, paying him $12,000 per year.

Employee eighteen, Gordon Moore, dropped like Hoerni from the rarefied ivory tower to join the hurry-scurry of commercial semiconductors. Moore had a Ph.D. in chemistry from Cal Tech. Shockley found him toiling in Baltimore as a kind of research gnome for the Applied Physics Laboratory at Johns Hopkins University—"conducting basic research on things nobody cared much about," as Moore later put it. His disenchantment had just brushed the bottom when Bulldog Drummond Shockley telephoned. "One day I found myself calculating the cost per word in the publications that were coming out, and wondering if the government was getting its money's worth—or frankly, if anybody was ever reading them. So I decided I ought to get into something a bit more practical."

In all, about a dozen well-schooled laborers came bursting with vigorous optimism, bristling to push past the borders that seemed able to restrain semiconductor science for only a moment longer. They wanted to be the first to break the barriers. They wanted the honor. They wanted the prestige. They wanted all the rewards. Let their names be known in science circles the way Shockley's name was known. To make better transistors was to make science while also making history. Their boss, newly minted Nobel laureate Bulldog Shockley (he received the prize in 1956 for having coinvented transistors in 1947), offered the best proof of that. It was all so pat because they also felt like contributors to the common cause, to the advancing culture. Just look at what transistors had accomplished already: the blinking, blipping gear aboard jet planes and on those sudden, fast-rising rockets; the encroachment of mammoth computers; those small, bleating radios. Shockley's workers believed unequivocally that they were improving the world while they pursued their first passion, laboring in white shirts with narrow ties, straight-cut trousers, and crews or maybe just a close crop of full, thick, densely waved hair like Robert Noyce—in this era social comity still stood above self-expression. Everything about the work was just so much fun. It engaged them. The puzzle. The hunt. The quandaries. The near-misses. The sudden small breakthroughs. Breathtaking flashes of illumination. But they hated their jobs.

"Working for Shockley proved to be a particular challenge," wrote Moore in the biographical sketch describing his former employer for another of *Time*'s tedious lists of noteworthies. "He extended his competitive nature even to his working relationships with the young physicists he supervised. Beyond that, he developed traits that we came to view as paranoid. He suspected that members of his staff were purposely trying to undermine the project and prohibited them from access to some of the work. He viewed several trivial events as malicious and assigned blame. He felt it necessary to check new results with his previous colleagues at Bell Labs and he generally made it difficult for us to work together."

The young organization fissured at last when Shockley insisted that his staff endure lie detector tests to get to the bottom of some petty, imagined offense. Mad-scientist Shockley also announced that the Semiconductor Lab wouldn't diffuse silicon transistors after all. Instead, Shockley said, it would change directions, making solid-state diodes, which were electronic devices that also did duty in circuits. But diodes lacked transistors' cachet. And the Shockley team, despite the obstructions of Shockley himself, felt themselves getting near the first goal. They didn't want to stop. They didn't want to discard the discoveries that had thwarted seasoned researchers before them. They wanted to make diffused silicon transistors. They felt outrage over the change. Eight of them defected as a group in 1957, just one year into their tenure. They set up Fairchild Semiconductor, aiming to complete the work they had begun. In addition to Hoerni, Moore, and Noyce, they included Julius Blank, Victor Grinich, Eugene Kleiner, Jay Last, and Sheldon Roberts. Six held Ph.D.s. Two were mechanical engineers.

Bill Shockley branded the group the traitorous eight. But in fact, the desertion by his star thinkers was really just another Shockley first. Just as the Bulldog himself set a certain high standard for the élan and esprit that would possess the best of the semicon seekers, the departures from his company established the industry's common pattern of business regeneration: The brightest researchers would run away with their best ideas to use as the basis to start their own companies. They weren't always driven away by dissatisfaction, as Shockley's eight had been. Often they were merely lured by opportunity. Ideas still ruled because the territory was still a wilderness, with large tracts unexplored and important discoveries still obscured. Any person with pluck enough could find space to sell a good idea. That encouraged the industry's ideamen to break free, forming new companies on the strength of abundant ideas—often ideas they conceived while they worked in the labs of high-flying contenders. Defections became the price that semcos paid for their success.

They were the price of failure too because talented scientists and engineers didn't need to cling to a company as it foundered. In Palo Alto, the Shockley Semiconductor Lab limped forward for a little while after the traitorous eight departed. An outfit called Clevite Transistor purchased it from Shockley in 1960. The doors closed for good in 1969. Shockley found residence as a senior don of science at Stanford University, the alma mater he'd left in 1932. He completed the sabotage of his own reputation with stunts like a run for the U.S. Senate as an advocate of controlled human breeding. Bill Shockley died from cancer in 1989. He had accomplished his life's work early, first by his semiconductor discoveries of the 1940s, then through the magnetism that pulled together the traitorous eight in '56 and '57. Technoscenti who encountered him even briefly while he lived remain awed to this day by his brilliance and sparkle.

The eight moved in at Fairchild just about when Jack Kilby was beginning his quest for life outside of Centralab. Kilby restricted his search to the semco powers. Fairchild at the moment was scarcely a hopeful whim. But the founders carried their zeal from Shockley Lab to their start-up. They also brought accumulated experience and a good many hunches about how to go about diffusing silicon to make transistors. Communicating at Shockley's with winks, nods, nudges, and wisecracks; huddling furtively behind vats and furnaces to whisper low-toned with excitement about sudden findings; smirking over their employer's latest outrage; comparing lab notes while sipping frosty beers at Dinah's Shack-up on the El Camino Real, the group had acquired conviction enough to support their bold resolve. Instead of running off individually to find separate jobs, the defectors stuck together because they believed they could accomplish the work that Bulldog had impeded.

None of the insurrectionists had much business experience. They were engineers and science dandies. They let Noyce take the lead because in addition to his keen analytical insight, Bob Noyce was a man of general abilities who seemed able to accomplish most anything he set his mind to. He was a natural leader anyway, charismatic, determined, strong-willed, confident, and wide-open generous.

Noyce finessed details with Fairchild Camera and Equipment, the company that put up the money to fund the new venture, covering its rent, payroll, attorney fees, office supplies, telephones, and all the rest of the pile-on expenses that bedevil a young company until it produces some goods it can sell. Fairchild Camera was an established East Coast firm from Syosset on Long Island. It made gear for aerial photography, selling most of it to the government. More important, Fairchild Camera was the creation of Sherman M. Fairchild, an inveterate inventor himself and also a financier who was accustomed to bankrolling ventures in obtuse new technologies. When the eight could find no other backers, Fairchild was willing to stick a toe into semiconductors.

Sherman Fairchild advanced the cash through the auspices of his Camera and Equipment company. Its collateral was the option to purchase the semiconductor operation outright, should Fairchild Semiconductor become successful. Each of the traitorous eight founders received ten percent ownership in the tenuous new venture, with the final twenty percent share going to Hayden, Stone & Company, the investment bank that had made the match with Fairchild. Eventually, Camera and Equipment would sink about $3.5 million into Fairchild Semiconductor. After twenty-four months, it would exercise its option, purchasing the operation outright.

But at the start, Fairchild Semiconductor ran on a shoestring. On October 2, 1957, Fairchild Camera Executive Vice President Richard Hodgson sent a $3,000 check to Noyce at his home on Lundy Lane in Los Altos, "as advance to you to cover necessary expenditures in setting up the semi-conductor operation until such time as the Corporation is formally organized." Hodgson reminded Noyce to save receipts so that Fairchild Camera could eventually get reimbursed the three grand front money. He offered the upstart "a sizable quantity of surplus shop equipment which you might be able to use." Young guys with families, the Fairchild founders worried over health insurance. Hodgson told Noyce they could likely latch into the group policy of Fairchild Camera. He'd get back with details.

At the beginning, the fledgling company belonged exclusively to the eight, and the group had definite ideas about the type of company they wanted to create. They wanted it to remain research-oriented, powered by ideas, energized by the boldness of its inquiries. They avoided government research contracts as a matter of deliberate policy. The founders had experience enough in the lab to recognize that they couldn't build the kind of company they wanted to build by accepting federal largesse. Just the opposite. Research for the government corrupted a company, enrolling it in a feast-and-famine cycle that left you at the beck of the funding agency, even when the agency's ideas turned daft.

"There were a lot of government contracts being thrown around," recalls Moore. "But their programs were what I call jumping through technological hoops. You know: can you make a transistor with these parameters? And you'd take a contract for a hundred thousand dollars and a year later you give 'em a transistor and they say, 'that's fine, now can you make one like this?' There was never any market behind the things. This was a business that was moving very, very rapidly, and you'd use your people inefficiently on contracts. You couldn't change directions, even though you might have two or three other, more appropriate avenues to pursue."

The founders preferred to keep Fairchild fast-moving and flexible, so it could chase promising opportunities as soon as they appeared and abandon its errors rather than wallow in them. Electro-tech encompassed the world to these young guys. They felt so excited by it, they felt so devoted to semiconductor innovation and ideas themselves, that they trusted that the right ideas wouldn't need any meddlesome assistance.

"We were really fairly naive in our business thinking in those days," says Moore. The organizing principle of Fairchild: "Build a better transistor and you'll find somebody who will buy it."

Thus infused with starry optimism, Fairchild Semiconductor Corporation opened shop in October 1957. It occupied a lackluster rented building on Charleston Street in Palo Alto when the town still was growing out of its rural doziness to become bona fide suburban. The company possessed little material means but a grand design: to make the diffused silicon that mad, brilliant Bill Shockley could not make. The entire new venture was based on uncertain technology in a field that wasn't very well established itself—although its newness was actually a benefit. Semiconductor technology was so raw, undetermined, and wide open that a bunch of youngsters with a good idea could easily enter and find room to play. The thoughts of the founders were Fairchild's only assets, along with their enthusiasm. The company's starting roster totaled thirteen people, five more than the Shockley deserters.

Jean Hoerni headed the physics section, which was a grander title than the position warranted because at the start he was also the only person in the physics section. While the new company was still in shipping crates, Hoerni went straight to work on the matter of refining the structure of transistors—in order to make them work more reliably—by sitting and thinking. Hoerni was the theoretician among the founders. That's Gordon Moore's polite way of saying that Hoerni liked to keep his hands clean.

"When we were setting up Fairchild initially, right after it was formed, we were all moving around diffusion furnaces and everything," he explains. "Jean was sitting at his desk just doodling."

At least that's how it looked to Moore and the rest. To vainglorious Hoerni, who held papers from not just one but two European universities, he was engaged in the nitty-gritty. "I became very interested in the final product of the company," he told an interviewer in 1986. "I said, well, if you're in industry, you'd better work on the product that the company is going to make, rather than stay as an academical expert."

Hoerni's specific concern was to find a way to keep finished transistors from short circuiting. It was tough enough just to make a diffused silicon semiconductor. It was excruciating just to diffuse only the right impurities into the flat disks of silicon in only the right concentrations to make the finished semiconductor behave the way you wanted it to behave. After subjecting wafers to the Kentucky smokehouse treatment, when finally you sawed them into the small flecks that would make separate transistors, only about a tenth of the devices worked. The other ninety percent were garbage.

But on top of that, out of that pitiful ten-percent yield—the process yielding only one working product out of every ten that it made—a lot of the finished transistors would short-circuit after they were assembled. Those became garbage too.

Assembly amounted to putting the semiconductor flakes in their little metal cans, like soup cans sized for a doll house. The silicon had to be wired as well, with three thin wires attached to each piece—one wire to deliver a current to the transistor, another to energize the transistor in a way that enabled it to control the current, and the third to collect and to carry the conditioned current from the device. The trio of wires sprawled out from the bottom of the cans like the legs of odd, metalloid insects. When the whole thing was assembled so that Fairchild could finally test it, a lot of the finished transistors failed because the small stray particles of dust trapped inside the cans stuck to the silicon and caused it to short out. Hoerni, doodling while his business partners hefted surplus lab equipment, wanted to come up with a way to insulate the silicon from the destructive stray bits of dust inside the cans.

One possibility was to use the oxide layer. That wasn't an original thought. Other researchers working elsewhere in semiconductors wondered about oxide too. Oxide is rust, created the same way rust forms on steel: by a reaction between the material and oxygen. A layer of oxide forms automatically on the surface of silicon, and at the time it was as undesirable as scale on steel and tarnish on silver. You had to remove it before diffusion, dissolving it away so that the impurities could seep into a silicon wafer. But the oxide layer was also an insulator: Electricity couldn't pass through it. Therefore, conceivably, a layer of oxide grown over a fully processed silicon semiconductor could shield it electrically from the particles that were causing Hoerni's troublesome short-circuits.

At least it was possible theoretically. The problem was getting the oxide to grow exactly the way you wanted it to grow, uniformly enough to provide a reliable barrier. Researchers at renowned Bell Laboratories, the birthplace of transistors, were trying to do just that at the same time Hoerni was doodling at his desk. Bell's interest alone was enough to scare away every other silicon experimenter: If the problem could be solved, Bell Labs would solve it, so there was no sense wasting your time. But Jean Hoerni thought differently.

"I always felt that Bell Labs, on the one hand, had obtained tremendous results," he explained. "But on the other one, there was no reason to believe they were going to be God forever." So Hoerni thought about silicon dioxide, and he doodled.

A transistor is monolithic—one piece of stone. But the chemical composition of the stone is not uniform through and through. It consists of different zones. The zones are created by diffusing different impurities into different sections of the silicon and by controlling the concentrations of the impurities. The work that goes on inside a solid transistor—the conditioning of electrical current—occurs at the junctions, which are the boundaries where one zone meets another.

In early diffused transistors, the zones were arranged in layers, like the parts of an Oreo cookie. Transistors had a base layer and a top layer, with a thinner middle layer sandwiched between. The pieces weren't physically separate. They were just chemical differences inside the material. The layered arrangement exposed the junctions on the thin sides of each flat little Oreo. Those thin sides were where the dust inside the cans stuck, shorting the junctions and debilitating the devices. But the oxide coating that could have insulated the junctions didn't adhere well to the sides. That was the nut that everyone was waiting for Bell Labs to crack—everyone except Hoerni.

Bell was trying to regrow the rust—the silicon dioxide—as a final step in transistor processing, after the zones had been created, just before the semiconductor was wired and put in a can. Hoerni essentially inverted that reasoning. Harness the insulating properties of the oxide first, he thought, before you turn the silicon into a transistor, by using the coating to control the location of the zones that will compose each transistor.

Usually the oxide was just stripped away to open the entire surface of a wafer for invasion by the impurities in the diffusion furnaces. But Hoerni figured you could remove just a small circle of oxide, leaving most of it on the surface of a wafer to block the impurities from infusing the silicon. That way, during diffusion, you'd create a separate zone only in one area, only where you'd removed the little circle of oxide, rather than across the whole wafer. Next you could reoxidize it, so the whole surface was insulated again. Then, Hoerni figured, he'd remove just a dot of the second oxide coating, exposing the center of the circular zone created by the first diffusion. Another diffusion produced the third zone he needed, in the spot where the dot had been removed. Thus, instead of three zones in a sandwich arrangement, top to bottom, he made three zones on the surface, level and nested one inside another. The transistor resided all on one plane, with the junctions all on the surface of the silicon flake, not on its sides. It was called a planar transistor.

With planar junctions, the flat top of a transistor could be easily insulated with a final growth of oxide. The insulation would stick tight to the plane. The design also made it a lot easier to connect the three wires to the device. You could attach them all to the top side.

Otherwise, Hoerni's planar transistors could be mass produced the way any diffused-junction transistors would be mass produced. You would lay out a bunch of them on a wafer of silicon, ranked and filed like the checks on a waffle (even though, at the time, the wafers measured only about three-quarters of an inch across). That way, you would make a whole batch of separate transistors in unison, sending the entire wafer through the tedious sequence of processing steps to steam in the impurities—although you would steam them only into the spots where the oxide coating had been removed, with one spot centered inside each waffle check that would later become a transistor. You would cut apart the checks and can them up to make separate transistors as a final step.

Meanwhile, Hoerni's teammates at Fairchild remained unaware of his work. The problems of silicon diffusion possessed them as they struggled to knead away the considerable kinks in their unyielding processes, desperate to make more than just one out of ten semiconductors that worked. To them, Hoerni's idea was nothing more than the aimless and infuriating doodles that had preoccupied him when they had set up the shop. Hoerni ran his planar experiments on the sly, at night, when he could get his hands on the evaporators, diffusion furnaces, vats, cauldrons, steamers, bubblers, flash booths, mashers, spinners, grinders, saws, and any other piece of mad-science lab gear the others used during the daylight hours. He built his first experimental planars as a bootleg project, without any piece of the research budget. "Lo and behold," he later boasted, "it worked basically the first time."

At the time, a transistor's final assessment came during the crudely effective tap test. You gingerly tapped the top of the can, then crossed your fingers and winced. The tap was meant to force the transistor to fail in the shop, if it was destined to fail, by dislodging any speck of dust that might later short out the junctions. When Hoerni showed his first planars to his colleagues at Fairchild, instead of a light tap with his finger, he whacked the cans with a hammer. "The transistors still worked," he later recounted. "That really impressed them."

☰ 3 ☰

First Contact

JEAN HOERNI DEMONSTRATED his first, lab-built planars right around the time Jack Kilby, marooned in the Dallas swelter, conceived of integrated silicon circuits. But at the time, Hoerni had no inkling toward integration. He figured his on-the-level transistors would be used the way all transistors were used in 1957 and 1958: as single, separate, and freestanding components. They would be attached by their three leggy wires to other separate transistors and to separate resistors and capacitors and the occasional odd diode, creating an electronic circuit for, say, a computer or maybe for some kind of measurement gear or a high-flying aviation gizmo.

But Fairchild made no immediate plans to begin manufacturing the nouveau transistors. In fact, when Hoerni first emerged vainly beaming after his solitary experiments to show off the design, no one at Fairchild—including Hoerni himself—had even a notion about how the company might turn planars into commercial products. No one knew how to mass produce them in quantities sufficient to sell to equipment makers. The newborn company had already taken teetering steps toward diffusing silicon in layers to make the Oreo-style transistors. The production equipment it had already purchased or, in some cases, built on its own couldn't perform all the steps that planar transistors would require. It couldn't etch away small circles of oxide in a waffle-board pattern upon a wafer, then diffuse impurities into those circles, then reoxidize the wafer so that its entire surface was insulated again, then etch little dots into the centers of the circles, aligning all the dots precisely so that they fell smack in the middle of the circles like little bull's-eyes, then diffuse the wafer again so that other impurities seeped in, doping the silicon at the etched-away dots inside each circle, then so on. The equipment could not master step after step of etching and diffusion and oxidation and a few others too; maintain precise and careful alignment of all the pieces through all the steps; and maintain all the exacting process controls on temperatures, pressures, chemical concentrations, and more. "We could no more make planar transistors than fly," says Gordon Moore, who at the time was in charge of manufacturing at Fairchild.

But they could see that the planar concept was indisputably brilliant, even if its timing was awkward. Therefore Fairchild took immediate measures to patent it. Even though the company couldn't use it right away, it moved to secure the design, tie it down, assert ownership. Protected by a patent, Fairchild could sit on Hoerni's bold invention while it focused all its energies and dedicated its scant resources to its original aim of making Oreos—technically they were called *double-diffused* silicon transistors. It would figure out on the fly where planar fit into its product portfolio. It would figure out how to make them when its small, overtaxed staff found a chance to draw a spare breath.

Robert Noyce got the job of compiling the patent application because Noyce directed the company's research and development. After they had set up Fairchild Semiconductor, after they had given Noyce the lead in negotiating terms with Fairchild Camera and Equipment and shouldering the early administrative burden, the eight had hired an experienced businessman named Ewart Baldwin to serve as general manager. That freed Noyce and the rest of the tech-savvy founders to play in the lab. Therefore when Hoerni's planar approach surfaced late in 1958, Noyce was the top manager no longer. He stuck exclusively to R&D.

The patent procedure was routine and straightforward. Fairchild's patent attorney, John Ralls, urged Noyce to write a broad patent, one that included other conceivable ways to use Hoerni's design. The planar structure was so innovative, so unprecedented, so outright revolutionary that it suggested new possibilities for transistors. If Noyce could codify some of those vague possibilities in advance and bundle them into the patent, Fairchild could eventually reap greater royalties. With a broad patent, not only would it be able to license the basic planar design to other semcos, but it would also have patent protection over variations it might later license as well. Thus, as the year 1959 began, Robert Noyce fixed his thoughts on planar transistors, contemplating permutations he might make upon Hoerni's innovation.

Destiny might have picked him for the job. If it did, it could not have made a better selection. Bob Noyce was brilliantly inventive. "Bob was a very creative guy," attests Gordon Moore. "Frustratingly so, because no matter what you were doing, he always had an idea that was so good you couldn't neglect it. He always had a lot more ideas than you could use."

Noyce was one of those rare individuals who combine an excess of scattered superlatives. He was exceedingly intelligent. He was an accomplished athlete—strength, power, grace, and energy were concentrated within his compact frame. He was congenial and charismatic. He was also unassuming, approachable, uncorrupted, and personable. Noyce was "quick to laugh," observed the interviewer Herbert Kleiman after he chatted two hours with the inventor in 1965. "Self-confidence is the epitome of Dr. Noyce," summed up Kleiman, who seemed outright awed by the man.

Noyce was born December 12, 1927, in Iowa, son of a Congregational minister. He graduated from Iowa's Grinnel College in 1949 and earned a Ph.D. in physics from MIT in 1953. Some say he was the brightest in a class of luminaries. His stint as research engineer at Philco lasted about two years. Then he skipped to the Shockley Semiconductor Lab. Then he set up Fairchild. Noyce died of a heart attack in July 1990 while swimming laps in the pool at his home in Austin, Texas. Today, a dozen years on, some people still line up to nominate him man of the year.

To author Tom Wolfe, whose hagiography "The Tinkerings of Robert Noyce" appeared in the December 1983 edition of *Esquire* magazine, Noyce represented a whole new ethic. He was the anti-East, an uncorrupted Midwestern kid who traveled to the far West to build what Wolfe called the new El Dorado, a land of legendary riches. Wolfe dismissed the whole Eastern power elite, businesses and universities especially, as feckless and ineffectual, crippled by a fawning self-regard that caused it to peer adoringly into its past rather than to look hopefully toward the future.

"In the 1940s," wrote Wolfe, "a bright youngster whose parents were not rich, such as Bob Noyce or his brother Donald, was far more likely to receive a superior education in Iowa than in Massachusetts. And if he was extremely bright, if he seemed to have the quality known as genius, he was infinitely more likely to go into engineering in Iowa, Illinois or Wisconsin, than anywhere in the East. Back east engineering was an unfashionable field. The east looked to Europe in matters of intellectual fashion, and in Europe the ancient aristocratic bias against manual labor lived on. Engineering was looked upon as nothing more than manual labor raised to the level of science . . . . This piece of European snobbery said that a scientist was lowering himself by going into commerce."

Noyce's spirit occupied the sensate universe, and to him divinity was not diminished by making things, like a wheel, which offered endless utility from a mere elemental form. He considered Hoerni's invention *aesthetic*. That was how Noyce conveyed that the design was self-contained and complete. It didn't need pasted-on, stopgap additions to remedy this little shortcoming or correct that little deficiency. A planar transistor was like an organic structure, built the way a transistor would be built if it grew naturally up from the soil. Its practical construction made the design easier to work with, with the transistor's vital junctions concentrated in one spot and accessible on the surface. Insulating oxide grew easily over the level plane. The entire transistor resided as a discrete, cleanly bordered device inside the silicon, rather than teetering like a cross-sectional slice from a hoagie.

In January 1959, Noyce called together his research staff to discuss the planar design. How else could we use this thing, they pondered. According to lore, during the meeting Noyce first saw with geometric clarity how the parts of transistors that had all of their features on the surface could be kind of pre-wired thin metal strips applied over the surface of the silicon. The metal pathways could approximate wires, but they'd be bonded to the surface, stuck down integrally on top of the silicon so that they became a part of the monolithic structure themselves. The insulating oxide layer on the top of the transistor—the same layer that protected it from stray dust particles— would prevent the metal pathways from touching the semiconductive zones of silicon beneath, so the metal would be insulated from the transistor at the same time that it was bonded to it. You could etch tiny points through that uppermost layer of oxide, aligning them precisely, so that the metal pathways flowed through the insulation to make contact only at the places you wanted them to touch the underlying transistors, thereby connecting to zones the way individual wires would connect to zones. But unlike wires, the pathways—the tiny metal strips—would be stuck fast to the silicon surface. They'd be part of the transistor itself, integral, built in during the same oxidizing and coating and masking and etching and bonding and all the other steps you were already using to make the device in the first place. To finish transistors, women on the production line wouldn't have to tediously solder wires to impossibly small, pinprick-sized connectors anymore.

And while you were at it, Noyce reasoned, why cut apart the transistors at all? You already made handfuls at once, all ranked and filed on a silicon wafer like the tread on a waffle. Because you were bonding tiny pathways on the top of individual transistors, why not run the integral metal stripes to the next transistor, and to the next one, and the next, and the next? Why not connect a bunch of transistors on one chip of silicon? The only trick then would be to isolate them somehow, one from the other so that the action of one transistor wouldn't bleed to the next. So that each little blinking transistor would keep its own place so that it would work singly, remain orderly and well controlled. But Noyce already had some ideas about how to isolate all those planar junctions. As certain as a block of geometry, he could see how he could use Hoerni's planar innovation to build an integrated circuit.

"So the elements of the idea for the IC are, one, the capability of running wires over the surface," Noyce later explained. "You couldn't do that with [a conventional transistor]. You had to have an insulator in there. Secondly, the idea of being able to cut things apart with junctions rather than physically cutting them apart. And then, obviously, just the realization that other circuit elements could be built into silicon—capacitors and resistors."

The idea of building those other circuit elements out of silicon had been Jack Kilby's starting point: If you can make them from the same material, then you can make them out of the same piece of that material. By the start of 1959, when Noyce and staff brainstormed his conception for integrating semiconductor circuits, Jack Kilby's parallel idea was already about six months old. Texas Instruments hadn't formally announced the concept, but the company had discussed it with some of the military researchers interested in miniaturization. Noyce may have heard whisperings. "I have kind of wondered in my own mind if Bob was aware of Kilby's work or not," says Moore. "But Bob saw how you could take the technology and make something that was remotely practical."

Noyce's concept for building whole circuits inside a single flake of silicon came from a fundamentally different direction. With the planar concept plunked in front of him, Noyce contemplated a radically new transistor type that invited integration. Grouping planar transistors was pat, simple. It was aesthetic. The idea was almost self-apparent. In fact, Hoerni hinted that the basic concept of integrating planar transistors was humming inside of Fairchild's research lab before Noyce codified it, officially making the entry in his laboratory notebook on January 23, 1959.

Jack Kilby did not have the planar advantage. Therefore his design lacked any adequate, inherent means to interconnect transistors and resistors and capacitors. His earliest concept remained vague about how to unite effectively those little devices once he'd fabricated them inside of a single semiconductor chip. Nevertheless, Kilby applied for a patent. Noyce did the same, independently, and a ten-year battle ensued over who really invented the IC.

The patent office and, eventually, the courts deliberated over issues ranging from the typical, like who got to the idea first (Kilby), to more arcane matters, such as whether specific terminology and illustrations in Kilby's application suggested interconnection enough to support legitimate integration. Eventually, late in 1969, Noyce won recognition for his deposited interconnection scheme. The following year, the Supreme Court refused to hear an appeal by Texas Instruments.

But the resolution was largely moot. Before the suit had even settled, Fairchild and TI worked out a royalty sharing arrangement in which both companies received payments from other semiconductor concerns that employed the integration concept to make silicon circuits. Neither Fairchild nor Texas Instruments held up development while the dispute crept toward a resolution. Rather than impeding the onward rush of circuit integration, the decade-long, Kilby-versus-Noyce patent wrangle caused only a distraction. Generally, informally, both Kilby and Noyce came to be regarded as coinventors of integrated circuits, even though they came to the invention separately. Yet among friends and allies, the dispute over absolute ownership of the idea simmered on. It raised so much rancor that some partisan supporters still stump for one man or the other, for Noyce or Kilby, eager to assure their guy's position in history by promoting him as the one true inventor of ICs.

In fact, historical circumstances encouraged the idea from both men. The competitive semiconductor business created those circumstances. Neither Noyce nor Kilby worked in isolation. Both had enrolled in the furious dash to reach ideas—the right ideas—before other racers reached them. Both were surrounded by the provoking, accumulating discoveries that the environment inspired.

Both Kilby and Noyce acknowledged antecedents that suggested their innovations. Kilby had the silk-screening process from Centralab. Noyce said his idea to top a chip with bonded metal pathways, replacing wires, came from a Fairchild research program called "expanded contact." The project sought to bond an aluminum film to Fairchild's silicon transistors, creating large contact areas so that women wielding tweezers and soldering points during final assembly steps would have an easier time attaching wires. His idea for isolating the separate transistors electrically on a chip, rather than physically—keeping the all-important junctions of one transistor clearly delineated from the next—recalled a concept just proposed by Kurt Lehovec, a Czech-born physicist working for the Sprague Electric Company.

Ideas were simply in the air. As early as 1952, at a gathering called the Electronics Components Symposium in Washington, D.C., the Englishman G. W. A. Dummer of the Royal Radar Establishment described his concept for compacting electronic circuits. It sounded an awful lot like the later ideas of both Kilby and Noyce.

The atmosphere in which the two men worked was charged, energized, and scintillated with hints, hunches, thoughts, theories, fragments, reports, gossip, threats, suspicions, and boasts. They came from all quarters. They came from coworkers, competitors, mutual customers, trade press reporters, conference speakers, and college professors. Kilby and Noyce operated in an inspired maelstrom. They existed in a competitive tumult.

"We were tremendously competitive people," explains Charles Sporck, the retired, long-reigning head of National Semiconductor. Sporck was a colleague of Noyce in the early, hurly-burly era of chip development. He worked for Noyce, joining Fairchild in 1959 as production manager, eventually advancing to executive VP and general manager before leaving to resuscitate a faltering company called National Semiconductor in 1967. "We'd read material like *Electronics News* to see who's doing what," Sporck says. "And there were always big arguments about whether this guy was really making a big mistake or whether he really had it made. The sales force would come in and say, 'God damn it, we just took an order away from TI,' and that was great stuff. After work we'd meet up at the Wagon Wheel, a bar up a block from Fairchild, and competitors would be in there and we'd all be bullshitting each other about what we were doing. It was like playing a football game."

☰ 4 ☰

Team Choices

FOOTBALL AND EVERY OTHER competitive endeavor differentiates losers as well as winners. Even with all the wide-open opportunities available in early semiconductors, with so much still undiscovered, contenders weren't assured success. They had to beat rivals who wanted to win just as badly.

Fairchild Semiconductor's early victories came from the exceptional qualities of its founders, beginning with Bob Noyce. For one thing, the team was intrepid, moving rapidly along paths that discoveries and innovations pointed to inexorably. Speed was essential because the technology advanced so quickly itself, pushed by so many jostling strivers trying out so many clever approaches to improve transistors. The companies with the better approaches trampled stragglers, arriving first at milestones and leaving very little room for latecomers.

But the bold resolve of Fairchild's leaders also worked alongside their peculiar brilliance for discovering and following just the best ways to improve their product. After all, daring, quick steps could be fatally foolish if they led a contender in a dead-end direction. With so many rivals trying out so many approaches and generating so many good ideas, a particular company's approach and ideas needed to be not just good but exceptional in order to rise above the competing rabble.

Still, even at Fairchild, the right choice was never clear until after the fact. Every idea seemed exceptional to its conceivers, especially when the idea was new and unsold, before impartial shoppers had an opportunity to select it or reject it. Thus, amid the fast-moving furor, even young Fairchild bumbled and nearly missed its shot to make semiconductor stardom.

As if to demonstrate the peril, the company's first business manager missed entirely because he jumped prematurely. He bet on a transistor-making method that appeared exceptional at the span of only a near horizon. His misjudgment made it pretty clear that Ewart M. Baldwin wasn't the business leader Fairchild's founders thought he would be when they hired him early in 1958, about six months after Fairchild had opened for business. The eight Shockley defectors had invited Baldwin to serve as their company's general manager, recruiting him from Hughes Semiconductor Division, the unit set up by Hughes Aircraft to make a run at the burgeoning semicon business. The eight took him as a concession to reigning business orthodoxy, which maintained that technology zealots should stay locked in the lab while a professional administrator addressed the non-technical aspects of corporate management—marketing, sales, purchasing, product distribution, and so on.

Baldwin thought that Fairchild had reached a technical end-point just one year after his arrival. Therefore when he defected from the company early in 1959, he took along its recipe book—the instructions on how to successfully make diffused-junction silicon transistors. Young, fragile Fairchild had just started making the products itself, an achievement no competitor had yet managed.

Baldwin also brought with him a group of eight other defectors from Fairchild. Together they set up Rheem Semi-conductor as a division of the Rheem Manufacturing Company, which made oil drums, furnaces, and water heaters. Semiconductors looked like a long stretch for the old-line industrial manufacturer. But the recipes tucked under Baldwin's arm appeared to give Rheem a sizable start over better-established companies.

But before the new semiconductor venture even found its legs, superior developments back at Fairchild threatened to make Rheem's up-to-the-minute, Oreo transistors—which were really Fairchild's up-to-the-minute, Oreo transistors—appear suddenly quaint. That threat could only materialize if Fairchild first made management steps to move the challenging concepts out of its research labs. Yet before it could make any kind of trenchant decisions, the company had to resolve its management crisis. Disillusioned by Baldwin's desertion, the team of Fairchild founders decided to stick this time with homegrown leadership. Naturally they picked Noyce. He became general manager of Fairchild Semiconductor just after he had conceived of integrated circuits early in 1959. Gordon Moore moved into Noyce's old job of R&D director.

The change placed Noyce forever outside the role of researcher. This doctor of physics from MIT, Bulldog's choice to run R&D at Shockley Lab, this coinventor of the integrated circuit (though at the time his creation was still a raw concept) suddenly became a businessman. His ascension seemed like another arrangement of destiny. Noyce moved back into the manager's office just as the outfit's first big make-or-break dilemma loomed. Fairchild at the time was still an unestablished company with only scant resources. Therefore it had to steer away from unproductive diversions that might exhaust those resources without bringing the company any tangible returns. The perplexing quandary confronting the new general manager and the rest of Fairchild early in 1959 concerned just how far it should pursue the serial inventions of proud Jean Hoerni and of Robert Noyce himself: unprecedented planar transistors and the integrated circuits they suggested.

At the moment no one could say with any authority whether the planar design would ever become practical on a commercial scale. In fact, outside of his first lab-crafted demonstration versions, Hoerni was finding it tough to produce planars according to a sustainable, repeatable manufacturing process.

Using prevailing processing methods, Fairchild laid out eighty transistors-to-be as a small grid on a silicon wafer that measured three-quarters of an inch across. After it endured all the pungent dousings and sweatings and burnishings that amounted to semiconductor processing, the little checkerboard was sawed into eighty pieces, with each individual fleck representing a separate transistor. During early experiments to make planar transistors, often only one out of each batch of eighty would work. By comparison, when making its standard double-diffused models, Fairchild produced about twenty good transistors from each batch of eighty. By the standards of the day, that twenty-five–percent success rate was pretty darn good.

After such an accomplishment, Fairchild certainly didn't need to risk ruin by pursuing uncertain fancies. The double-diffused silicon transistors it had just begun to ship to customers looked promising enough to catapult the company to a pinnacle of technical achievement. Certainly Ed Baldwin thought so when he ran off to stake his own new venture on the double-diffused approach. Therefore factions at Fairchild argued against the pursuit of planar. This wasn't the time to fuss around with an untested improbability, they protested. Fairchild was already mortally invested in double-diffused transistors, they said. It should make a run with its most promising product and forego the quixotic distraction that planars presented.

"That was actually a difficult problem for Fairchild," related Hoerni in an interview in 1986, "because Fairchild had at the time a monopoly on the so-called mesa transistors"—a term describing the layered, bumped-up shape of double-diffused Oreos. "Fairchild was doing very well," said Hoerni.

It had brought out its first commercial transistors late in 1958, a fast twelve months after the company's founding. That year the hopeful firm sold just $500,000 worth of the products. But in 1959—the year Noyce took over as general manager—its sales reached about $7 million, a fourteen-fold increase in one year. By then Fairchild employed more than 1,000 people, mostly women in prim white blouses working its assembly lines—the long rows of sturdy tables where the assemblers, seated, bent to peer through binocular microscopes at the small silicon specks they affixed with wires.

Fairchild had instantly become the industry's star producer of diffused silicon semiconductors. These were high-speed, premium transistors that sold at $18 apiece, the highest price in the business. Therefore they were supremely profitable despite the low production yields that still plagued semiconductor manufacturing. Virtually all of Fairchild's first transistors were used in computers—the big, lumbering computers that required thousands and thousands of the things. Within two short years from Fairchild's inception, its product was the envy of the industry, and other semcos raced to catch up. "Almost every transistor maker is rushing to produce the devices," reported *Business Week* in a March 26, 1960, special report. "More than 20 companies will include facilities to turn them out in new plants under construction or in advanced planning."

But no matter how noteworthy its technical achievement and how promising its early start, in 1959 Fairchild was still a small and tenuous company operating amid some sizable brutes. Looking over its shoulder, it saw Texas Instruments, which sold about $90 million worth of semiconductors annually. Both General Electric and the independent semco Transitron Electric Corporation, near Boston, sold more than $30 million in semiconductors a year. Other biggies, including RCA, Westinghouse, Hughes Aircraft, Philco, Sylvania, and Raytheon, were well-established companies. They possessed technical resources, cash, and suitable boardroom gravitas. Although none yet made diffused-junction silicon, they were swaggering confidently just off Fairchild's tail. Noyce later commented that if TI had moved into diffusion two years sooner than it did, Fairchild would have vanished.

Therefore to the anti-planar faction inside Fairchild, this hardly seemed the time to squander corporate resources on a daring and iffy new venture, especially with the company's prospects and performance in high-flying, double-diffused mesas improving all the time. "The management at the time had a difficult decision," Hoerni stated. "To the credit of Bob Noyce, he overruled the rest of his staff and said, 'we are going to make transistors this way.'"

Similarly, Noyce did not debate or dither for long over integrating circuits. "It was the next interesting thing to do," explains Gordon Moore. "There was enough interest from the military in small electronics. This made a lot of sense. It was kind of a logical step, and if other people couldn't see it right away, we thought that eventually they would."

The decisions came naturally. To Noyce and many of the other, eager young zealots working in Palo Alto, staying on the technical advance was their way to participate in the biggest, the most significant and exciting competitive scrum they had ever witnessed, involving a science that—as if it wasn't already interesting enough!—let them touch every breathtaking new gad that swirled in the world around them: space flight and satellites; cars tailing high, pointy fins; radios clamoring; computers fulminating; jets with throaty air scoops booming through the sound barrier. All of that and so much more was partly theirs as long as they made semiconductors.

Fairchild's top cadre, Noyce especially, also recognized that while entrepreneurial enthusiasm and competitive impulses advanced their art, it also improved their company's business prospects. To keep the corporation alive, they had to keep ahead of the next advance in the technology and the next one after that and the next one after that. They had to set the pace of the innovations. If they only kept up, other innovators would squeeze them out. Fairchild's most valuable assets were break-throughs and one-of-a-kind technologies that could pioneer whole new markets with new and better goods that other, big-ger, bullying companies didn't sell. Even after Fairchild grew large enough to achieve corporate security, Noyce worried over ways to keep the successful organization energized by the same sense of small-company urgency.

Thus the ideas of planar transistors and integrated circuits landed in a place that had not just the braininess to make some-thing out of them, but that also felt powerful incentives to do so. Those incentives were vital because a lot of patient, painstaking engineering still was required to turn the concepts into usable products.

Determined to see his idea succeed, Hoerni even moved his office from the laboratory to Fairchild's manufacturing section to make sure the production managers found solutions to all of the processing problems that held up his planars. Mostly that involved painstaking, excruciating attention to the manufactur-ing process. Production specialists had to discover the precise recipes for penetrating a series of changes into the silicon with unerring precision, to build up minute structures by sequen-tially layering chemical change upon chemical change, creating nested zones arrayed in perfect alignment within solid material. They had to develop equipment like laminar-flow hoods and fine-sieve filters just to keep out the ordinary dust that fouled the process. They had to learn photolithographic techniques that applied the etching methods of printmakers on an infini-tesimally smaller scale, shielding areas while exposing only microscopic spots to the chemical processes that affected the properties of the material. All told, Fairchild spent about two years translating Hoerni's planar concept into a salable product. The advertisement introducing the 2N1613 diffused silicon planar transistor announced "another Fairchild first," run in the April 22, 1960, issue of *Electronics* magazine.

Similarly with ICs, "there was just a heck of a lot to do to make structures like that," says Moore. For example, "junction isolation was non-trivial." Fairchild's perseverance paid off. Although Kilby had conceived of the concept six months ahead of Noyce, Fairchild officially beat Texas Instruments to market with the first practical microchips. It transferred integrated circuits out of the lab and into commercial production in April 1961, one year after the public introduction of planar transistors. Fairchild's first line of silicon microchips, trade named Micrologic devices, contained only eight transistors.

Of course, the race was far from finished—although nobody yet recognized what direction it would take or how far it would travel. These early ICs with their few transistors still stood a far distance from resembling any kind of computer on a chip. They were still just components, comprising only parts of circuits. To make useful equipment, you still had to gang a bunch together. Electronic gear, it was thought, would still consist of interwoven circuits assembled from big fistfuls of parts fastened with wires and tabs. There would be fewer parts for sure because integrated circuits would consolidate whole groups of transistors and resistors and capacitors. That was a big improvement alone, especially in exotic places like jets, missiles, satellites, and spacecraft where hard-working, complicated circuits also had to be compact.

By the time Fairchild brought out its first eight-transistor Micrologic chips in 1961, the company's business in discrete, nonintegrated electronic elements was bounding. It had added silicon diodes to its product list. It had opened a new plant up in San Rafael, north of the Golden Gate. It had added space to make more transistors near its new home on 545 Whisman Road in Mountainview, a bit further down the peninsula, where the company had taken larger quarters. Fairchild considered itself first and foremost a transistor maker. It also had high expectations for ICs, but no one imagined that these uncertain, solid amalgams were capable, once refined, of reordering human endeavors.

"After we got the first family of integrated circuits transferred into production," recollects Gordon Moore, "I assembled our senior people in the lab and said, okay, we've done integrated circuits. What will we do next? And we started looking for new phenomena that had different electronic properties and the like. I had no idea that we had just scratched the surface of something as important as this. It's amazing how naive I was."

☰ 5 ☰

Chipping Away

FAIRCHILD HAD WON the race to produce the first practical IC, but not by much. In fact, Texas Instruments had even started advertising the concept one year ahead of Fairchild's debut, with a March 1960 bleat in *BusinessWeek*. The ad screamed *one-hundred-to-one miniaturization* in banner type across the top of the page. It promoted what TI called its Type 502 Solid Circuit, described as a "semiconductor network" consisting of not quite a dozen elements inside a package one quarter inch long. One Solid Circuit, the ad read, could "realize such electronic functions as amplification, pulse formation, switching, attenuation, and rectification." But they were crude devices offered as curiosity pieces for $450 each. Their biggest shortcoming: They lacked the advantage of planar transistors. "People just bought one or two to see what it looked like," Kilby later explained. TI's first practical commercial microchips came out more than a year later, in August 1961, tailing Fairchild's by about four months. By that time, it had acquired the right to employ the planar approach from Fairchild. Using Jean Hoerni's technique to construct the chips, TI sold its Series 51 for less than $100 per integrated circuit.

But the price still seemed high to equipment makers who, after all, didn't need to buy ready-made circuits. Equipment makers already specialized in circuit construction, and for that reason they felt powerful incentives to reject the new consolidated circuits-on-a-chip. Circuit building was their turf. The honor belonged to them, and their skilled, specialized circuit designers weren't about to accept substitutes made by the mere semiconductor manufacturers who sold them transistors. Thus equipment companies and the circuit designers they employed greeted the first microchips with jeering skepticism and even disdain.

Fairchild, Texas Instruments, and the other semcos that soon joined the crusade found the technical delicacies of their new microchips challenging enough. Now they faced a second daunting obstacle in the early resistance the idea encountered. As they struggled against finicky, unyielding manufacturing processes, they also fought a marketing battle, searching for places where they could prove their products' worth as they endeavored ever so desperately to sell them.

Jack Kilby and his colleague Harvey Cragon experienced the rancor personally when they presented the concept at a technical meeting not long after the first microchips had reached the market. The assembly turned so raucous that if people had brought rotten fruit to throw, they might have let loose with a battered apple or maybe a festering peach. Kilby has hands that can deflect missiles. But Harvey Cragon is not a large man. There's no telling how he might have withstood an attack of overripe edibles.

Kilby and Cragon were two of the early emissaries sent out by Texas Instruments to sell the idea of integrated circuits. They were speaking to about two dozen engineers and university know-alls at a workshop in Seattle in 1962. The city was also hosting a world's fair that year, a whiz and wonder event titled the Century 21 Exposition. Its most enduring feature was the Space Needle, Seattle's 607-foot alien saucer stuck up on gandy legs. But the exposition also attempted a serious celebration of science. NASA displayed the funnel-shaped Mercury capsule that had cradled John Glenn for three perilous spins around the Earth on February 20, 1962, just 60 days before the fair opened. Sperry Rand brought one of its million-dollar UNIVAC computers, imperiously occupying a ten-by-ten pad and programmed to spit out excerpts from literature. World-of-tomorrow technologies on display included a direct-dial telephone system—no more Thelma-Lou operators connecting callers by poking cords at switchboards.

But the irate conference-goers confronting Cragon and Kilby hadn't come to Seattle for razzle-dazzle alone. These guys were plotting the very high-watt future that the nearby exposition promised. They'd come to a technical meeting to hone the circuit-making skills they needed to deliver it. They sought newer, better ways to knit together transistors, resistors, capacitors, and even some vacuum tubes. ICs had been available for scarcely a year. The technology was still so new that Kilby, the guy who invented it, was out making the pitch. A lot of the circuit builders who perched on meeting-room chairs were hearing about it for the first time. The concept didn't impress this audience. Cragon remembers the small crowd all but hooting him from the podium, shouting "get out of here, you idiot. That can't be the way the world is going to go."

Meanwhile, at Fairchild Gordon Moore heard people dismiss microchips with the certainty of irrefutable math. It was already tough enough for semiconductor companies to make even one transistor that worked, they mocked. Now they wanted to integrate a handful of them prearranged as a circuit? Because at least one of the eight transistors on Fairchild's early Micrologic chips were bound to fail, critics chided that only 0.1^8 percent of the ICs would work. That amounted to one good chip out of every ten million or so produced, "which meant you couldn't make 'em at all," says Moore. "When we tried to sell these things, we did not run into a receptive audience."

The small-scale integration available in the first microchips from Fairchild and Texas Instruments scarcely changed the piece-by-piece, transistor-by-transistor approach to circuit building that equipment makers already knew well. Still, people found reasons to dislike them because even these early, inadequate, low-density ICs bucked the conforming order and violated its comfortably established practices.

Electronic equipment makers already employed armies of people trained and oiled to assemble from scattered components radios and record players, computers, controllers, clocks and digital counters, guidance gear, probers, sequencers, and all such manner of devices. Circuit designers labored as a proud professional class, striving to select just the right variety of transistor, resistor, diode, tube, and capacitor. They strained to group them in just the right combination, to order them carefully in just the right sequence, in order to make gizmos that were less expensive, more efficient, slicker, more clever, more elegant, better functioning, and more profound than the competing gizmos made by other companies. Gordon Moore ran into one aeronautics firm that used something like sixteen different configurations of commonplace circuits called flip-flops in the gear it made. Each flip-flop configuration was deemed so important that it had a separate circuit designer assigned to shepherd and refine it. So much for buying flip-flops preconfigured and ready to use inside a silicon chip.

What's more, to assure that their products would work as designed, electronics companies qualified every component they used. Test specialists tortured every piece rigorously to see how consistently a particular transistor stood up to the wear and tear of everyday use or maybe to find the temperature at which one brand of resistor wandered out of its operating range. Now, suddenly, suppliers that made nothing more than transistors were knocking and saying, *Here, use these little chips instead. They contain a bunch of transistors already clustered together. They contain some resistors and capacitors too. See, they look like miniature dominoes, except that they have these bent metal tabs sticking out the sides like caterpillar legs. All you have to do is solder the legs onto your circuit boards instead of soldering on all the three-prong wire connectors for the dozen or so transistors each little chip replaces.*

But what could a company's test engineers do with ICs? They couldn't even see the individual components. They had no way to examine them. If they used parts that they couldn't probe and measure, how could they know with confidence how their finished circuits would perform?

And so what if the chips contained built-in resistors and capacitors. Everyone knew that silicon semiconductors made lousy resistors and lousy capacitors. Why patch together circuits out of these matte, miniature dominoes with their metal crab legs when they contained crummy resistors and crummy capacitors? Why not just use the real things?

"We old designers that did discrete-components design just found it difficult to understand the integrated circuit," recounts Rex Fritts, an electrical engineer who started designing equipment in 1959 for Collins Radio in Cedar Rapids, Iowa. Back then Fritts used separate transistors and even some vacuum tubes to lay out the workings for aircraft navigation and communication gear. "You always tended to want to see the circuit inside the integrated circuit so you could understand what was goin' on," he explains. "We didn't just want to do current in and current out, you know. We wanted to design the whole thing. We were more familiar with the whole thing."

It didn't help that the semcos had to sell their new concept to the circuit designers themselves. But it was the designers, and their managers especially, who most often specified which components a company would buy to include in their piece-by-piece equipment layouts. Microchips, as ready-made circuits themselves—or at least, at this stage, ready-made parts of circuits—threatened their livelihoods. They threatened whole fiefdoms inside the equipment companies, where managers reigned indomitably over component testers and specifiers, circuit-design engineers, and populous subcastes of technicians involved in designing electronic products.

They had an excuse to ignore them too. Early ICs were expensive. They were brand new, after all, and therefore their makers had to charge higher prices to recover their investments in research and to pay for all the new plant equipment they bought to make the products. What's more, with no demand yet for microchips, both Fairchild and TI had a long way to go to reach anything approaching the coveted economies of scale that would help them drive down their prices. For that to happen, the companies needed to sell vast numbers of chips, enough to keep their production lines operating at furious, round-the-clock rates. Exercising economies of scale, a company could lower the price it charged per piece but still make enough to cover its research and manufacturing investments by selling many, many pieces. Of course, the lower prices would encourage even more sales, which would require more products from the production equipment, which would reduce the cost per piece even more, thereby spiraling the cycle upward: greater consumption, lower prices, yet more consumption, prices going lower still, encouraging more consumption.

But when the first products appeared to upset the electronic status quo at the start of the 1960s, the microchip market—or rather, the potential market—looked a long way from supporting any kind of manufacturing economies.

The most that chip advocates had going for them was the Cold War. In the United States, the military standoff created acute demand for any technology that could make weapons more capable than the brutish clubs the Soviets waved.

The Cold War was a cultural event of the 1950s, permeating the thoughts and influencing the actions of just about everybody who lived in the United States. Its start in 1953 coincided with the cessation of combat in Korea, leaving the stalemate that divided that country north and south along the ideological lines that delineated the war's two main combatants: the democratic, each-to-his-own Yanks versus the communist central planners who owned everything and promised to distribute their bounty equitably. Latent fears became tangible with the orchestrated ascension of Nikita Khrushchev as Soviet premier. His rise began with the death of Joseph Stalin in March 1953. Gap-toothed, potato-faced, and bellicose, Khrushchev preached peaceful coexistence with capitalist democracies while he turned Soviet guns on students protesting for freedom in Budapest in 1956. In September 1960 he took off his shoe to gavel its heel at the United Nations in New York, shouting that he would conquer the West. He started sneaking nuclear weapons into Cuba that year. In 1962 he ordered the slaughter of picketing workers in Russia's own Novocherkassk. America's Cold War weapons programs were well financed from the fear people felt.

They expected the Red Menace to strike from aircraft and spacecraft. Therefore weaponry went high-tech to counter the hidden, high-altitude threats. Gradually, a growing sense of security sustained the electronic progress that engendered it. After a March 1960 exhibition by the IRE, the Institute of Radio Engineers, the trade magazine *Electronics* beamed that "the so-called missile gap . . . may have been a blessing in disguise. The reason: Lack of high-thrust rockets as the space era began forced rapid microminiaturization to make the best of the limited propulsion capability available." As a consequence, the report read, "the Soviet advantage could be nullified by the sheer volume of instruments in later U.S. boosters."

The same microminiaturization had been the stimulus that had delivered Kilby to Dallas in 1958. He had conceived of integrated circuits as TI's entrée into the debate. Of course, even by then each military branch had ventured well into its own fevered quest for a microelectronic technology, with the Army developing its Lego-like micro-modules, the Air Force straining to discover obscure molecular electronics, and the Navy boosting a concept just as arcane. Silicon microchips didn't match any of them. But just the same, with the military so eagerly embracing micro concepts, TI had immediately approached the Army, Navy, and Air Force, before its commercial ICs were even available, begging for dollars to support further development of Jack Kilby's innovation. The move turned out to be a good one because—more than the money it placed in the pockets of Texas Instruments—it ended up stamping the concept with the imprimatur of an institution that wielded considerable muscle in electronics.

Not that the sale had been easy. TI's tirelessly ambitions president, Patrick Haggerty, first pitched the idea to the Army and Navy in November and December 1958, just two months after Kilby had first tested his hand-carved lab chips on September 12. Haggerty was an ace of a salesman who transferred enthusiasm like a contagion. But the Army and Navy had turned him away. Jack Kilby and Willis Adcock, TI's semiconductor R&D chief, together called on the Air Force in early December that year. The airmen bought the idea.

An integrated circuit wasn't quite what the branch had in mind, but it also wasn't too far a departure from molecular electronics. The molec-elec concept was so vaguely defined that the Air Force never adequately explained exactly what it was after anyway—although old-guard Westinghouse, the idea's biggest advocate, merrily pocketed a lot of funding for hook-or-crook research to make something, anything, that was molecularly electronic. "Their existence theorem was a quartz crystal, which acted like an inductor and a capacitor without being either of them," explains Kilby. Because quartz worked as a radio tuner, the theory went, other materials could be invented or discovered that would inherently perform electronic or electronic-like operations, without any of the separate pieces that made up an ordinary electronic circuit.

At least Kilby's new integrated circuit was made from silicon crystal. And it came as a single piece besides. But it was still a circuit. It didn't replace transistors and their supporting components through some alchemy involving molecular makeup, which seemed to be what the Air Force sought. In fact, an integrated circuit still contained all the conventional circuit devices. Transistors, resistors, diodes, and capacitors still existed as structures within each little chip. But they were integrated: The chip remained a solid, diminutive speck.

That was close enough for Richard Alberts. He was a civilian administrator working in the molec-elec program at Wright Field, a sprawling research complex run by the Air Force at Wright-Patterson Air Force Base in Dayton, Ohio—an auspiciously fitting spot to inaugurate integrated circuits publicly. Both Wright Field and the encompassing Wright-Patterson base were named for Orville and Wilbur, Dayton's most famous sons. The air base had grown up around Huffman Prairie Flying Field, where the brothers had repaired for aerial experiments in 1904, right after they had pioneered powered flight at Kill Devil Hills, five miles south of Kitty Hawk, North Carolina. At Huffman Prairie in 1905 the Wrights launched Flyer III, considered the world's first practical plane. It could turn figure eights. The U.S. military moved to the site permanently in 1917, establishing a flight school for young dashers shipping to Europe to fight the kaiser. During World War II, Wright Field led radar and communications development for the Army Air Corps. It remained the service's center of avionics experimentation, including the quixotic inquiries into molecular phenomena.

Alberts backed TI's solid-circuit concept even though he recognized that it was not the same as the Air Force's hazy notion of molecular electronics. He finagled a $1.5 million contract for TI in June 1959 to further develop the devices. The Texas-bred business starlet received a follow-up contract in January 1961, granting it $2.8 million. In return, TI had eighteen months to build a pilot production line that could turn out 500 integrated circuits daily for at least ten consecutive days. Also, TI had nine months to build a computer made entirely from its circuit consolidating chips. That gave it only until the start of autumn 1961. The Air Force wanted some early evidence that the things could be put to productive work. The job of building the 500-chip fabrication line fell to Jack Kilby at the Semiconductor Components Division. Harvey Cragon got the computer-building assignment, which would make him the first person actually to make something useful from integrated circuits.

Cragon was an engineer in TI's Equipment Division, which handled mostly government jobs, making products like large-scale surveillance radar and small-scale radar probes to pack aboard planes. The group also made gear for rockets, like an electronic launch timer that sent out the signals setting up a craft's takeoff. The equipment had to be small.

Thus Harvey Cragon was a Cold War equipment designer, the class of engineer who would have to embrace microchips eventually by building them into the products he made, if the devices were ever going to go anyplace. Of course, Cragon already worked for Texas Instruments, a company that in 1959 not only had an inside track on the technology but that was also its loud-shouting advocate. Still, as a designer in TI's equipment-building branch, he was archetypal of the electronicists who had to pick up the next phase of the silicon transformation by putting microchips to work. He was from the class of electronic engineers who saw the gadgets first, at the same time that the group found itself newly empowered to make weapons to fight the Cold War.

Before the Cold War, in 1950 when Cragon graduated as an electrical engineer from the Louisiana Polytechnic Institute in Ruston, Louisiana, his professional prospects had been dismal. Electronic research and development had gone latent after World War II. Accordingly, Cragon's first job was to route telephone lines for the New Orleans phone company.

But in 1953, after he returned from a two-year stint in a tank battalion during the Korean War, Cragon found that the stand-off between the U.S. and the Soviets had encouraged a resurgence in electronics research. He took a job as a junior design engineer for the Hughes Aircraft Company in Los Angeles. His team built fire-control computers for jet fighters: Radar aboard a plane locked it onto an enemy bomber, steering the craft to keep it on target while it launched missiles to intercept the intruder. The system used vacuum tubes that were as thick as a pencil and as long as a pinkie—miniature by the prevailing standard.

From there he moved east to Tullahoma, Tennessee, where the Arnold Engineering Development Center of the U.S. Air Force performed flight simulations inside cavernous wind tunnels, testing both aircraft and spacecraft. Cragon designed improvements to the big 1950s-flavor computers that drew conclusions from the tests performed in Arnold's gaping caves. Finally, in late 1958, at age twenty-nine, Cragon moved to Dallas to design equipment for Texas Instruments. He arrived about two months after Jack Kilby had demonstrated his first solid circuits in the North Dallas lab.

The assignment to build the first microchip-powered computer should warrant him at least a footnote in history. Using ICs and ICs alone, Cragon made the thinking machine smaller than any of his contemporary computer-circuit designers could have imagined. Assisted by another engineer, Joe Watson, and a few lab technicians, he hand-built the machine, carefully connecting three hundred delicate, specially encased crude early microchips. The team paid no heed to real-world concerns such as how such an implement might be manufactured in large numbers. They didn't have to. Cragon's 1961 Air Force computer was a one-of-a-kind demonstration. "It was a tour de force that was made to impress people," he explains.

As the world's first computer made from integrated circuits, it was a marvel of compression. In an era when computers were unapproachably complex and most often so large they filled rooms, Cragon's synthetic thinker was about the size of a transistor radio. Its three hundred integrated circuits were stacked sardine-style in columns ten high, with the columns shoehorned five deep and six across into a black metal case. They were simple, first-of-the-genus ICs, each containing only a handful of capacitors, resistors, and transistors. The computer was programmed to perform simple math: addition, subtraction, multiplication. You would tap in a problem using mechanical keys and watch the answer flip up behind a small glass window on the so-called Manual Control Unit—a box that looked to all the world like a chunky cash register, standing separate from the trim, slim computer and more than fifty times larger.

The control box was just a translator. The magic occurred inside the small computer. The only other machine that could do math then—aside from a gargantuan computer—was a weighty, mechanical accountant's adder that was packed densely with intermeshed gears, pinions, rods, and levers, all intricately cut, balanced, and assembled. Cragon's tiny computer contained no moving parts. It used electronic pulses alone, manipulating them to perform rigidly structured logic. The pulses represented binary numbers, the long, incomprehensible strings of ones and zeros arrayed in sequences that computers read as present or absent, on or off, go or no go. The binaries match the two possible states of transistors: on or off, pass or don't pass, go or don't go. Thus Cragon's computer, like computers today, handed off each pulse to transistors arrayed as gates or switches, which flicked on or flicked off according to the internal logic of the machine in order to send the pulsing current to another switch. That switch would pass it on to another or maybe block it in order to direct the current down a different path to a different switch, which would in turn send the pulse this way or that, and so on until a conclusion was reached with alacrity approaching the speed of light.

The computer gave off only heat as evidence that its little chips passed data—although it gave off plenty of that. Cragon instructed his workbench technicians to bolt it to the center of a big aluminum plate one-quarter-inch thick, meant to radiate away heat so the machine wouldn't cook. The showpiece needed a display panel anyway. Therefore the plate bore the lettering: Experimental Molecular Electronic Computer.

TI stuck with the molecular electronics name for a few years to come, in obsequious homage for the Air Force contracts it took. The Air Force and Westinghouse used the term even longer, at least through 1965. But no matter what name was attached to them, integrated circuits were launched with Cragon's computer. The machine made a triumphal tour, accompanied by Haggerty and Kilby, Cragon, and other TI emissaries, including Charlie Phipps and the engineer Joe Watson. They went to Wright Field first, in tribute. Next they traveled to Washington, D.C. Last they visited Los Angeles. The itinerary brought the computer only to military men and to the electronics firms that made gear for them.

But the idea was out, legitimated inside a working machine, waved under the noses of scientists, engineers, and technicians—the sort of circuit creators who might be the first to employ it. Still, their initial resistance was fierce—with circuit builders riled enough to roust Cragon and Kilby from a dais in Seattle in 1962—because microchips just didn't mesh with their established ways of working. Winning their embrace of ICs clearly would require more than whistle-stop tours by curiosity-piece computers and more than magazine ads and all the other standard issue of marketing and promotional campaigns. To popularize their new product, the chipsters needed to place them in critical roles that would demonstrate dramatically that silicon chips were something more than just the sum of their transistors and a few other parts. They needed to show that equipment made with integrated circuits could outperform the piecemeal assemblies of established methods. Such demonstrations began to accrue as microchips found uses where necessity dictated—in applications where chips and chips alone would work.

Shortly after Cragon returned from the molec-elec tour, space explorer Dr. James Van Allen called in Dallas, shopping for a special-order instrument that could measure radiation encircling the Earth. Earlier, on January 31, 1958, Van Allen had launched a craft he called Explorer aboard a Redstone rocket to probe the ether beyond the atmosphere. But the belts of atomic energy he discovered—today they bear his name, the Van Allen Belts—were so loaded with radiation that the conventional instruments aboard Explorer I could not measure it. Using integrated circuits, packaging them densely the way he had packaged them for the molecular electronic computer, Cragon made a small, compact instrument that withstood the rigors of launch and the extremes of space flight while it counted the radiation that had saturated Van Allen's earlier equipment.

As jobs dribbled in, the microchip makers honed their manufacturing abilities. In mid-1962, Texas Instruments began a six-month program to make ICs for Autonetics, a division of North American Aviation that was building a gadget named the D37B guidance and control computer for Minuteman missiles. During the 180-day program span, TI created eighteen new configurations of integrated circuits, containing anywhere from twelve to forty components arranged in layouts that hadn't been rendered into solid silicon before. Kilby calls such programs "stressful" because to make the chips, TI had to improve its chip-making processes on the fly. It had to finish the order with better manufacturing processes than it started with.

Meanwhile, significant orders began to arrive in support of more significant programs, like the buildup of Minuteman missiles. Beginning around 1963, both TI and Fairchild sold chips for use in the Minuteman II series. As an intercontinental ballistic missile (ICBM), Minuteman had to launch into outer space, soar part way around the planet, then drop onto a pre-determined rooftop. Its electronic guidance and control systems were made to put it on course and to keep it there. The second-generation Minuteman II packed aboard more electronics than its predecessors, like jammers and such to help it penetrate radar sites and antiballistic defenses. The sophistication of U.S. electronics ended up making missiles so capable that when the United States and the Soviet Union got around to negotiating arms limits in 1972, the Soviet's got 1,618 ICBM missiles compared to America's 1,054. The United States could make do with fewer because the microelectronics in its Minutemen simply made them more accurate.

Fairchild also supplied ICs for equipment used in the Apollo moon program, which started in 1963. NASA boasted that the lunar probe's navigation computer, built with silicon chips, was so reliable that the craft would not carry a redundant backup. Earlier spacemen had brought along two computers in case something in the first one jiggled loose.

As their processing abilities improved, as acceptance by high-profile programs like Apollo and Minuteman kicked the new solid circuits toward legitimacy, the IC makers pushed relentlessly to place their products in broader markets. At the start of 1965, for example, a Fairchild advertisement promised a $550 Scott hi-fi stereo amplifier (built with Fairchild's planar transistors, the ad noted) to the engineer who came up with the best new use for its model A702 Operational Amplifier integrated circuit. Any application in space and defense, commercial, or industrial equipment was eligible.

While other semiconductor companies joined Fairchild and TI in making microchips, equipment companies began to catch on to ways to use the devices. On May 3, 1965, *Electronics* magazine reported that Scientific Data Systems, a computer maker, had made history by placing the world's first million-dollar order for integrated circuits. Its model SDS 92 would be the first commercial computer to use microchips in its logic circuits, and Scientific Data was developing a computer that would employ ICs exclusively—not intermixed with other parts—for logic processing. Fairchild supplied the chips.

On June 14, *Electronics* reported that Honeywell was setting up a solid-state design center in Minneapolis. The facility would unite all of its integrated circuit specialists for speedier conversion to ICs in Honeywell's computers.

Nuclear-Chicago Corporation announced that its scintillation-counting system—used to measure radiation—would be "one of the first large instruments to be made commercially with integrated circuits." Inside the machine, 350 ICs from Signetics Corporation would replace the 6,000 separate transistors found in an earlier model. Because the new product would cost the company less to assemble, Nuclear-Chicago planned to use the savings to pack more features into the device. Its new chip-powered scintillator would include the data calculator and the printer built right into the instrument. Before ICs, they had been extra-cost options.

Westinghouse Electric revealed that its new Model 20 numerical controller would be the first factory controller to use microchips. Introduced in September 1965, Model 20 sold for half the price, at $5,000, and used one-sixth the number of electronic components than an earlier pre-IC model.

As the technology made such gains, the semcos rushing into ICs awaited a bounteous payoff from the growing demand. A 1965 survey of microchip makers showed abundant optimism. Collectively they expected to sell $60 million worth of their gadgets that year, almost twice the amount they had sold in 1964. By 1968, the semcos guessed, equipment makers would take more than $150 million worth of ICs.

But the encouraging demand still wasn't enough to support every hopeful. Therefore in 1965 only a few microchip makers were profiting. Raytheon did okay, and Fairchild and TI together accounted for about seventy percent of all microchips sold. But small-fry like Micro-Electronics Corporation and Molectro Corporation found themselves begging for funds just to stay afloat until the anticipated bonanza arrived.

Steep prices for silicon chips still held back a lot of buyers. "Although the price for integrated circuits seems to be low enough for the military," reported *Electronics* on January 11, 1965, "it's still too expensive for most industrial customers."

Therefore there must have been at least a measure of desperation behind Bob Noyce's decision at Fairchild to cut prices below the bare bones. "He told them he would sell them the integrated circuit for less than they could buy the individual components to build it themselves—which was far below our cost for building them," relates Gordon Moore. "He said, 'look, use these. It's cheaper.' That got the interest of people who previously were pushing these things aside."

Take a loss at first, the reasoning went. By stimulating demand, the lower prices would enable Fairchild to crank up manufacturing, thereby approaching an economy of scale, profiting by high volume rather than by high prices. But according to Moore, the greater strength of the decision was the long-term and lasting precedent it set for the chip industry at large. Noyce established that microchips would compete on the basis of price, appealing to mass markets in which semcos could place vast quantities of the products.

"That thinking permeated our industry," says Moore. "It's become the one driving factor that is really different about this business. The standard solution to any problem has been to lower the price. The net result is that we've never seen another industry where the cost of the product has gone down this much. If the industry had gone the other way and tried to charge per transistor or something, and held the price up— which would have been a natural way to think about it—this progress wouldn't have happened."

But through the first half of the 1960s, after Harvey Cragon had led circuit builders to accept the little wonders, no sort of pervasive mass market loomed. ICs certainly had advanced, but they still remained stuck in special-interest obscurity. Scintillation counters were never going to amount to a commercial bonanza.

But the ambitious and inspired technologues hustling the products hadn't spoken their last. Patrick Haggerty, for one, irrepressible as president of far-bounding Texas Instruments, wasn't about to let his sales calls to the military stand as his last attempt to pitch ICs. Therefore in 1965 he launched a grand effort not just to use microchips but to popularize them.

☰ 6 ☰

Calculated Gains

PATRICK HAGGERTY WANTED to use microchips to make a pocket calculator. At the time, in 1965, the idea was unprecedented. Calculators were not mass-market products, and they certainly weren't portable. They were bulky business tools used by book-keepers and accountants, auditors, actuaries, scientists, mathematicians, engineers, and any other professional who mashed numbers. They were still mostly mechanical. Some had motors like electric typewriters to provide a little power assist, and a couple of cutting-edge models used transistors.

But for the most part calculators were awkward contraptions: big, heavy boxes that sat upright on a desk and accomplished addition and subtraction through the gnashings of intricately intermeshed gears and levers. To multiply, these pre-electronic machines repetitively added. To divide, they repetitively subtracted. You could spend $5,000 to buy one from one of the entrenched and established patriarchs who controlled the field. Status attached to brand names like Friden and Marchant—companies that had learned through decades of experience how to build the machines reliably and efficiently.

As early as 1939, the Marchant Company had crowed that it could stamp out the intricate metal gears that drove its mechanical adders for a mere penny per gear. A single machine contained a thousand of them. Its manufacturing had grown as precise as a watchmaker's.

But Haggerty had a knack for dreaming up new, transformational products that subverted the status quo. He saw them as mechanisms for popularizing the semiconductors upon which his company was building its future. He thought a portable calculator—a slick bit of moon-launch technology that any ol' person could own, could hold in his or her hand, and set conspicuously on his or her desk blotter—might create a big new market for the microchips TI felt so eager to sell. It didn't matter to Haggerty that the technical means to create such a calculator did not yet exist. The concept was seductively compelling for its promise alone.

Besides, ideas shook out of Haggerty like nervous shudders, flung from the turbulent commixture of his wide-ranging intelligence and his restless energy. Haggerty is remembered as a technical visionary. He was also an accomplished executive. Both technology and management acumen provided the means to sate his ample ambition.

"This was a period when TI was considered a model company, written up in every business journal in the country every month or so," recollects Jack Kilby. "He had a lot of attention. I think he enjoyed it. He also saw new technology as a way to grow the company, which was the reason for being in the first place."

Haggerty had joined TI after serving apprenticeships that had only hinted at how far his ebullient ambition could carry him. Born in 1914 in Harvey, North Dakota, Haggerty learned electrical engineering at Marquette University in Milwaukee. While a student, he learned business management by working a co-op job at Milwaukee's Badger Carton Company, a box maker. He became a production manager at Badger in 1936 after graduating from Marquette. A year later, Haggerty was running the company's engineering, manufacturing, and administrative operations. He left to join the war effort in 1942. As an officer at the Navy's Bureau of Aeronautics in Washington, the irrepressible young Haggerty evaluated and purchased airborne electronic equipment for the service.

There he encountered Texas Instruments (at the time it was called Geophysical Service Incorporated), which had come to the capital to sell equipment for finding enemy subs. Haggerty joined the company after the war, in November 1945. He started as general manager of its Laboratory and Manufacturing Division, the operation that had grown out of TI's experience building scientific instruments. He became executive vice president of Texas Instruments in 1951. He served as president from 1958 to 1966 and as chairman of the board from 1958 until his retirement in 1976. Haggerty died of cancer on October 1, 1980.

His notion in 1965 to make a portable calculator was a reprieve of the Regency transistor radio from one decade before. Regency was the world's first fully transistorized, portable radio, and it had represented a crowning achievement for Pat Haggerty.

He was executive vice president at TI when he launched the Regency program in 1953. At the time, transistors were still new enough to attract suspicion. They were still unexplored and largely unknown beyond tech-initiates. To change that, Haggerty directed TI engineers to design a little radio. Their creation operated on four germanium transistors, powered by a battery that hid inconspicuously inside its case. It measured only five inches tall by three inches wide by one and a quarter inches thick. With the design in hand, Haggerty went shopping for a business partner: a radio maker that would manufacture and market the diminutive tuner, using transistors supplied by TI.

But the format—pocket-size, with untethered portability from a self-contained battery—seemed daft to the people who built consumer appliances in the mid-1950s. General Electric, Sylvania, and some other reigning monarchs of radio manufacturing flatly rejected it. They scoffed. Transistors were tiny all right. And sure, they sipped so little power that you could energize them with only a small, hidden battery. But the things were still darn expensive. Save them for jet planes and rocket ships, and maybe for some of those big, hyperthyroid computers too. But nobody, sniffed the radio-making establishment, nobody was going to pay fifty dollars for a receiver this small when for a mere twenty bucks he or she could buy a handsome, fully refined tabletop model. And exactly who was this saucy little pipsqueak of a company anyway, making its sub detectors and its seismic recorders? Who did these Texans think they were, bringing a radio design to the titans of the industry?

Finally, Industrial Development Engineering Associates Inc., an Indianapolis company, took the project—after TI agreed to cut the price drastically of the transistors it would supply for the portable. Industrial Development's Regency Division turned the plans into the Regency radio, trim and angular like the cant of Sinatra's fedora, the epitome of the moment's style. The Regency was the world's first all-transistor portable. Stores in Los Angeles and New York began selling it in late October 1954, kicking off the Christmas shopping binge. Elvis Presley had cut his first record just three months before, at age nineteen. In an October 18 press release from TI, Haggerty remarked, "with the introduction of this first mass production item replacing the fragile vacuum tube with the tiny transistor, electronics enters a new era." According to the scuttle around the industry, TI spent $2 million to develop the radio. But on the strength of the reputation it thereby acquired, the Texan soon found itself supplying transistors not just to Regency but also to IBM for use in its gargantuan computers. Some TI alumni claim that Haggerty aimed all along to use the radio to grab the computer maker's attention.

Just as the Regency had introduced ordinary consumers to newfangled transistors one decade earlier, in 1965 Haggerty wanted his pocket-size adding machine to open a huge new market for microchips. His technological vision was not abstract, detached, or isolated from his practical concerns as a business manager. Pat Haggerty's concept of corporate health and commercial success required TI to grow from within, organically, accumulating new customers by exercising its abilities, the way a body builder builds muscles by flexing them. Therefore he peered energetically into the future to make sure his company arrived there first, developing popular new uses for particular technologies that would enable TI to grow and prosper by capturing new customers.

But it wasn't all just business, either. Haggerty, along with other chip advocates—mostly some of the leaders of the handful of companies that made them—could have entered another field if they merely cared to jockey corporate balance sheets. Haggerty could have remained a box maker, building his empire of cardboard. But semiconductors also offered them adventure and the adrenal jolt of discovery, even inside their executive offices. Their work engaged them. It excited them. They still believed that the technology's power and capability weren't well appreciated yet. Outside their circle, the devices weren't approached as transformational. They hadn't yet sparked the kind of fundamental breakthrough their advocates envisioned. These early ICs were regarded more as mere multi-transistor packs that were useful in machines that would have used many transistors in any case. Machines such as scintillation counters weren't likely to make any grand contribution to culture at large.

Nor would the computers of the mid-1960s, which were still unwieldy, esoteric, shamefully expensive, and rather far outside of ordinary experience, contribute to culture. Some attempts to reduce their bulk had produced scaled-down machines with severely limited capabilities. In 1960 the Burroughs Corporation started selling its model E–101 "desk-size computer" that businesses could use for chores like bookkeeping and payroll processing. It was the size of a hefty desk. An operator sitting down at the standard gray cabinet—a color as common in offices as olive drab in the Army—might have been sitting behind a disembodied automobile dash. E–101 sold for $38,000, and its memory ran out after 220 words.

At the time, people outside of the semiconductor elect did not even accept the idea that silicon microchips offered the best means for expanding the influence of microelectronics. One popular rival method for miniaturizing circuits used the stone chips in only a supporting role. Called hybrid circuits, they were a throwback technology based on the silk-screen methods first devised during World War II by Centralab and the fuse makers at Harry Diamond. Capacitors, resistors, and wire-like pathways connecting them were built up in printed layers, with space left among the parts to place transistors and maybe even some silicon ICs that consolidated a group of transistors into one part. Hybrids provided a way to make more complicated electronic circuits—circuits made up of more parts—than early ICs could amalgamate inside their single piece of silicon. But by 1965, IC advocates were pulling hard to advance new microchip approaches that integrated hundreds of circuit parts. That would enable a single IC to do much more demanding work. But hybrids undermined the argument for such large-scale integration. Hybrids already provided the means to consolidate a lot of circuit elements. And they were cheaper than the super ICs then stumbling out of semiconductor development labs.

Thus under assault by competing approaches to circuit miniaturization, feeling their product poorly appreciated, IC advocates felt a competitive urgency to popularize the concept. Therefore they proselytized. In the December 1964 *Proceedings of the IEEE* (Institute of Electrical and Electronics Engineers) Haggerty wrote, "the basic knowledge and the tools of electronics are so pertinent to the needs of our kind of society that the products and services which are the result of the knowledge and tools have nearly unlimited usefulness and can contribute in a major way across our entire social structure."

Others were more explicit and even fanciful. In the April 1965 edition of *Electronics* magazine, amid all the dense technical notes and all the news about business wheelings, one of the industry's most energetic visionaries, Daniel E. Noble of Motorola, wrote stunning predictions about the influence that microcircuits would one day exert on everyday life.

"In the future," he opined, "we can expect electronics to find new applications for the consumer in communications, comfort, convenience, computation and credit. To these we can add fun and games, health, and education."

Noble was the long-reigning technical executive who built Motorola into a world-leading microchip maker. In *Electronics* in 1965, he stuck a twenty-five to fifty–year horizon on his predictions, anticipating that home computers would become commonplace within that span, that automobiles "will use more and more electronic devices," and that "electronic ignition will become standard equipment." He also presaged the World Wide Web, predicting that "the housewife will sit at home and shop by dialing the selected store for information about the merchandise wanted."

The same issue of *Electronics* carried an article by Fairchild's Gordon Moore, from which later acolytes distilled the idea that became known as Moore's Law: every eighteen months chip density (the number of transistors per chip) will double while the price shrinks by half. Moore makes clear that he didn't put it that way in the 1965 article. The so-called law, he says, was kind of read into his text. Its main point was simply that microchip capabilities were improving, and improving fast. Still, the specific forecast that's known as Moore's

Law has proven to be remarkably accurate. When it was written, the prophecy was desperate propaganda. Moore was addressing electronic equipment makers, the consumers of his company's microcircuits, telling them, *Hold on a while longer. We're getting there. If you just look at my numbers here, you'll see that these little chips of ours are soon going to get quite capable, while the cost per transistor gets remarkably low.* The article's sub-headline confided that "With unit costs falling as the number of components per circuit rises, by 1975 economics may dictate squeezing as many as 65,000 components on a single silicon chip."

But those semiconductor seers were doing more than simply spinning words. They were also hustling to place their products. Haggerty tuned his kinetic mind to dream up a few stunning gizmos and gadgets that, Regency-like, might popularize ICs, placing the tiny stone circuits inside common people's pockets. He spilled out his musings to Jack Kilby while the two shared a row on a business flight to New York. "Haggerty was something of a philosopher," Kilby attests. "He liked to explain his ideas to people, and did so, with a lot of people, at almost every opportunity. It was his style to throw out ideas. You could pick 'em up or walk away from 'em, as you choose." By this time, Haggerty had advanced from executive VP to president of Texas Instruments. Kilby had moved into the job of deputy director of semiconductor research, as a follow-up to his landmark invention of an integrated circuit. Now, as deputy director, IC innovation was his specific concern. Willis Adcock still ran the semiconductor research lab as a whole.

Kilby dismissed a couple of his boss's airborne notions out of hand. They were far-fetched and impossible. But the concept of a portable personal calculator stuck. In a manner of thought very different from the fast, unformed flashes of Patrick Haggerty, exercising care and plodding patience, Kilby wrapped some ganglia around the notion of a small computing machine that could drop into a pocket, run on a battery, and perform simple math. To be self-contained it would need to incorporate a key pad for punching in problems and a window of some sort to show solutions. Even the big computers of the day didn't bundle together all their parts like that. Instead they sprawled, agglomerating racks and cabinets that included separate, free-standing readers that fed in questions and separate writers set on stands that printed out replies. Haggerty's little adder would even conceal its own power source, thereby copying the most innovative aspect of Regency: It would require no cord.

Still, such a product was almost as impossible as the concepts from Haggerty that Kilby had already discarded. About the only electric button in use at the time was a doorbell. Big computers didn't yet use electric keyboards, and even electric typewriters relied on mechanical buttons and levers. The motor just gave them a boost. To show numbers, the best instruments relied on Nixie tubes. Nixies were glass cylinders that looked like vacuum tubes. They were filled with small neon lamps shaped as numerals and superimposed, one ahead of another, so that when one numeral illuminated it would show through the tube. Nixies were too big to use in any kind of tagalong calculator. And they gobbled up too much power anyway. You'd never light a bank of Nixies using a battery. And what kind of battery could possibly power Haggerty's pocket adder anyway? The chips alone required more electricity than you were likely to get from any small battery of the day. And, speaking of silicon, none of the commercially manufactured microchips from Texas Instruments or any of the industry's other hopefuls packed transistors enough to perform even the logic required simply to add, subtract, multiply, and divide. They did not even come close.

Yet the idea remained fast in Kilby's thinking. While he undertook the ordinary duties of deputy research directorship, his mind ruminated more on the possibility of a portable calculator. He constructed technical scenarios. He played through possible solutions to the thorniest problems. He kept his mind engaged in the inquiry even though he approached it obliquely, which was the way he approached all the rich mysteries of semiconductor research: Lank, laconic Jack Kilby followed his own idiosyncrasies toward the task of making better microchips.

"You'd be workin' at your desk and pretty soon there'd be a big shoe right there on the desk beside you and it's Kilby. He's using your desk as a footstool," recounts Jerry Merryman, a researcher who started under Kilby at Texas Instruments in March 1963. "Kilby would walk through the lab and talk to people all the time." He'd chat over technical papers. He'd inquire about progress. He'd bring up ideas, theories, hunches, discoveries, new directions. He'd toss down a concept and maybe solicit a reply. He'd listen to your response with a stoic stillness that made his intentions tough and often just plain impossible to read.

Once, Merryman recalls, "he handed me a paper that'd been written at Bell Labs." In the brief, Bell proposed a new kind of shift register, which is an electronic assembly that works as a computer's short-term memory. "He says, 'What do you think of this?' and I just looked at it casually. He said, 'Why don't you look at that and tell me what you think?' I said okay. But I was workin' on some other things and he came back in about a week and he said 'What did you think about that Bell Labs paper?' I realized this time that he was serious about it. So I said, 'Well, I, you know, I glanced at it that time that you were here, and I don't think that's the way you ought to do it. I think I could do some better things than that.' He said, 'Okay.'" And that was how Merryman received an assignment to develop a new semiconductor shift register at Texas Instruments.

Therefore Merryman suspected that a matter more extraordinary might be in the air when he was summoned to an actual office meeting on October 20, 1965. He found a few of the company's brightest assembled in Kilby's office. Present were Vernon Hardy and L. J. Sevin, semiconductor researchers like Merryman. Harvey Cragon sat a little bit off to the side because he wasn't a member of Kilby's team. He still worked nearby as resident computer expert in the company's Equipment Group. Cragon's role that day in Kilby's office was simply to offer advice. Kilby's main aim was to pick a researcher who could push ICs past their current limits by packing them inside a pocket-size math machine.

"Kilby had a little book on his desk," Merryman recalls. "I think it was a little red book, maybe four-by-six inches and maybe three-quarters of an inch thick—not too unlike some modern calculators. A little larger maybe. But you could put it in your pocket. He was saying something like, 'Well, Pat and I have been talking.' Now, he meant Pat Haggerty, and you've read the story many times that Haggerty would go off on an airplane and come back with several ideas and most of 'em would be nutty but every once in a while there was somethin' you needed to follow up on.

"Kilby said, 'We want some kind of personal computer, and it would be nice if it was no bigger than this book. And of course, it'll have to run on batteries. And it will have to have some buttons or somethin' on it for you to tell it a problem. And it'll have to have some neon lights or somethin' to tell you the answer.'

"And then," says Merryman, "there was probably not more than ten seconds of silence, because engineers don't laugh at absurdities. When you tell 'em you want to do something, they just give it their best shot."

At the time the thought of building a portable, handheld electronic calculator was so absurd that no such machine was under development anywhere. The word *calculator* wasn't even in parlance yet. Kilby called the object a *sliderule computer* because it would mimic some of the simplest functions of the slide rules that every engineer wore dangling in a holster like a lawman's revolver. The product's only near precedent was a little mechanical adding machine called the Curta that came from Germany. The Curta looked more like a fishing reel than a paperback, but you could hold it in one hand while you spun numbers with the other. It performed only the rudimentary, entry-level mathematics that any third or fourth grader of the era had already mastered. But even simple math—addition, subtraction, multiplication, and division—required more electronic logic than a few of the best ICs packed in a box as small as a book could perform in 1965.

A few days after the exploratory October 20 meeting, Kilby officially gave Merryman the job of overcoming all the impossibilities that the idea implied. "Jerry was probably closer to being a Renaissance man than anybody we've had around here for a good while," Kilby observes.

Yet according to their paper credentials, Jerry Merryman was the least likely of the three men to win the assignment. He didn't even have a college degree. On the other hand, L. J. Sevin would eventually demonstrate pluck enough to leave TI, in 1969, to set up his own pioneering semco, Mostek Corporation. Later, in 1981, he would establish the Sevin Rosen Funds, a venture capital firm that helped finance later generations of ambitious entrepreneurs—it funded the start of Compaq Computer, for one.

But Kilby saw in Merryman the kind of grubbing, get-it-done talents such a project required. Merryman had become a semiconductor researcher by disposition and by active intelligence, rather than through schooling. He had entered the electronics trade in 1944, when he was twelve years old, making radio repairs at an appliance shop in his little hometown of Hearne, Texas. His technical schooling started with a secondhand copy of the 1937 edition of *Radio Engineering*, a groundbreaking book by Frederick Terman. The experience began a habit of exploration and self-education that became so comprehensive that, by the time Merryman reached Texas A&M University, the electronics coursework couldn't hold him. "I grew restive and went out to measure the world," he says. Undegreed, he acquired enough on-the-job expertise to land a research position with the world's top semiconductor company. He joined Texas Instruments in March 1963.

Restless energy animated Merryman. He was clever, fast, original, and self-reliant. He preferred to think independently about problems, calling on his own experience and insight rather than sticking his nose into technical papers to see what other people thought. Merryman was a handyman. He didn't spin grand hypotheses, and he avoided unworkable theories no matter how pat and pretty they appeared to the intellect. All of his traits would be tested by this program.

As calculator project manager, he had eighteen months to make one prototype handheld that used ICs to perform simple math. Armed with that model, the company hoped to sell the concept—as it had sold the transistor radio concept—to an equipment manufacturer that would then become a big buyer of Texas chips. After the initial meetings of October 1965, the program picked up the code name Cal Tech, ostensibly named after the Pasadena university.

It was a complete engineering project. Cal Tech fully occupied four engineers and technicians under Merryman, with occasional assistance from outside the group—such as John McCrady, who built a nightmarish testing jig with 226 tiny tungsten wire probes meant to descend simultaneously like fingers upon the 226 metal contacts that splayed from all four sides of the ICs that were specially made for Merryman's adding machine.

The calculator's case had to be specially designed by a mechanical engineer and milled out of a solid block of aluminum. To create a key pad, engineer James Van Tassel plated copper dots on a thick sheet of flexible plastic that he positioned under the keys. Pressing a numbered key on the face of the finished calculator forced a dot on the copper-spotted plastic to contact another dot on a printed circuit board that was layered beneath it.

At the same time, Merryman searched inside TI to find a workable method to display answers. None of the lighted approaches, such as light-emitting diodes (LEDs), were close to commercial readiness. But he found a development team that was honing a technique called thermal printing for National Cash Register. New and unknown at the time, the method scrolled heat-sensitive paper beneath an electronically controlled printing head that could be programmed to produce words, not just numbers on cash register receipts. For his calculator, Merryman used just a small band of the thermal paper, narrow quarter-inch tape on a wide, flat roll like ribbon that spooled out of the side of Cal Tech. Numbers were printed along the length of the paper tape. Merryman carefully parsed the electricity that the mechanism sucked to feed the tape and to burn in the imprint in order to make batteries last longer.

But the biggest difficulty by far was making the microchips. They needed to do more than commercial chips of the era were capable of doing. Merryman started by simplifying the sequence of operations that the circuit would have to perform. He rejected the common binary notations used by digital computers because his calculators wouldn't have enough transistors to manipulate binary digits effectively. Instead he worked out number representations that enabled the circuit to perform mathematics more intuitively. His calculator logic handled addition and subtraction the way kids learn to do it in grade school, stacking the numbers and then working from the right, carrying or borrowing values from one column to the next.

But even his simplified logic would require far more computations than he could get from standard-issue ICs. Merryman needed something like 4,000 transistors. At the time, common commercial microchips contained only about twenty. He couldn't gang together a bunch of low-density chips—the way conventional equipment was made—because he'd never find room inside a case the size of a paperback, especially not when he added all the interconnections he'd need to string the chips together.

Therefore Merryman designed mega-chips: circuits made from an entire silicon wafer. Instead of dicing the wafers into separate, individual chips after processing, he used them whole, creating a monolithic silicon circuit about one-inch across that was packed with transistors and accessory circuit parts. In the semiconductor trade it was called a full slice because it used the whole slice of silicon that was usually subdivided into separate ICs.

Even so, Merryman needed four of the full-slice wafers to get the number of transistors he needed. He drew up a plan that divided the computations among the four so that each big chip performed only a portion of the work. A calculation might start on big-chip A, which would then pass off some conclusions to big-chip B for further processing, and so on.

But even four full-slice mega chips couldn't handle the computing load. Although each held 3,072 transistors, Merryman could count on getting only about 750 usable transistors per wafer. That was because only about twenty-five percent of the parts made by the crude, immature processing techniques of the day were good. To get a higher yield—that is, a higher percentage of working parts per wafer—Merryman designed the circuits so that the silicon would be particularly easy to manufacture.

"I went down to where they did the diffusion and masking processes," he says, "to where they made the wafers, and I told 'em that I wanted an eighty-three percent yield. And they fell out laughing. They said, 'Why, the simplest product we ever made is about twenty-five percent yield. How do you expect us to get eighty-three percent?' I said, 'I'm gonna design for eighty-three percent. It's gonna use low voltage and low current and wide tolerances and big transistors and big leads and big contacts, and I'm gonna build it out of tolerant, forgiving parts, such that it's gonna work.'"

That approach would have been inappropriate if Merryman was designing ordinary ICs, to be laid out as subdivisions on a wafer and later cut apart. But for his one-of-a-kind, full-slice circuits, his easy-to-process configuration came as a gift to the fabricators. They exceeded the high-yield target.

Yet even using four full-slice chips specially designed with forgiving wide-body parts, Merryman had to perform still more contortions to coax simple mathematics from the circuits. TI's fabrication line delivered just over fifty-inch–wide silicon slices with about eighty-five percent of their circuit parts working. But the bad spots, although they were down to only fifteen percent of the total, still fell randomly over the surface of each silicon slice. Ordinarily, when wafers were sawed into standard-size ICs, the bad chips were simply discarded. But because Merryman was using the whole slice, he had to devise interconnection patterns that would tie together only the working components while bridging over the bad ones as if they weren't even there. And because his calculator required four unique circuits, he needed four distinct interconnection patterns.

Therefore Merryman made fingerprints of each wafer in the fifty-wafer group, recording the exact positions of their bum transistors. Then he turned the problem of channel-routing—laying out the interconnections within each chip—to an IBM mainframe that was shared among TI units. The computer was enshrined in a separate building and operated by data-processing specialists. To run a job, you had to pick a number and wait for the specialists to call your turn. "It was a room full of big stuff," Merryman describes. "It used up kilowatts and it used up air conditioning." Whenever his rotation came up, Merryman crossed the North Dallas campus carrying two shoe boxes filled with the punched cards that contained the programming and the data he needed to have fed into the machine. A few times the IBM grew confused. Merryman intervened manually, restringing bits of the circuit to straighten a tangle. "Sometimes the computer just couldn't do it," he says.

Yet even simplified computations, distributed over four full-slice mega chips that were filled with forgiving wide-body parts that were eighty-five percent functional could not produce one working calculator. After the interconnecting metal was evaporated onto the chips and etched to produce the layouts that had been determined (mostly) by the big IBM, not one out of fifty-two completed circuits worked. They required reconstructive surgery. Merryman and team peered through microscopes to spot damages. They used a dental drill to poke through the epoxy that had been coated over the wafers to protect them, connecting hair-like gold wires as jumpers that intervened at each flaw.

One Cal Tech sliderule computer, a black aluminum box studded with numbered keys the size of sugar cubes, the whole assembly closer in bulk to a hardcover than a paperback, was finished in December 1967. The development had spanned two years, six months beyond its original eighteen-month target. According to papers Merryman pushed around as project head, the cost of Cal Tech ran to $240,000. But he figures that additional support came out of general research funds available to Kilby.

But the calculator finally presented to Pat Haggerty didn't meet the executive's expectations. As configured, Cal Tech couldn't possibly launch ICs the way the Regency had placed transistors in just about everyone's pockets. Merryman and his crew had indeed succeeded in making one working prototype that is heralded as the world's first cordless, portable calculator. The project showed how much an astute and dedicated engineering team could accomplish when the resources of a corporate powerhouse stood behind it. But the program failed to make a mass-consumable calculator. It succeeded in showing how far TI's ambitions outstripped its present abilities.

As a demonstration project, Cal Tech showed too clearly that TI's microchips weren't ready to support portability economically. They did not contain enough processing power, and they did not compress the processing power they did contain into small enough dimensions. And they still required far too much nursing and nurturing to produce. One of the original Cal Tech team members, Edmund Ward, dramatically underlined those shortcomings early in 1966 when the program was just building momentum. Ward calculated that the integrated circuits planned for the machine would cost something like $15,000 each. Stick in four of them, and you were talking a $60,000 portable calculator. It was folly. Ward quit out of consternation. He went back to school to study for a Ph.D. at Purdue.

He was premature. The technical barriers that had battered the Cal Tech team for two full years soon fell away as competing chip-makers pushed their products to perform better. Three years after Merryman built the prototype, a facsimile of Cal Tech went on sale for only about $350. Ward had overestimated its price by about seventeen thousand percent.

≡ 7 ≡

Adding Contenders

ED WARD HAD SIMPLY BET too soon that chip technology could not support popularly priced products. He had based his calculator cost analysis on the capabilities of the moment, which had made the adder's logic circuits impossibly difficult to mass produce. Pessimistically, he had failed to account for improvements that were already arriving when the Cal Tech calculator project started. In the mid-1960s, the wheel of progress was hard into another big turn. The chips used in Cal Tech were bipolar semiconductors, containing the layered Oreo-cookie kind of transistors. But breakthroughs in manufacturing methods were already delivering a new-breed IC called metal-oxide semiconductors. It provided both the compressed processing power and the economy that mass-market products required.

Metal-oxide semiconductors were an essential innovation that arrived as a product of the industry at large rather than as a single, discrete invention. They seemed to appear spontaneously from multiple sources, growing out of the competitive tumult that characterized semiconductor development in the 1960s. But because they came late, when bipolar chips were already filling productive roles, they needed a vehicle—some means to prove their value—in order to cement and to assure their ascendance.

Chips made of metal-oxide semiconductors—called MOS— weren't available to Merryman at TI because they were still only emerging when his calculator project began in 1965. They weren't mainstream micros yet. Instead they resided among the entrepreneurs at a few upstart companies that were striving to make a name and a fortune by being the first to sell the desirable new product. Remarkably, Texas Instruments, the place where ICs had been invented just seven years earlier, was already a part of the old-guard, established order. Its bipolar microchips represented the mainstream. TI had helped make them mainstream by sinking a whole lot of investments into manufacturing processes that could provide a reliable supply of the minicircuits. But in the near future, as MOS became established, the Texan chip would teeter toward irrelevance and obsolescence as the better idea supplanted bipolars.

It was not a very new idea. MOS chips were based on a different transistor type, called a field-effect transistor—abbreviated FET, naturally. Field effects had been conceived by Bill Shockley back in the middle 1940s. Since then, researchers had made them experimentally, beginning in 1960 with John Atalla, a Bell Labs scientist who worked from Shockley's original theories. But no one had figured out how to manufacture them consistently enough to turn them into useful products. "They could make a few, and that is what whetted people's appetite," says Jay Lathrop, a chip fabrication specialist who helped build TI's early chip manufacturing processes. "So there wasn't a question about whether or not it was going to work. They had sort of proved that it would work—*if* we could get 'em all to look like the good ones."

The field effect is an electrical property surrounding a zone of specially treated semiconductor material: The silicon spot creates a field when it's energized by an electric current. The field can be made either to attract or to repel a second current flowing nearby by varying the electricity fed to the spot that creates it. To make a field-effect transistor, the energized spot nests inside a surrounding layer of semiconductor that can carry the second current. The field then acts like a clamp either to turn on or to turn off the transistor: In its repellent state, the field squeezes down to block the nearby flow of electricity; in its attractive state, it opens up to allow the flow.

Through the 1960s, enterprising researchers and the businesses behind them had begun to overcome the obstacles to making field-effect transistors. The biggest obstacle fell in 1962 at Fairchild when the scientist Frank Wanlass fiddled with a new piece of production equipment, a high-energy ray gun called an electron-beam evaporator that turned metals to mist. It provided a better way to vaporize materials so that they could be deposited in a thin layer on silicon wafers to make the conductive pathways that connected transistors. Wanlass discovered that he could make the field effect work reliably when he used the ray gun but not when he tried other, older methods to evaporate metals on his way to making MOS devices. The riddle set up a chain of reasoning that sent him pondering back to his doctoral research at the University of Utah, where he had studied material contamination. Wanlass reasoned that the ray-gun evaporator obliterated certain impurities that lower-temperature alternatives did not destroy. From that he deduced that sodium, an element as common as sweat, was the culprit that fouled MOS chips. After Wanlass revealed that piece of insight, semcos began to make MOS circuits successfully by scouring away the places where sodium sneaked into their manufacturing processes to befoul their products.

MOS chips gave them a few strong incentives to eliminate all the sources diligently. The field-effect transistors in MOS circuits were smaller, simpler, easier to manufacture, and they burned less electricity than layered, bipolar transistors. When the Cal Tech project was just beginning in late 1965, the Silicon Valley start-up General Micro-electronics was already making chips with field-effect transistors just five percent the size of conventional bipolars. Therefore General Micro could pack a lot more of the tiny dynamos into an integrated circuit, providing more transistors per chip to accomplish more complex logic. While Merryman was resorting to big full-slice wafers to provide all the transistors he needed for Cal Tech, General Micro-electronics was making single MOS chips that contained 615 transistors—a staggering leap from the 20 or so in TI's standard bipolars. At the same time, General Micro's rival, the General Instrument Corporation, was doing even better, making an 800-transistor chip. The two companies were the pioneers in making commercial MOS microchips. Both bragged loudly about the approach of 1,000-transistor ICs.

Another big advantage was the low electrical needs of field-effect transistors: You didn't have to drive through as much energy to make them operate. That meant that they shed less heat as a by-product. Therefore MOS chips didn't cook themselves the way bipolars did. You got more transistors *and* cooler equipment. What's more, their electrical efficiency paid a nice dividend in longer battery life when they were used in portable machines.

And there was more. Mostly because they required fewer processing steps—38 compared to 130—MOS microcircuits were cheaper to make. The fewer steps also left fewer opportunities for manufacturing errors to sneak in. Therefore the MOS-making process yielded a much higher percentage of working chips, helping to reduce their prices even more.

At the same time, because the microcircuits were more densely integrated, machine makers could use fewer chips, yet still get abundant transistors for building intricate logic engines. The lower chip count made their products easier to assemble, with fewer parts to interconnect. General Micro-electronics estimated in 1965 that electronic gear could be built at one-tenth the cost using MOS chips.

Field-effect transistors didn't fire as fast as bipolars, and therefore some critics complained that they were poorly suited for such products as computers, which could keep you waiting too long for an answer if their transistors didn't blink like rapid bug eyes through all their innumerable sequences. But in the end, the sheer density of transistors on MOS chips made up for the slower action of each transistor. The electrical impulses didn't have to travel as far between transistors, saving time in transit. And they could do all or at least a lot of their work while remaining inside a single IC. The many chip-to-chip jumps in an assembly of multiple, bipolar chips slowed down processing.

When their advantages were added up, MOS microchips brought the kind of discontinuity that encouraged the formation of new companies. Their capabilities were so superior that you could count on customers to buy them, but none of the established suppliers were selling them yet. In fact, the established companies were struggling to figure out the manufacturing techniques themselves—if they weren't already committed, as was Texas Instruments, to the Oreo approach entirely. The MOS market was wide open for enterprising technologists who also wanted to be their own bosses.

Therefore when microchips made of metal-oxide semiconductors arrived at the same time that bipolars were demonstrating their inadequacies to the Cal Tech crew, a cascade of new business activity accompanied the new-style chips. Anxious to set up their own bold new ventures, defectors fled from semcos that were just getting established themselves. General Micro-electronics, the early leader in MOS, had been created by a team that left Fairchild in 1963, setting up shop next door in Santa Clara. Frank Wanlass himself had briefly joined that venture. Then he skipped off to the second new MOS hopeful, General Instrument. L. J. Sevin's departure from TI to create

Mostek in 1969 was motivated by the opportunity to make MOS chips. During the same period, establishment firms stretched resources to get into the new technology. In 1965 both Fairchild and Stewart-Warner Microcircuits were making some special-order MOS designs, while RCA made plans to introduce a line of ready-to-use metal oxides. And some equipment makers that ran their own IC operations, including Autonetics and Hughes Aircraft, dashed into metal oxide so they could build better chips to use in their machinery.

In 1965, a microchip of any kind was still an obscure entity, struggling to win over skeptics. The chip-making industry was still only nascent. But already it was reforming around this fundamental breakthrough that would soon render earlier approaches to the technology—which were still new themselves—obsolete for most advanced applications.

Cal Tech had begun at the beginning of the changeover when bipolar Oreos still reigned as the dominant chip configuration. The new approach ICs with their clamp-like field effect were just growing out of experimentation and development. Accordingly, they still suffered from the same sort of special-interest obscurity that afflicted ICs at large. The first MOS circuits sold mostly to NASA and the military. The space agency used them in some ground-support equipment, and it built MOS-filled computers to launch aboard scientific satellites called Imps—interplanetary monitoring platforms. The Army used the new ICs in timers for artillery fuses, while the Light Military Electronics department of General Electric built battlefield computers containing the chips.

The break toward popularity occurred because calculators—which at the time were more likely to be called adding machines, comptometers, or numericators—were eagerly prepped and awaiting the sort of transformation that MOS capabilities could deliver. Just as integrated circuits were straining to burst their barriers and spill into wider use, the common accountant's helper was also undergoing a fundamental format change. MOS microcircuits, with their greater capabilities, brought them that means, while calculators in their turn provided the kind of popularizing outlet that integrated circuits sought.

Thus the reorganization and reordering in semiconductors fueled the same situation in calculators: A technology renewal enabled new-coming companies to challenge the established hierarchy. Like the yin and the yang, each supported and was supported by the other. Pat Haggerty didn't start that. His Cal Tech project was merely coincidental with the fundamental format change that had already begun to infect calculators.

By the mid-1960s, with Cal Tech just getting started in Dallas, electronics had already begun to transform the mechanical contraptions then known as adding machines. A few all-transistor models, such as the Friden EC130 and the Sharp CS10A, appeared in 1964. They were hardly portable, as the small machine Pat Haggerty envisioned would be. They weighed as much as a German shepherd and cost as much as a family car. But that same year, General Micro-electronics started designing densely integrated MOS circuits for a new calculator by the Victor Comptometer Corporation that aimed to break the mold. The idea was to compress most of the logic onto a single chip, to produce an adder that would be much smaller and simpler than any of its contemporaries. Victor showed prototypes of the machine at a business expo in New York in 1965.

That was only the first small chink in the armor. MOS microcircuits presented an opportunity to change number machines radically enough to challenge the entire old-guard hierarchy that built them. Energetic and aggressive companies like Sharp, Canon, Sony, and Casio—all Japanese equipment makers— latched onto microelectronics as a vehicle into a business that was otherwise walled off. The only way they could war against the fortified status quo was by changing the rules. They did that by changing the nature of calculators, using MOS chips to make machines that were more desirable. The race they started in the 1960s was all about making calculators that were smaller, more capable, and less expensive than the last one.

MOS circuits fed the frenzy. In fact, MOS-powered calculators grew so small and efficient so rapidly that the idea to make them portable became plainly apparent not long after the inspiration had occurred to Haggerty—who was by then out trying to find an equipment-making partner to build the Cal Tech calculator. In 1969 the Japanese company Canon eagerly teamed with TI and began spinning the prototype into a model it called Pocketronic. It imitated the form of Merryman's creation on the outside, but on the inside Pocketronic used more suitable chips made of metal-oxide semiconductors.

By the end of the 1960s, the head start that TI had gained by beginning its Cal Tech project in 1965 had been erased by ambitious rivals. Pocketronic wasn't even the first portable calculator to reach stores. That honor went to a Sharp model called the QT–8B. It was a modification of an existing model, made by sticking batteries into Sharp's QT–8, a smallish plug-in desktop adder that was the first calculator to use large-scale-integration MOS chips. The U.S. company Rockwell supplied the ICs. Their consolidated processing power and low electrical drain made the cordless conversion possible. The Canon Pocketronic followed it by a few months, going on sale in Japan in the autumn of 1970. The United States saw it in February 1971.

Other basic four-function, portable handhelds appeared in 1970, including the Sanyo ICC–0081, another Sharp, the EL–8, and the Busicom LE–120. Busicom's model used an all-in-one chip supplied by L. J. Sevin's Mostek Corporation. It was the first "calculator on a chip": a single, condensed microcircuit that performed all of a math machine's functions within its confines. Before that, even calculators made with denser MOS microcircuits required a ganging of chips to get through their simple add-subtract-multiply-divide computations. Therefore the Mostek chip marked a milestone achievement, signaling that integrated circuits had acquired enough transistor density—and therefore enough capability—to work solo. Inside the single-chip calculator, ICs were no longer just circuit components. Instead, one IC was the circuit, self-contained, complete, and entire.

But it was still a special-built circuit designed to perform only one task: school-kid math. Soon a more significant innovation would occur at another striving start-up company called Intel. The newcomer would harness the high density of MOS to create a much more versatile microchip with computing capability that made a calculator-only chip appear timid.

But in the meantime, before that development occurred, the commercial one-upmanship and cutthroat frenzy in calculators gave microchip makers the taste of mass markets that they sought. The very early portables were expensive, with prices hovering around $400 and higher. But the price barrier began to topple almost as soon as the size barrier was breached. In 1971, the U.S. company Bowmar—formerly a maker of the light-emitting diode (LED) display bars used in many of the first portables—started selling a truly pocketable model, about the size of a cigarette pack, for $240. It assembled its 901B from chips and keypads purchased from Texas Instruments, which by that time had caught up in MOS. Within a year, dozens of companies began rushing out pocket adders to satisfy the explosion in demand as prices plummeted. Hewlett-Packard started selling the first portable that could perform more complex mathematics like logarithms. The race to make math machines that were smaller, simpler, and less expensive was bubbling into a competitive frenzy.

By the end of 1972, the average price for a basic four-function calculator stood around $150, with a few selling below $100. By 1974 pocket machines routinely sold for under $100, and price competition was starting to squeeze some once-eager equipment makers out of the business. In 1975 teachers began to complain prophetically that kids would never again memorize addition and multiplication tables as calculators priced under $20 began to appear in classrooms. Competitive pressure grew more intense.

Even Bowmar, the fast-rising one-time leader in portable calculators, began to falter. By this time its principle supplier of chips, Texas Instruments, was doing a brisk business selling its own models—it had brought out its first Texas Instruments brand model in 1972. As prices fell lower and, therefore, more consumers bought small calculators, IC makers struggled to keep up with burgeoning demand. TI kept more of the chips it made for its own calculators, siphoning away the silicon Bowmar relied upon to develop and sell updated, ever-more-desirable models. Bowmar thereby fell into bankruptcy in 1976, vanishing into obscurity as quickly as the company had risen to stardom as the top maker and seller of the machines in the United States. By 1978, compact calculators sold for under $10. Soon they'd be given away as premiums to entice people to buy more profitable products.

The commercial turmoil among calculator builders ran alongside a complementary tussle among their chip-making partners. An early free romp in the developing MOS market didn't assure a company's success. General Micro-electronics, the field's pioneer, couldn't quite master the difficulties of microchip manufacturing. It never delivered the chips meant to power the vaunted Victor Comptometer desktop model 3900, the machine that had been hyped in 1965 as the first to use densely integrated MOS chips. The 3900 was never built. General Micro eventually foundered.

In the meantime, Texas Instruments raced to a lead position in calculators. Jerry Merryman's pioneering first try, the Cal Tech, had shown the company its limits soon enough for it to accomplish a quick change. By stretching TI's chip-making approach to its farthest extent, Merryman had shown its inadequacy in time for the company to adapt.

$\equiv$ 8 $\equiv$

Common Ground

THE CALCULATOR ON A CHIP that Mostek Corporation made for Busicom in 1970 signaled a high point in circuit integration: One microchip contained transistors enough to perform calculations solo. You no longer needed to gang together a group of ICs to make a functional piece of equipment. But the Mostek chip was still very limited in the functions it performed. It made a dandy add-subtract-multiply-divide calculator. It was useless for anything else.

To go further, to penetrate deeper into the routine patterns of casual experience, chips had to become more versatile. Of course, no one at the time was actively working to make microcircuits supremely versatile. Mostek's all-in-one calculator chip already seemed achievement aplenty.

But a computer scientist named Ted Hoff swiftly turned the whole semiconductor crowd toward multifunctional microchips. Hoff did it almost inadvertently. He was merely following his nose. Exercising his intellectual curiosity. Appeasing his distaste of half measures and wasteful inefficiency.

In fact, by rights Ted Hoff should have never even unrolled the big paper sheets that showed the circuit plans that stirred his thoughts so restlessly. It was not his job. At the brand new company called Intel, Hoff's assignment was to promote products *after* they were developed. But the plans he curiously peeked at were far from finished. The drawings showed the operations of a future line of microchips. They were supposed to go to the circuit designers, who would use the diagrams as guides when they laid out the chips' geographies. They would make twelve chips in all. The designers would map each one, locating each transistor and meshing out all the whispering interlinks to make the chips perform the operations that the plans specified. That work didn't require Hoff's meddling.

The plans had come over from Japan about two weeks earlier, carried by the three engineers who had drawn them. The trio worked for Intel's newest customer, the Japanese calculator company Busicom. Just as Busicom had hired Mostek to supply the chip for its handheld calculator, it retained Intel to make the ICs it needed to fire a flashy new line of desktop number machines.

Although Hoff wasn't involved in the work, he'd been appointed Intel's goodwill ambassador, assigned to answer questions for the visitors and to help them negotiate the company's unfamiliar hallways. Accordingly, he was waiting at 8:00 A.M. at the San Francisco airport when they arrived on June 20, 1969, a Friday. Lightened by enthusiasm, lifted by the achievement that their twelve dense circuit schematics represented—although both those impulses were masked somewhat by the formal diffidence of their culture—the engineers had come to Santa Clara to oversee the transfer of their markings into silicon. They'd stay in furnished rooms that Intel had arranged at the Mountain Bay Apartments. Hoff discovered only when they arrived that the complex didn't provide linens. Secretaries scrambled out to buy bed sheets and towels. Later that same evening, Hoff himself winged away for a vacation in Tahiti. Now he was just back, and after the absence, you would have thought he had enough of his own work to catch up on. But he peeked at Busicom's plans anyway. "Being a curious sort," he explains, "I couldn't resist trying to find out more about what they were doing, and trying to understand more about it. And that's when I began to have some concerns about the design."

It was hopelessly complicated. Twelve chips! Did they really need twelve chips? And each of those twelve was a tangled morass. They'd require more transistors than Intel could possibly pack into an IC. And then the chips would have to be potted inside expensive little cases that were daunting complexities themselves. Through every step, manufacturing would be a nightmare. The expense would be debilitating. "We were a young company," says Hoff. "We didn't want to go bust because of our first project." He chuckles at the recollection.

But at the time he couldn't abide the clumsy inefficiency of Busicom's plans. It violated his personal sense of propriety. Hoff took his worries to his boss. He said that he thought he could create a more reasonable design. His boss, Bob Noyce, said okay, give it a whirl. Thus began the project that showed that the ultimate in miniaturization had arrived: an entire, programmable computer could be reduced to a single chip.

Just like his first peek at the plans, the corrective logic design Hoff then undertook stepped far outside his ordinary responsibilities at Intel. Officially, Marican "Ted" Hoff was manager of applications research, a job he had held since joining the company at its founding the prior summer as employee number twelve. Like Gordon Moore and Jean Hoerni, he had busted out of academe. Hoff's sojourn in the ivory tower had lasted for fourteen years. In 1958 he had earned a bachelor's in electrical engineering from Rensselaer Polytechnic Institute. In 1962 he had completed a Ph.D. at Stanford. Then he had stayed at Stanford for six years longer as a research associate conducting computer studies in what's called adaptive systems—trying to make trainable computers that could learn from experience, like people.

As Intel's manager of applications research, Hoff's main job was to come up with enticing ways to use the memory ICs that the new company was eager to move out of its lab and into production. The idea was to show equipment companies how they could use the new breed of data storage chips, thereby encouraging them to buy the things. Scratching out the circuit pattern for a calculator departed substantially from that.

But then, the whole assignment was a departure for Intel. It was more of a quick-grab, fast-money job than an undertaking that fit with the company's ambitious business strategy. Intel simply needed the cash.

At the time Intel was just another uncertain new semco set up by a band of defectors. In this case they were rather prominent defectors: Robert Noyce and Gordon Moore, two of the leaders who had built up Fairchild Semiconductor. (Another of Fairchild's leaders, Charlie Sporck, had left before them, taking over as chief executive of National Semiconductor, a moribund company that Sporck salvaged and revived, making it a billion-dollar enterprise by 1981 and eventually purchasing Fairchild in 1987.) Noyce and Moore were encouraged by the same boomtown ethos that encouraged so many other semiconductor start-ups: They understood that the field was so raw and so rapidly changing that it provided opportunities aplenty for eager zealots with bright new ideas. Therefore when the situation at Fairchild had turned sour, they saw no reason to stay.

After its fast rise to prominence, Fairchild simply failed to give its core team of talented technologues sufficient reason to stay. By the late 1960s, Noyce had been elevated from general manager of the semiconductor unit to group vice president of the parent company, Fairchild Camera and Equipment. Yet when Camera went hunting for a new chief, the family-owned outfit overlooked Noyce. By 1968 it had already overlooked him twice, burning through two top managers in less than a year. When it began recruiting a third, Noyce took the hint.

"They set up a three-man committee of the board to run the company and started looking on the outside. So Bob kind of got ticked off," recalls Gordon Moore. Early in 1968, Noyce told his friend and colleague that he was getting out. He invited Moore to join him. At first Moore declined. But by May, while Noyce made his way to the door, Moore reconsidered. "I could see things would change fairly dramatically if somebody came in from the outside," he relates.

Thus on July 18, 1968, the two former employees of Fairchild Semiconductor incorporated as Intel Corporation. The name came from a clever combination of the words *integrated* and *electronics*. Robert Noyce started as president and chief executive officer. Gordon Moore was executive vice president. The money behind the group came from venture capitalist Arthur Rock, who grew into a Silicon Valley icon for the start-ups he bankrolled.

The new company's business plan was uncomplicated. It would make densely integrated microchips—that is, chips containing a lot of transistors—and it would make them in designs that it could sell to a lot of different customers. That way, the founders hoped, the ICs would sell in vast quantities.

The strategy reflected both the progress that had occurred in microchips since 1965 and the prevailing worry over development expense that threatened to stall their advance. By the time Intel was founded in 1968, the technical obstacles to large-scale transistor integration were falling rapidly. In addition, industry leaders no longer fretted as much about placing their products. Silicon ICs were rapidly winning the argument, attracting more and more equipment companies. The looming revamp of calculators from gear boxes to electronic engines promised to place microchips in far wider circulation than space ships and big army guns ever could. The Victor Comptometer Corporation was already showing off its prototype that used whizbang

MOS chips from General Micro-electronics. The tech set even adopted the acronym LSI to denote the concept of large-scale integration, as if a quick-draw utterance would help legitimate the concept.

But skeptics complained that the economics still didn't add up. Semcos could never sell LSI chips profitably, they said. Why bother making products that drove their producers to bankruptcy?

The problem began with the fact that electronics companies hadn't grown past the old practice of designing a special circuit for every individual piece of equipment and machinery they built. A computer company planning to use LSI chips in its product wanted unique LSI chips laid out according to its own specifications. Similarly, each calculator company wanted uniquely designed chips. So did makers of oscillators, scintillators, calibrators, and most other bits of oddball gear that might use densely integrated circuits. The so-called "calculator on a chip" that Mostek began making for Busicom in 1969—squeezing all the logic required by a four-function add-subtract-multiply-divide calculator onto one IC—was still a single-purpose custom design. The chip could only function as a calculator. What's more, that particular calculator chip would only be used in Busicom's rendition of a handheld. For the most part, semcos operated like for-hire fabricators, taking design drawings from the equipment makers and rendering them into monolithic silicon.

But that rendering was expensive. In the late 1960s, the engineering required to develop a complex silicon circuit averaged around $50,000. Add in the cost to manufacture the things, and LSI expenses looked outright impossible to recover. A semco would simply sell too few of each special-purpose chip it created. Computers and other electronic wares were still pricey rarities reserved for special jobs. Sales were far from bounteous. A hot-selling computer might sell just 2,000 units. Semiconductor suppliers couldn't earn a living by making batches of only 2,000 chips before they had to retool and start all over again on a different design.

Intel's founding plan was to alter those economics. It aimed to escape the prevailing industry practice of making a few of this circuit, a few of that circuit, and then running through the whole expensive hassle of designing yet another circuit layout, only to sell just a few of those. By making LSI chips that could be used in many places, it would recover its design and manufacturing investments because it would make more money selling the same design over and over and over again.

"The idea was, we were going to find complex circuits we can build in large volume," says Gordon Moore. "And the first thing we see is semiconductor memory. It was the only place where you could define a complex integrated circuit that you could make in large volumes, so you could really amortize your design costs."

Memory circuits lacked some of the glamour and distinction of logic circuits, such as the logic circuits that powered, say, calculators. Memory circuits played supporting roles. But they were still essential elements inside electronic implements— especially inside a programmable computer, which needed a place to hold the instructions that told it how to function. Logic circuits made the actual computations. They mauled and manipulated incoming electronic impulses in ways that produced considered replies. The Mostek calculator on a chip was a logic circuit. The core of the chips Busicom wanted from Intel were to comprise logic circuits, similarly configured to solve math problems. By contrast, memory circuits simply held electronically coded information until it was called for by a logic circuit prepared to go to work on it. Therefore memory didn't have to be custom configured to perform a specific task. Its task was always the same. A memory circuit that worked in one device would do just as well in another. That's why Intel expected to make one version of a memory microchip that it could sell for many, many uses.

But the plan possessed one flaw: Semiconductor memory didn't yet exist. At the time of Intel's founding in 1968, computers stored information in complicated, cumbersome assemblages called memory cores. Their main component was a small metal doughnut, the "core." Each core was suspended by small wires. It could be electrically magnetized, demagnetized, and magnetized again, each time with its polarity—the orientation of its magnetic field—pointing either one direction or the other. Therefore it could designate either a binary numeral one, if pointing one way, or a zero, if pointing the other. Enough cores strung together could designate computer words amounting to instructions, or programming, that told a logic processor what steps to follow. They could also hold information, stockpiling the data that a computer processed.

A memory bank could contain thousands and thousands of the little rings, strung together in sheets like iron fabric or like nouveau coats of mail. With wires suspending the cores and wires to magnetize the cores and wires to read the direction of their magnetic fields, the things were big, awkward tangles. But in the late 1960s, they were the only game going.

Transistors, little on/off, one/zero switches themselves, could also store binary digits. But early chips didn't contain enough transistors to provide practical mass memory. Intel's founders staked the company on their certainty that they could find a way to integrate enough transistors on a chip to make semiconductor memory a practical reality, coat-of-mail cores and every other entrenched approach be damned. "The major advances in this industry have always been technology driven," observes Moore. "The market never knows it needs these things till after it sees them."

But first Intel had to figure out exactly how to make its mass-producible memory chips. In the meantime, to help support itself, the company shopped for the same sort of custom-designed circuit jobs it had been organized to avoid. That led it to Busicom. In April 1969, Intel signed on to design and supply the set of calculator microcircuits for the Japanese concern. They would be special-purpose logic chips, not the multipurpose memory chips that Intel was staking its future upon. But the job paid ready cash, which the start-up company badly needed at the moment.

The deal was like dancing with the last girl standing at the punch bowl. Busicom—its actual name was Nihon Keisanki, or Japanese Calculator, but it was commonly called by its product name, Busicom—was a new company, just like Intel. By 1969, with the frenzy to make electronic number machines fully a-shiver, established calculator companies had already paired with established semiconductor companies. Busicom had already joined with Mostek—at the time a newborn company too—to make the all-in-one calculator on a chip that would power Busicom's handheld. But it still needed a chip supplier for the line of powerful desktop calculators it planned. For those it found tiny Intel, alone and late to the dance.

Intel was still so small that Ted Hoff's immediate supervisor was Bob Noyce, the chief executive. But that arrangement wasn't for austerity alone. From lessons learned at Fairchild, Intel's bosses believed a technology company had to remain lean so that it would be flexible and fast-acting enough to make inevitable changes. Managers had to be involved, not aloof. They had to keep the troops energized and engaged. Sclerosis at any level might cause a company to miss an unanticipated change, and thereby miss a big chance.

Corporate flexibility also meant that workers were allowed to operate with a wide range of freedom. People had assigned responsibilities, but they could also wander into other inquiries, as long as they wandered productively.

Therefore Bob Noyce didn't flinch when Ted Hoff came from out of the blue in July 1969 to worry over Busicom's mixed up circuit sketches. "I explained what some of my concerns were, and I said I thought there might be some ways to improve the design. And he said, 'Well, if you think there's a way, why not? Go ahead and pursue it.' He said, 'It's always nice to have an insurance policy.'"

Hoff squeezed in the design rehab as a side project, fitting it among his regular obligations as manager of applications research. His computer studies at Stanford had prepared him well for the task. In fact, at Intel at the time Hoff was uniquely qualified for the undertaking. He was about the only researcher who knew how to set up the dominoes to fall logically inside a computer. The others were mostly all physicists and chemists, the sorts who made semiconducting silicon give up its secrets.

He started from scratch. The logic inside Busicom's originals was simply too messy and meandering. Even with the work divided up and apportioned among a dozen ICs, the Busicom plan called for chips of unprecedented complexity. Most calculators of the era contained only about a half-dozen stone circuits, with each circuit containing between 600 to 1,000 transistors. Intel, ambitious in its own right, figured it could make chips containing 2,000 transistors. But each of Busicom's twelve ICs would need up to 5,000 transistors to perform the operations the company envisioned. What's more, each chip would require some thirty-six or forty metal connectors—the "leads" that stick out like insect legs to bind an IC into the electronic system that surrounds it. Intel was only a year old. It wasn't even making any ready-for-market memory chips yet. It couldn't possibly make these things at the prices that Busicom expected to pay. According to the contract, Intel would let the chips go at about four to five dollars apiece. "That was my initial concern: that we wouldn't be able to manufacture these things to the price targets," recalls Hoff.

But as much as he felt professionally impelled to fix the design, he was also just personally bothered by the ponderousness and the sloppy inefficiency of Busicom's design. Its logic was split up, segmented, slap-dash, convoluted. It was unaesthetic. "The trick is to get logical chunks of stuff together," he insists, "because the minute you try to start splitting it up you end up with a God-awful number of wires running back and forth between the chips." Tall, long-framed, and lank, his pens standing at the ready inside a plastic pocket protector, Hoff looks the type that school-yard shrills might call a science nerd. But the label would simply misinterpret his stubborn insistence on rightness and order.

He worked through July and August, cobbling logic and blocking out simpler computing sequences that could still achieve Busicom's aims. He boiled down, streamlined, simplified. He added provisions like sub routines, simplifying operations that helped eliminate some of the mush and tangle. Hoff knew sub routines as a carryover lesson from his computing days at Stanford. They streamlined the logic by taking out certain repetitive procedures that popped up over and over again during the course of computations. Treating them as sub routines, he could write each operation only once and then send out to retrieve the appropriate one at all the places that the main process needed to perform the routine.

He hacked out encumbering wires, mapped orderly sequences of operations, and colocated logical chunks of stuff. He consolidated. He shortened the pathways electrical impulses would trace. He struggled to make single integrated circuits perform heaping loads of the work unaided, keeping calculations on one chip alone, to reduce the whole knotted network to fewer chips, to more elegant and efficient chips that would need just sixteen leads instead of the thirty-six or forty that Busicom planned to use to import and export signals.

For the first couple of months he worked unaided. Then in September Stanley Mazor joined Hoff's application development department. Mazor was a computer guy like Hoff, with some prior experience in the field. He contributed to the circuit design, becoming a collaborator as well as a scientific soul mate and sounding board for Hoff. "This was really the first time I had somebody to bounce ideas off of," Hoff says.

The Busicom circuit rehab wasn't the only moonlight project that Manager of Applications Research Ted Hoff undertook at the time. He also worked on a process to automate mask cutting at Intel. Masks were the all-important stencils that blocked out particular portions of bald silicon wafers during photolithography, the manufacturing step that laid out the transistors-to-be, as well as defined the pathways among them for the interconnecting strips of metal that would be bonded into a chip. Typically the masks were cut by hand. But Intel's upcoming memory chips would be laid out in orderly and repetitive patterns. Its early 256-bit memory IC consisted of 256 identical cells arrayed symmetrically in ranks and files upon the chip. Why pay some poor guy to plot and to cut out precisely a template of 256 identical cells when a motor-driven cutter could produce more accurate masks?

Intel paid about $10,000 for a PDP–8 minicomputer from Digital Equipment Corporation to control the cutter's path. Minis were a new concept in computing, so named because they were smaller than mainframes. They were built according to the prevailing method of computer construction, assembled from manifold electronic components. But minis were also less ponderous, easier to operate, and much less expensive than mainframes.

In Intel's lab, the PDP–8 also made a fun toy for researchers. Paul Brasseur, a technician working for Hoff, loaded a software program called Focal, which turned the general-purpose mini into a math machine, doing duties that everyone with a science degree could appreciate. "It made this computer look like it was a big, powerful calculator," says Hoff, "because you could write out equations and then it would just execute 'em on the spot."

So why, wondered Hoff, was he simultaneously sketching plans for special-purpose chips for Busicom that would perform calculations only? The PDP worked as a calculator today, but tomorrow, following a different set of instructions, it might drive, say, a mask-cutting coordinatograph.

Thoughts enmeshed. Hoff walked down the hallway to the marketing department to ask the sales experts why people bought big expensive desktop calculators if they already had computers at hand that could solve the same equations. The marketers reminded Hoff that computers first needed to be programmed before they would behave like a calculator. Programming was a pain, they said. People didn't want to bother with cards or punched tape to feed in the instructions computers needed just to solve math problems. Therefore they would spend, say, $5,000—a going rate before microchips made calculators throwaway consumables—for a machine that did only arithmetic.

But a link had occurred in Hoff's thoughts. The synthesis had begun. Like everyone else in the business, Hoff had heard all the starry predictions about how semiconductor companies would one day build a whole computer on a single chip. They would miniaturize a complex logic circuit enough to fit it entirely inside the confines of a single silicon speck. The feat merely required very dense, very large-scale integrated chips that contained enough transistors and things to carry out all the computations solo. In fact, in a way Mostek was attempting to do just that, working for Busicom's other hand, at that very moment.

But Mostek was making only a calculator on a chip, and although that chip would consolidate all the special-purpose functions onto a single sliver of silicon, it would still be a special-purpose device. It would be smaller, sure, but it would be as inflexible as the calculators that hogged a whole big corner of peoples' desks to do only math. So why not make a single chip that worked like the PDP instead? It could be a calculator when you wanted to calculate, but it could also perform any other computing job you wrote instructions for. Hoff's all-in-one chip would be a general-purpose device. He had already knocked down, compressed, streamlined, and simplified the architecture of his Busicom circuit. He was already getting close to a single chip. Why stop? If he structured the logic carefully enough, if he sequenced the operations efficiently enough, he could design a monolith that would perform all of a computer's processing tasks within its sole confines. Memory chips, soon to be Intel's signature products, could store programming in a space as tidy as the logic chip. They could keep handy any instructions such a solo-processor would need to perform an assigned duty. That way Busicom would still get its calculator. It would simply have to program the chip to work as a calculator, the same way Digital Equipment's PDP–8 could be programmed to solve equations.

As a computer, Hoff's IC would be general purpose. You wouldn't need to design and make a different chip to do every little this and that anymore. One IC—done, designed, in the bag, and ready to use—could be put to work in all sorts of different ways. Hoff thought of coordinating elevators, maybe, or timing traffic lights. You could come up with thousands of places to embed such a controller. They weren't places that would support the design and development of a single-purpose LSI circuit. But if an LSI control circuit was already available, awaiting only programming, all sorts of possibilities opened up.

Custom-made logic chips would remain in use, especially in places where a general-purpose, programmable micro wasn't capable enough to accomplish a task, or where sales volumes were already high enough to capture the expense incurred in making a custom chip. But overall, programmable micros promised to encourage the distribution of synthesized intelligence to every far corner.

"Our industry generally is driven by volumes," attests Les Vadasz, the Intel manager who would soon be tasked with figuring out how to manufacture Hoff's concept. "The investment in design and development has to be a small fraction of the total cost" of making the product. "The only way that can happen is if the volume is high. Especially as the cost of development goes up. I mean, today we have multi-hundred-million-transistor chips. The only way you can get to that at an economic level is if there is enough volume associated with the total market."

Hoff's first microprocessor—the name the industry gave to full-function computers on a chip—didn't come close to containing that many transistors. But he established the concept, marrying programmable computers and semiconductor structure. It was an act of synthesis, creating a single, more powerful entity from two separate technologies.

Explains Vadasz: "You had a computer concept over here which was progressing on its own, with its transistors and diodes and core storage and all those things. And over there is a semiconductor technology which is moving on its own toward more and more complex integration. Then Ted just put the two together and said, hey, I don't care if there are huge boxes full of transistors out there doing much more general-purpose applications. I just want to use this technology to do a limited set of applications that nobody can do right now, and he put the two together."

To Gordon Moore, Hoff's innovation was a matter of prescient good timing. "People had talked about a computer on a chip for years," he says. "But it was always way out there in the future. What Ted saw was that, with the complexity with which we were already working, you could actually make an integrated circuit like that now. That was the real conceptual breakthrough."

But to the visiting Busicom engineers in the summer of 1969, Hoff's concept was nothing more than a challenge. They were not pleased to see that their prized creation might be preempted. Therefore, working separately from Hoff but at the same time, they undertook a revision of their own. They did not comprehend *simplification* quite as comprehensively as Hoff. They clung to their grand original, only whittling it down. They reduced the number of transistors per chip to around 2,000 from the original 5,000. But the plan still required twelve chips, still with thirty-six to forty pins sticking out of each, and therefore all those infernal wires still running among them.

By contrast, Hoff proposed a three-chip design (later a fourth was added). His microprocessor acted as a lone central-processing unit—the computer on a chip. He supported it with a read-only memory chip, ROM, to store the programming that would turn the microprocessor, in Busicom's case, into a calculator. Next to that, a random-access memory chip, RAM, kept at hand the data that the central processor juggled during computations. All the circuits would be in simple sixteen-pin packages—only sixteen bug's legs instead of forty to attach each chip to its surroundings.

On September 16, 1969, Intel sent a formal letter to Busicom suggesting Hoff's alternative. In October, Busicom senior executives came to California to sit as judges in the computer chip bake-off pitting their own engineers' revision against the stunning innovation by Hoff. They had to determine which approach Intel would pursue to fulfill the original development contract. After watching both presentations, the execs chose Hoff's programmable computer on a chip.

Great Debates

THERE WAS STILL A CHANCE that Ted Hoff's versatile, multifunctional computer on a chip would turn into nothing more than the cerebrum inside just another calculator. There was a chance it would miss history by missing its opportunity to become the world's first programmable, chip-size computer—the stimulant that would suddenly salt the idea among every other envious semicon striver. Busicom still owned Hoff's brainwork. He had created the all-in-one microprocessor under the original development contract. Busicom had put up $60,000 to cover design and engineering, with a commitment to purchase the ICs from Intel once manufacturing started.

Certain powers inside Intel were happy to leave the situation like that. Let Busicom have the blasted thing so that Intel could sell memory ICs without distraction. Silicon computer storage was itself an unfamiliar concept, they argued. The last thing Intel's sales and marketing staff needed now was another new and unfamiliar concept—this microprocessor thing—to sell alongside memories. Even ambitious, lean, and agile technology companies can miss opportunities. In 1970 and 1971, Intel was about to miss the opportunity to introduce microprocessors because the tenuous young upstart was afraid to spread its resources too thin.

At the same time, competitive cross-fertilization was spreading the idea. A computer terminal maker called Datapoint picked it up while doing business at Intel. Then it flit like a bee to Texas Instruments, where it left the concept for TI to begin developing on its own. Eventually, the kinetic interplay produced by the companies' rivalries kicked the idea out into the daylight.

Datapoint had first lit on Intel in 1969, while Hoff and Mazor were still working out the sequence of instructions for the Busicom microprocessor. (At the time, Datapoint went by its original name, Computer Terminals Corporation.) Datapoint didn't care about that. It was interested in using Intel's upcoming memory ICs inside a new line of thinking computer terminals then on Datapoint's drawing board. Terminals had become the sensory organs of big computers, the stations where people entered requests and viewed a computer's replies. Datapoint aimed to build some intelligence into its upcoming line of Datapoint 2200 keyboards and screens so that the terminals could handle information faster. Semiconductor memory would be perfect for that because the little chips would fit so handily inside a terminal, yet they'd still provide the cache needed for incoming and outgoing information.

But after that innovative interest in silicon memory, Datapoint reverted to the customary practice for the logic chips it planned to pack inside its terminals. It would have some ICs specially designed, tailored to perform precisely the functions its terminals required. It would go elsewhere for those. With Intel it talked only memory.

In order to determine how its memories might work within the Datapoint system, Intel needed to see the terminal's entire electro-schemat. The plans crossed the desks of Hoff and Mazor right when they flushed with enthusiasm for their all-in-one chip. Their reaction: Why the devil did Datapoint want special logic circuits? They could do it all with one programmable flake, just like the one that Hoff and Mazor had in the works for Busicom. The pair wrote out a technical specification to show Datapoint exactly what they meant. They didn't expect their idea to travel.

But according to the Intel account, Datapoint, a Texas company, was at the same time talking to TI about supplying the logic microcircuits for its dream terminals. It carried Hoff and Mazor's schematic down to Dallas, where the idea began to grow into a development program inside TI's semiconductor lab.

Intel didn't know that the cross-pollination had occurred. As a young company with scant resources, it was having enough trouble just finishing the Busicom job. Hoff and Mazor's one-chip design had been selected in the standoff of 1969, but that design consisted of only the computing sequences that would permit single-chip data processing. The work of translating those sequences into microscopic silicon—a wholly separate discipline—still remained.

To put the project on a crash course toward completion, Intel went back to its well: Fairchild Semiconductor. In April 1970 it hired away Federico Faggin. Thirty-nine years old, Faggin had a Ph.D. in physics from the University of Padua in his native Italy. At Fairchild he had pioneered a process for making metal-oxide microcircuits called silicon gate—it used silicon to create the field effect rather than the metal used by other companies to make field-effect transistors on MOS chips. Faggin understood monolithic structures the way Hoff understood computing sequences. His first assignment at Intel was to translate the Busicom micro into a speck of silicon.

Faggin took Hoff's conceptual design and started to sprint. As he translated the scheme into semiconductor structures, he also modified it where he saw opportunities to improve it. He tore through the project in a mere nine months, considered a lightning pace by people in the trade. By February 1971, Busicom received early samples of its microprocessor-cum-calculator chip. When it was eventually awarded, the final patent for the invention, awkwardly called a Memory System for a Multi-Chip Digital Computer, went to the trio of Faggin, Hoff, and Mazor.

Those technologists saw clearly how their product neatly meshed with Intel's business approach. As a general-purpose computing chip capable of changing functions with a simple change of software, it promised the same advantage as memory chips: After you sweated through the engineering chores just once, you could set up the manufacturing process for that single design and let it cruise, making a product that would work in all sorts of places, so that you could sell it all over the place.

Yet Intel hesitated, stuck in the debate about what to do with the new concept. The issue wasn't just ownership—the fact was that Busicom, not Intel, held rights to the design. The larger controversy swirled around the fundamental concept itself. What good was a single-chip computer? Marketers arrayed against the technophiles. Faggin, Hoff, and Mazor felt eager to spread the new micro around. But the marketers, the people sent out to pump Intel's products, wanted just to call it a calculator and let Busicom keep it.

"They said, 'We'll never sell it to anybody else. It's just too much work,'" Hoff recalls. They argued that the company couldn't support a microchip so radically different. For one thing, the salespeople wouldn't even know how to explain the new concept, let alone promote it. "The expression I heard was, 'We've got diode salesmen out there trying to sell memories, and now you expect them to sell computers! You're crazy.'"

The marketing mavens worked up sales estimates to support their case. They overlooked Hoff's idea that a programmable chip could end up as a controller embedded in all sorts of machines, in traffic lights and elevators, for instance. It was a computer chip, so the marketers zoomed to computers as the machines most likely to use it. Computers were still an uncommon, ethereal species, even though minicomputers like the Digital PDP–8 were making them more accessible. The current demand for minicomputers totaled only about 20,000 a year. If Intel's IC sneaked into ten percent of them—a handsome penetration—that would still only tally to sales of 2,000 microprocessors annually. Why bother?

Software arose as another issue. Coming up with programming to make the chip work inside of Busicom's calculators wouldn't pose too grave a challenge because it would require only a one-time effort. But selling the chip for use far and wide implied that Intel would also have to provide a whole lot of software to support it. You couldn't sell a programmable device without also providing programming. That's how the system worked in the early 1970s. Software was often a give-away, thrown in as an enticement by a hardware company when it sold a computer. Often the seller even sent out a technician to set up a new computer and smooth away wrinkles to settle the machine comfortably into its workday routine.

"It's one thing when you're selling a ten-thousand dollar box," says Hoff. "You can afford to send a guy out there to hold the engineer's hand for a while. But not if it's a fifty-dollar or a hundred-dollar chip. You don't want the same, ten-thousand-dollar hassle."

Intel didn't have any programmers anyway. Intel couldn't even hire any programmers. "The prestige of the programmer was always based on how big a computer they let him screw up," says Hoff. "I had one fellow come in and his first question for me was, 'What size Three-sixty am I going to get to work on?'" He meant the IBM Three-sixty, the premier monstrosity of the day. "I said, 'We're talking about something much, much smaller.' He said, 'I don't really think I'm interested.'"

"The general feeling of so many people at Intel was that this was such a big step and such a change in direction for the company," Hoff elaborates. "Should we really do it? How do we do it? What are we getting ourselves into? There was just a constant agony.

"I remember one meeting with Bob Noyce, where Bob said, 'We've got a tiger by the tail. We don't know what to do.'" Hoff chuckles. "He said, 'We're not ready to make a decision to go ahead with this.' And I said to him, 'Every time you put it off you have made a decision. You've made a decision *not* to announce.' And I said, 'We're going to lose this.' In other words, somebody else is eventually gonna come out with this thing."

Noyce, as Intel's chief executive, could droop to a managerial nadir when he stood between warring parties. Robert Noyce is best remembered for his incongruous combination of stunning brilliance and unassuming, guy-next-door graciousness. He could make you think you were as smart as he was. Therefore he was warmly admired, like a trophied team captain who made you want to play alongside his luster. But when his team argued, the affable charismat could try too hard to stay on the two sides at once.

"He couldn't say no," says Charlie Sporck, the Fairchild alum who turned National Semiconductor into one of the industry's victors. Sporck honed his own management prowess while working under Noyce at Fairchild, and he remained a friend and admirer after their paths diverged. Before that, in their formative Fairchild days, the two men used to bring together their families for Sunday dinners. Sporck remembers his colleague's hands-on, inquisitive energy. He remembers the afternoon when Noyce came by and saw that Sporck had a barbecue grill half finished in his backyard. Charlie was stuck and couldn't decide where to lay the next brick. Bob rushed home to fetch his masonry tools, and the two men finished the project together. But on the job, Sporck saw his friend's soft spots too. "I could go in and get something from him. You know: *I want to buy this or buy that. Yes.* And somebody else would come in and say, *he shouldn't do that.* He'd say, *yes.* Or you'd go in and say, *Bob, I think we ought to replace the plant manager up there at the diode up in San Rafael*. He'd say, *Well, Charlie, if you really think so*. And somebody else would come in and say, *Jesus, we can't do that, Bob*. And he would go, *Oh, no, we can't*. I mean, that was Bob: he just could not be a bad guy."

Thus in 1970 and 1971, as he led the early ascendancy of Intel, the foresight and the inspired leadership Noyce had demonstrated a decade earlier at Fairchild, when he had rallied the company around planar transistors and around his own IC innovation, seemed to falter. Noyce was as uncertain as anyone about what to do with the Hoff/Mazor/Faggin microprocessor. He scarcely had time to consider the controversy anyway. All around him Intel's seams were stretching from the heft of early success. The company's memory chips were out in the market and rapidly winning converts. By July 1970, encouraged by demand for the products, Intel set up the Canadian company Microsystems International Limited to make some of the circuits so that equipment makers would find an ample supply. That sale of manufacturing rights and know-how also brought Intel more than $2 million.

By August 1971, Intel was selling memory circuits to more than 500 customers for use in mainframe computers, test and measurement equipment, calculators, and other such gear. Whereas most of its buyers resided in the United States, business had also spread to Europe, the Middle East, and Japan. By September 1971 Intel ICs sold at a rate of more than $1 million per month, more than double the sales rate from one year earlier. The company had just moved into new offices on Bowers Avenue in Santa Clara, housing an 18-member administrative and executive staff, 34 sales and marketing people, most of its 88 researchers and engineers, and some of the 242 workers it employed in manufacturing and testing. Intel ran a second manufacturing site in nearby Mountain View. It paid independent companies in Tijuana, Mexico, and in Hong Kong to perform final assembly of its chips—encapsulating the silicon in protective packages. And it was preparing to admit outside stockholders in the fall, becoming a publicly traded company.

Noyce was busy. The whole damn company was bustling. And the quandary over what to do about microprocessors still roiled. Then, in May 1971, an opportunity arrived from Japan. Just when the all-in-one logic chips were getting ready to ship, Busicom hit a financial snag. The calculator wars had begun, and competition had grown bruising. Busicom asked Intel to reduce the price of the chips. As Intel marketers prepared to cross the Pacific to renegotiate terms, Faggin, Hoff, and Mazor pestered them. "We said, 'For God sakes, if you can't get anything else from them, get the rights to sell to other people,'" recounts Hoff. Thus, despite their reluctance to peddle the product far and wide, they bought back the rights. For the favor, Intel returned Busicom's $60,000 development fee. (The refund didn't go far enough: Busicom died in bankruptcy a few years later.)

Yet even after it obtained ownership, the chip-maker haggled internally about what to do with the microprocessor. The rancor raged three months longer, until competitive cross-fertilization returned to settle the argument, traveling back from Dallas to Santa Clara. This time the stimulus wasn't a technical specification like the one Datapoint had spirited to TI. It was more generalized business intelligence, carried in the person of Ed Gelbach, who was hired away from Texas Instruments to serve as Intel's new marketing director in August 1971. The hire was a coup for Intel because TI was then the prime mover in semiconductors.

Before Gelbach had left Dallas, TI had silently developed its own version of a programmable, single-chip computer. Aiming to power the Datapoint terminal, TI's Gary Boone designed and patented his own take on a microprocessor, finishing soon enough to demonstrate a working model in March 1971. That actually beat the Intel chip that Federico Faggin was simultaneously sculpting because Busicom didn't see working silicon samples till May of that year.

In addition to his insider's perspective from TI, the new marketing director also brought an outsider's perspective to Intel's argument over its microprocessor. Gelbach arrived feeling eager to make marks with the striving young company. Like every other astute combatant in semiconductors, he held a high regard for the market-creating magic that a useful, hitherto undiscovered concept could work. He realized, as Hoff had warned earlier, that other semcos were close behind Intel with the idea. "I've always felt that Ed never got the credit that he deserved for making that gutsy decision" to sell the microprocessor, says Hoff. When Noyce later recounted the microprocessor's development, he wrote that Gelbach "realized the [product's] potential was not as a replacement for minicomputers but as a way to insert intelligence into many products for the first time."

By the autumn of 1971, about a month after Ed Gelbach arrived, Intel was plotting its microprocessor sales strategy. The first advertisement for a ready-to-use microprocessor appeared in the November 15 edition of the trade journal *Electronic News*.

TI, in the meantime, let the idea drop. Datapoint didn't use Boone's IC in its terminal, and the Texan didn't take other measures to rush out a microprocessor. "The issue as I understand it and remember it," says Harvey Cragon, the TI alum, "was that TI had a lot of business on its plate at that time, and this did not seem to be a fruitful way to spend resources. In any company like TI, or Intel, or anybody, there's essentially an infinite demand for resources, but a finite supply. And so somebody has gotta say, we're going to do this and we're not going to do that."

At Intel, that somebody was Gelbach. The company called the new product the MSC–4. It consisted of four chips: the central processor, random-access memory, read-only memory, and register memory for short-term storage. The central processor was clearly the star. It was designated the 4004. The half-inch

long, sixteen-legged mechanoid bug packed as much computing power as the first ENIAC computer, a machine that had
filled a room.

The announcement in *Electronic News* proclaimed that the
4004, when combined with the appropriate memory chips,
would "provide complete computing and control functions for
host systems, data terminals, billing machines, measuring systems, numerical control systems and process control systems."
It mentioned nothing about traffic lights or elevators, but people who made and used machines soon started thinking for
themselves. For one, there was the meat packer who telephoned
Les Vadasz looking for help weighing bacon. To put together
one-pound packages, his meat cutters had to take great pains to
trim the last piece, slicing it maybe a little larger, maybe a little
smaller, to bring the package weight to exactly one pound. The
hog butcher wondered if he could attach a chip-based controller to a scale and a slicer to automatically adjust the thickness of the last slice to tally one pound. "I thought it was brilliant," says Vadasz. "Those are the kind of things that suddenly
were possible."

Noyce wrote of a Dutch engineer who had been isolated for
twelve months while teaching math in Kenya. Late in 1972,
after his return, the engineer sent a letter to Intel expressing
amazement that microprocessors had changed electronics so
unalterably during his one-year absence.

Intel established education and training programs to prose-
lytize for microprocessors and to help equipment makers put
them to work. To address the issue of software—to get Intel off
the hook for all the niggling programming its chips would
require as they ventured far and wide—the company developed
and sold programming tools to help people create their own
computer code as they adapted microprocessors to specific
uses. Other single-chip computers quickly followed the pioneering 4004. Intel introduced a more capable model, the 8008,
in April 1972, offering twice the computing power as the 4004.

The 8008 was the heir to the early brainwork that Hoff and Mazor had done for the Datapoint terminal. When Noyce and Hoff listed the pantheon of groundbreaking microprocessors in a paper they published in 1981, they included seven Intel models, plus others like the 6800 from Motorola, the TMS 1000 from Texas Instruments, National Semiconductor's Pace chip, and the 1802 from Motorola, all unveiled in 1974.

Successions of improved all-in-one processors appeared as Intel and every other chiptopian visionary of the semiconductor industry adopted the mantra *smaller, faster, cheaper*. They relentlessly applied technical refinements to make transistors tinier, to pack them together more densely, to make them fire more rapidly. They devised better microstructures. They discovered more effective material treatments. They beat down costs by improving production methods. In 1974, Intel's 8080 provided the brains for the first personal computer, a $395 mail-order kit called Altair that sold tens of thousands within months. By 1985, Intel was packing 275,000 transistors into its new model 286 microprocessor. Its Pentium II, released in 1997, contained 7.5 million. Three years later, in 2000, the first version of Intel's Pentium 4 appeared in personal computers with 42 million transistors. Its circuitry was fine-tuned to handle communications carried over the spontaneous, ubiquitous, democratic computer network called the Internet. It could flash TV-like video onto computer screens, support instant audio and video conversations, show three-dimensional drawings, process photos, and encode music for MP3 players.

By the time Pentium 4 appeared, the bold prophecies that Motorola's Dan Noble had made in *Electronics* in 1965 still had fifteen years to run, but already they looked timid.

≡ PART TWO ≡

Building the House

≡ 10 ≡

Changing Guards

BY THE TIME TED HOFF'S first microprocessor arrived in 1971 to trigger so much transcendent computer innovation, circuit wizards had already advanced far toward fulfilling their wish to get ICs into common circulation. The microprocessor provided a last necessary encouragement to equipment developers. With general-purpose computing chips ready-made and at their fingertips, the engineers who crafted familiar commodities could cleverly transform their products. Like the meat packer who telephoned Les Vadasz, ordinary merchandisers took up the hunt for popular places to employ ICs.

The calculator wars that then raged in full fury gave an early first hint that semiconductor companies didn't have to provide the chips *and* the applications. If they only created compelling new tools, people scattered in other trades would pick them up independently and use them to advance their private positions. In 1965 in Dallas, Patrick Haggerty had simply been impatient when he'd urged his engineers to invent compelling new gadgets that could sneak silicon circuits into widespread use. The Canon Pocketronic—heir to the Cal Tech calculator that had consumed Jerry Merryman and a handful of Texas Instruments' researchers for two tough years—was quickly eclipsed by more capable models made by companies like Bowman, Sanyo, and Sharp, which made better calculators simply because their livelihoods depended on it. Those companies established the format that TI adopted when it moved in to manufacture calculators on its own.

Similarly, subversive agents in other businesses welcomed microchips as a means to assert themselves against old-guard establishment powers that wouldn't embrace new ways simply because they had perfected the old ways. At one such established player, a company called Essex International, an aggressive engineer named Robert Fosnough used Intel's first 4004 microprocessor in his attack against the creaking, ancient hierarchy that ruled home appliances.

Essex was located in Logansport, a Midwestern city far from the bustling hubs of semiconductor foment, situated amid Indiana's corn and soy fields some 1,000 miles north of Dallas and 2,300 miles east of Silicon Valley. But even at such a far remove, people at Essex International sidled into microelectronics to protect the lucrative position they held in switches, solenoids, relays, and related electrical parts. Those were all old-line products, called *electro-mechanical* because they turned electrical energy into mechanical action, or movement. They were heavier and far more muscular than the petite semiconductor elements that operated on mere whispers of current and that were more likely in 1970 to come from such places as Dallas and Silicon Valley. Relays pass heavy loads through fat wires, managing electrical currents that would burn through lesser junctions. They are behind-the-panel parts used just about every place electricity performs physical labor. Relays send current to the starters that crank automobile engines. When a home thermostat kicks on, its faint signal tells relays to shunt power to pumps and fan motors down at the furnace. A person who switches on a microwave to reheat leftovers for lunch activates a hidden relay that sends juice to a power-sucking magnetron, the part that generates the rays that pierce the food inside the oven.

Essex had been at the relay trade for a while. It began making electric current controls in Logansport before World War II, selling most of them to automakers. Starting in the late 1940s, the company ventured into other markets, especially appliances. Essex then made relays for washers, dryers, refrigerators, air conditioners, and every other sort of big machine that people bolted into their homes.

But by the end of the 1960s, the company could see an intruder rumbling around the border of its comfortably established business. Makers of heaters and air conditioners began asking what contributions electronics might make to their products. Heating systems and cooling systems might do a lot more for people, they figured, if they had some flexibility built into them. Their products might become more useful, and therefore more popular, they thought, if maybe they could be programmed to provide more than mere on/off, start/stop operation. But people who made chillers and furnaces didn't know anything about chips and transistors. So they brought their questions to Essex because Essex made the parts that made up their current controls, providing the relays and such that worked behind the dials and buttons and levers on their operating panels.

To answer the challenge, in 1970 Essex set up an electronics team, called its appliance controls group. "We wanted to get into electronic controls to protect what we had," explains William Hopkins, a Logansport native who was then vice president of marketing. "Since 1949 we had built relays for Whirlpool, GE, Trane—for every air conditioning and appliance manufacturer. Naturally we tried to keep our ear open. We wanted to protect what controls we had, and some of those controls were affected by the approach of electronics. We saw the market going that way."

The company hired Bob Fosnough as engineering manager
of the new operation. Fosnough was a 1965 electrical engineering grad from Purdue. He joined Essex from a Magnavox operation in Fort Wayne, Indiana, where he'd worked for five years
behind a vault door, designing military electronics that he still
can't talk about. "I sort of wanted to take some of that technology and try it someplace else," he says.

But at Essex he felt frustrated. The company seemed stuck
in a warp as a mid-century relay maker. Relays paid its bills,
after all. Its plant managers already knew how to make relays.
Its sales and marketing people already knew how to sell them.
Its engineers knew how to design them. Acknowledging the
looming threat of micro-controls required mere words. And setting up an electronics operation took just a smattered investment. But violating the reflexive habits of a large, unwieldy corporate apparatus demanded much more. For all his ambition,
Bob Fosnough was an invisible come-lately. The thousands of
other people who equaled Essex felt predisposed to do their
jobs the way they'd always done them. Penetrating their
thoughts would require some shock and spectacle. Essex was
already successful, after all. What incentive would anyone feel
to depart substantially from a workday formula that worked?

Fosnough wasn't alone in his slow-simmering frustration.
Max Nelson, who handled product development, felt it too. So
did Larry Long, who worked in sales. One morning in the
spring of 1971, after a staff meeting of routine tedium, the trio
lingered in the conference room, drawn together by a mutual
resolve to *do* something. They were kindred thinkers. Young,
perceptive, striving, impatient, they saw the opportunity all
around them. Electronics was making everything new. Large
changes waited right on the threshold of the room where they
sat. But at the same time they felt restrained by the go-slow cau-
tion of a corporation that had dipped only a toe into the undertaking, whereas the great weighty bulk of its established ways
rolled blindly with the power of unconscious inertia. They

couldn't just sit and wait while Essex idled. Nothing would come to them if they did—at least nothing would come fast enough for them to seize opportunities that moved so swiftly they might easily wash past or be caught first by someone else. If they waited, if they only rode the momentum of the appliance business, they might miss the unformed changes they glimpsed ahead of them. Ambitious, anxious, desperate, hopeful, slouching thoughtfully and uncomfortably in conference-room chairs, they recognized that they had to move proactively. They had to make a thing, something, some product that would bust electronic controls beyond mere good intentions at Essex. They needed to place the opportunity out where everybody else in the company could see it as clearly as they saw it.

Fosnough already knew how to put together electronic timers and clocks, and he figured he could parlay those devices into some sort of a full-fledged appliance control box. Larry Long knew appliance needs from selling relays to manufacturers. "So we said, well, maybe we can make an electronic controller to replace wind-up controllers in microwave ovens," Fosnough recounts. "That seemed like it might be a good idea. A microwave oven was an immature product," which meant that it still possessed ample room for improvement. "It had a big price tag on it, so it could afford some expensive electronics in it. And the technology was right on the cusp of being able to do it."

Recalling the secretive ways of Magnavox, Fosnough taped paper over the hall windows of the small lab while he built his prototype controller. He didn't want the idea to leak out into the wider appliance world. Essex engineers spent a lot of time calling on customers, kibitzing with kindred engineers who made washers, dryers, air conditioners, refrigerators, ranges, and microwaves. The visits kept them current so that Essex could create ever more effective relays and switches. But business intelligence seeped both ways, and Fosnough worried that if the rest of Essex R&D knew what he was up to, some loose-lipped staffer might say too much as he bent over plans and product drafts at an appliance company. Once an appliance engineer got wind of it, he'd mention it to every other control company he traded with. Fosnough reckoned that Essex competitors would be sure to copy the concept. The idea was too good not to copy.

The developers' most daunting challenge was to devise timing and control circuitry that fit unobtrusively behind an oven's narrow side panel. Therefore they needed micro-logic. But paying an IC house to make a custom chip for a single, one-of-a-kind, uncertain prototype was out of the question. The project was pure speculation, funded wholly by Essex, lacking any firm prospects for payoff. Heck, microwave ovens weren't even particularly popular at the time. Home versions had been around only a few years, and most people still didn't know what to make of them. Therefore most of the high powers at Essex already looked askance at the project. They didn't see any future for it. Fosnough and his coconspirators would have never even won the chance to try their venture if they hadn't already struck up a friendship with the vice president who ran their division, a fellow named Gary Probst, who happened to be the son of the president of Essex. Therefore the brass beneath Probst had to go along, but they didn't like it. Fosnough felt harried, beset, unsupported.

His dilemma presented a perfect opportunity for Intel's 4004 microprocessor to prove its value. The adaptable chip could provide all the logic-processing power that Fosnough's prototype controller required. And it came at a small fraction of the price he'd pay for custom silicon. He could drop the ready-made logic chip into the model for a price cheap enough to assuage the belligerent brass glowering askance at his aspiration. He built the sample using the newly introduced Intel 4004 microprocessor, along with its three sidekick memory chips. The chips nestled in a circuit board that hid behind the number pad people would use to punch in cooking times. A bar of red, tiki-stick numerals at the top of the controller counted down the timer.

Fosnough, Long, and Nelson brought their invention to Litton Industries up in Minneapolis, Minnesota. Litton ran alongside Amana Refrigeration in home microwaves, with the two companies selling more ovens by far than anyone else. But of the two, only Litton was known as the techy innovator. After all, it was owned by the California aerospace concern that bore the same name. The flash-and-dazzle aura of rocketry rubbed into Litton appliances. If any mere oven-making outfit was going to go for a computerized control panel, Litton would go for it. How could the Fosnough team miss?

But Litton slammed the door on the idea. The chief engineer at the appliance maker, Verle Blaha, decreed that consumers would never buy such a thing. He said the mock-up looked like some sort of game, a slot machine maybe. In fact, it looked like nothing so much as a disembodied calculator. It could control a microwave oven, but so what? Litton didn't want it. Even moonbaby Litton felt content to stay electro-mechanical. The big-thinking developers from Essex felt deflated. When returning to Logansport—550 miles from Minneapolis—the only fact that any of them knew with certainty was that they would hear a lot of I-told-you-sos back at the relay plant.

Computers for Cooks

AMANA REFRIGERATION had introduced the world to practical home microwaves in 1967, but by 1971 the appliance branch of Litton had caught up to Amana in sales. Neither moved a bounty of the newfangled cookers. The appliance was only four years into its existence, and it still attracted more curious gawkers than it did actual buyers. Amana and Litton each sold about 100,000 ovens in the United States in 1971, together accounting for half of the models that moved out of shops, while General Electric and a handful of Japanese names shared the bottom half of the market. But Amana still led its rival in experience. It still led in name recognition. Because it had been selling them the longest, it still had more ovens at work on countertops than had any other microwave maker.

Yet over at Essex, Bob Fosnough had dismissed Amana when he first sized his prospects for selling a computerized controller. The appliance industry as a whole may have seemed like an ancient regime alongside the sculptors of silicon microdots, but internally the business recognized its own order. The chieftains of home appliances considered Amana a small, snoozing company that just nibbled at small pieces of business. To them it was a rube's outpost, tucked remotely into small-town Amana, Iowa. Therefore Fosnough assumed that Amana wasn't innovative enough to try a computerized control box.

Yet while Fosnough was still only assembling his sample, Amana was already out courting semcos in Silicon Valley and Dallas, looking to create a microchip controller of its own. The competitive imperative to improve its product had driven Amana's enterprising oven experts out to seek the chipsters. At the start of their search, Richard Foerstner, the engineer who had midwifed home microwaves just a handful of years earlier, and Dan McConnell, the marketer-cum-technologist charged with pushing Amana's ovens into more kitchens, knew so little about silicon circuits that they might have reinforced Amana's backwoods reputation. But driven by a powerful compulsion to learn about electronic control, Foerstner and McConnell picked up a technical education in the course of their journey. Their big problem was finding a semiconductor company willing to take Amana seriously enough to take it on as a partner. For all their bluster about popularizing obscure ICs, microchip makers overlooked the rich possibility that Foerstner and McConnell presented to them: Microwave cookers could lead ordinary consumers to miniature electronics.

The semcos were following their own agenda. They explored more highfalutin territories for their products, looking to place them inside math machines and such to perform computing jobs already familiar to the microscenti. Kitchen wares? That was an unknown country. Besides, semcos weren't quite capable of giving Amana everything it needed. They made miniature stone circuits. Amana needed the chips plus everything that wrapped around a chip to comprise a full-fledged control box.

In the end, it took Amana's survival instincts and its intimate understanding of the wants and needs of everyday folk to complete the marriage of the old order and the new. It took the unblinking determination of McConnell and Foerstner to intersect microelectronic management with domestic life, introducing the flashing numerals, the easy-touch number pads, and the screaming beeps that became fixtures in every household.

Beginning in 1966, Richard Foerstner, a mechanical engineer from the University of Iowa, had spent better than a year shuttling between Amana, Iowa, and Hooksett, New Hampshire, where the company Raytheon made the magnetrons that generate cooking rays. After his countertop adaptation of a microwave cooker reached store shelves in the autumn of 1967, Foerstner remained engineer in charge of the product, responsible for its ongoing improvement. That began immediately. He tightened up the door latch, for instance, and improved its seal to help allay fears about stray cooking rays.

Dan McConnell was an electrical engineer from MIT who had moved to Amana from Raytheon in 1970. He started as the microwave product manager and climbed quickly to become Amana's vice president in charge of product planning. McConnell directed the search for a micro-control partner.

Their motives to computerize cookers grew from a few sources. The first was archrival Litton. Despite the disdain it showed to Essex, Litton was happy to sell the electronic look. It made a big marketing splash with a microwave oven that featured a kind of built-in digital stopwatch. Ordinary ovens used electro-mechanical controls that featured marked dials used to set cooking time. Better ovens had two. One dial was marked in minutes for setting longer cooking times. The other was marked in seconds for quick hits. Litton's electro-look oven still used traditional electro-mechanicals, and it still featured a twist knob to set cooking times. But instead of showing the settings as numbers etched onto a dial, the oven flashed the time as showy electronic numerals. The timer itself, the mechanism actually controlling the cooking span, was still a mechanical wind-up. Therefore the oven didn't provide any greater cooking accuracy than conventional models. But it looked cool. It looked techy.

The executives at Amana considered it a sham and a hoax. But the feature helped Litton sell ovens. They recognized that they needed a counter measure. A legitimate, computerized control panel would certainly trump Litton's simpering time display. Even though Amana wouldn't sell a lot of them—after all, computer-equipped ovens would cost more than the standard models—the flashy showpiece would win over buyers to the brand.

Sales by innovation was an unrecognized Amana trait, but it nevertheless provided another big motive for going electronic. The company cultivated a culture of innovation—a hidden habit that belied the stodgy image that dogged Amana inside the appliance business. Its innovative spirit went unnoticed because as long as Amana remained a small, privately owned operation, as long as it made mostly just fridges and freezers, it simply didn't sell enough merchandise to make the rest of the industry pay much attention. Even at the start of the 1970s, when Amana was the microwave leader alongside Litton, the makers of more commonplace appliances overshadowed it. Next to, say, GE and Whirlpool, Amana was a speck. But it maintained a comfortable position in its market niches by wooing fussy, image-conscious consumers who preferred—and who could afford—top performance over basement prices.

The company polished its image through advertising that aimed to make Amana a status symbol. It stayed away from mass retailers, placing its products in upper-scale appliance stores instead. Most of all, Amana attracted buyers by getting out ahead with new features that neighbors across the showroom aisles didn't yet offer. In 1947 it began selling the first upright freezer for homes. In 1949 it brought out fridge-and-freezer combinations with the two chests aligned side by side. The models could be hyped for convenience because they reduced stooping and bending.

The impulse to innovate came straight from Amana's ebullient and irrepressible proprietor, George Foerstner. The senior Foerstner ran his company boldly and cleverly, recognizing consumer wants before people quite realized themselves that they wanted an innovation. He maintained a stubborn commitment to corporate image and brand-name notoriety. Foerstner also played bridge masterfully enough to land on television with Charles Henry Goren, a gamemaster who hosted airwave tourneys back when TVs were still all black and white. He applied the same astute gamesmanship to his business, engaging in dealings that kept his corporate attorney sprinting like an Olympian.

Foerstner had started Amana Refrigeration in 1934 for the Amana Society—a kind of member-owned corporation that emerged from the bust up of the Amana Colony of the Community of True Inspiration. Today a lot of locals remember the colony as a communist endeavor. But it was organized as a commune only to discourage materialism and to inculcate members in its founding principles of piety and spirituality. The Community of True Inspiration came to the United States from Germany in 1843 to escape religious discrimination. The Amana Colony went capitalist in 1932 by issuing shares of its communally run enterprises to church members. Foerstner ran the refrigeration business for the corporation until 1950, when he purchased it with the aid of some local investors.

In 1965 Foerstner sold Amana Refrigeration to the Raytheon Company, a technologically accomplished defense contractor that had made a name making radar. Raytheon bought because it wanted to expand into other businesses, to escape dependency on government work. Foerstner sold to get cash to expand his appliance trade. But he made Amana a Raytheon subsidiary under the proviso that he'd continue to run the place.

Home microwaves grew serendipitously when the talents of Foerstner bumped into Raytheon. The defense company had introduced the world's first microwave cooker, its Radarange, in 1945. The product was a civilian adaptation of radar, infiltrating food with waves of energy from scaled-down versions of the magnetrons that beamed rays into the atmosphere to spot aircraft. But the first Radaranges were hardly fit for homes. They were refrigerator-sized appliances priced at a few thousand dollars apiece and sold only to commercial kitchens. Only a few home cooks living around the Boston suburb of Lexington, where Raytheon kept its headquarters, had any experience with the products because some Raytheon engineers had installed the galootish ovens in their kitchens. Foerstner found out about them while he poked around the place to acquaint himself with Amana's new proprietor. He discovered that the engineer's wives loved the things.

Always alert to new opportunities, George Foerstner returned to Iowa inspired to scale down microwaves for consumers. Understanding the dynamics of home kitchens, he insisted the devices sit upon a countertop and that their price remain below $500. Amana carried over Raytheon's Radarange brand name to its glittering new line of consumer ovens.

Wonder, awe, and fascination also helped launch Amana's microelectronic odyssey in 1971. The appliance engineers in Iowa had never designed anything that used electronics, but they certainly had experienced it. As the alluring technology grew more pervasive, it showed up at the lab inside their scopes, meters, oscillators, modulators, amplifiers, superheterodynes, and other mad-scientist stage properties. They were familiar enough with computers too. At least they knew computers as they were commonly conceived then, as otherworldly oracles hidden inside a hushed corporate sanctum called the data-processing department. If they wanted a riddle solved, they had to wait in line like everybody else in the company until the white-robed computer attendants were ready to run their numbers.

Still, micro-capabilities had grown familiar enough to excite and to engage the engineering crew at Amana. Dick Foerstner bought an HP–35 hand calculator right after the model came out in February 1972. The 35, the first portable available from the fabled instrument maker Hewlett-Packard, was more than a common four-function add-subtract-multiply-divide calculator. It's been called the world's first electronic slide rule because it was the first handheld that could handle all the functions of the most capable slide rule, including the deep math performed by scientists and engineers, figuring logarithms and working trigonometric functions with easy keystrokes. Foerstner marveled at the thing. As he contemplated the tidy palmful of keys that spoke back to him through trim, red-glowing tiki-sticks alight in an orderly bar, as he considered the unseen interior actions occurring on silicon inside the trim plastic box, the chip's instant propagation of atomic particles in controlled patterns that instantly concocted flawless sums of numbers, as he reveled over the calculator's plush mysteries, the impulse he could not suppress was, *I could use something just like this to control Dad's oven.*

Amana's product planners knew enough to recognize that chip technology, no matter how esoteric, provided control capabilities too powerful to pass up. "It was just the absolute best application for digital control that you could possibly think of," says Dick Foerstner. By intelligently manipulating a magnetron's power, a computerized controller could finally make microwaves deliver on their promise of ultra-convenience, creating freezer-to-table cookers that prepared foods more quickly and far more easily than any method home chefs had known before.

The early microwaves were just plain limited by the shortcomings of their clunky dials. Not only were the electromechanical timers imprecise but they also provided power at only an all-or-nothing level that wasn't friendly enough to frozen foods. A frozen mass reacts differently to microwave energy, heating at a slower rate than it will heat after it's thawed. Therefore once a microwave oven thawed a small spot in the center of a cube of, say, frozen beef, the inside could cook entirely while the outside remained a meaty glacier. Therefore Amana aimed to use its chip-built controller to cycle

the power on and off, on and off, on and off repeatedly, letting
the microwaves penetrate frozen foods for only a few seconds,
then cutting them off to let the warm spots expand for a few
seconds, then jolting on the magnetron again to repeat the
cycle. An oven could even follow that on/off thaw cycle with a
regular cooking cycle that zapped the oven's contents at a
steady rate to speed up cooking after the ice had melted. The
controller could also provide low and high power levels, with
gradients in between.

"What we wanted was more features. We wanted to be able
to do sequential cooking. And, of course, some people were
puttin' in temperature probes and things like that. It's best to
have a little bit of electronics in there," explains Rex Fritts, an
unassuming electrical engineer who joined Amana in 1971 to
help with the Radarange's computerization. Fritts had worked
for twelve years at the Collins Radio Company in neighboring
Cedar Rapids, Iowa, designing circuits and systems used in air-
liner navigation and communication. Amana wanted him for
his experience in making circuitry that managed high power,
such as the power needed to energize a magnetron.

At about the same time over at Logansport, the inspired
team at Essex—Bob Fosnough, Larry Long, and Max Nelson—
had also recognized the advantages of electro-control. But Fosnough's crew aimed at space-star Litton, whereas Amana
started its search in 1971 by going straight to the front, to the
semiconductor companies themselves.

"The trail was fairly long," recounts Dan McConnell. He and
Fosnough began naively by running down a company that
made the timer that ticked inside digital clocks, which were
new contraptions then. The timer didn't approach the sophistication Amana sought. "We came to realize early that the
requirements we needed were pretty complicated," says
McConnell. Amana's mechanism would have to work some
logic to provide cooking options. In other words, it needed to
make computations. "So we started to look at ICs."

A connection at the University of Iowa sent them straight to the top of Intel to talk to Bob Noyce, an Iowan who was already in the running for the state's favorite-son award. Noyce felt intrigued by Amana's idea. And Foerstner and McConnell obtained needed schooling in the technology during their visits to ascendant Intel. But ultimately the Silicon Valley icon-to-be didn't take the job. Intel made chips; it didn't build the finished assemblies that used them.

The Amanans received a similar reception nearby from Fairchild: interest, some preliminary discussions that helped them hone expectations for their intended controller, but ultimately no deal. Fairchild figured demand for microwave ovens was too scant ever to pay it back for the engineering Amana's controller would require.

After all, at the time, Amana moved barely 100,000 ovens per year. It figured only a fraction of those would incorporate any costly new electro-controller. For every-which-way semcos that saw alluring possibilities in so many directions, the opportunity to design not just the chip but the whole box as well—the backplate, the display window, the buttons, the wiring, and the other accessory pieces, all tucked into an enclosure that would screw into an oven's side panel as handily as a lamp cord plugged into the wall—only to sell just 20,000 or 30,000 of them a year was not an enticing temptation.

The engineering work wouldn't be trivial either. "When we started looking around, there was absolutely nothing like what we had in mind," says McConnell. Microelectronics was attached mostly just to commercial or industrial equipment and to elite military gear. In their ordinary, at-home experiences, people were just starting to see digital clocks and pocket calculators. The Hamilton Watch Company was just bringing out its Pulsar "solid-state wrist computer," the first digital watch, announced in 1970 but not produced in earnest till 1971. When promoting the new gadget, Hamilton had to describe what it meant by *digital*: "PULSAR's most striking physical difference is that it has no hands. Its time is computed and displayed electronically, utilizing computer logic circuitry."

But down in Dallas, Texas Instruments was already adept at the sort of complete systems engineering that Amana's ready-to-use control box required. With its Cal Tech calculator and even going all the way back to the Regency transistor radio, TI had signaled that it would sell semiconductors by devising whole products that used them. Thus when Foerstner and McConnell finally visited Dallas, they discovered that Texas Instruments had already set up an appliance-control team to investigate possibilities. Amana had found its development partner.

By the time the two companies hooked up at the start of 1973, Amana's education had taken it further than TI had gone in its probes of the appliance business. Amana saw very clearly where its product needs intersected with the capabilities of microelectronics. "We had to educate them in terms of the application," says McConnell. "They didn't know anything about microwave ovens, or what we wanted to do or why it was even worth doing."

Together TI and Amana developed the concept into a workable design. In Iowa, Amana made plans for its plant to build ovens incorporating electronic control boxes shipped up from Texas. But the microwave lessons TI took from Amana convinced the ambitious semco that it could do better selling not just the controllers but the entire appliance. Texas Instruments was reaching to extend its prowess the same as it had recently done in calculators, building its own plum models to compete against the likes of Bowmar, which purchased chips and other parts from TI. "They decided they were going to build their own microwave oven," states McConnell. "We found to our shock that they had set up a recruiting shop in a hotel right next to Amana. We severed all connections with TI."

The double cross occurred late in 1973, and in the end it cost Amana about a year. But at the time the company felt stuck. Its prospects of finding another partner looked poor. Amana had already exhausted the best possibilities during its first search. It had burned through months of inquiries and discussions before it had finally found TI. "It was hard to convince people that this was worth investing in," McConnell reiterates. "It would have taken too long to start all over again." Then Essex knocked unexpectedly at its door.

After the rebuff from Litton, Robert Fosnough and his few embattled allies at Essex felt they had run out of good options. They shrugged. "We said, well, there's this stodgy old company out in Amana, Iowa. They're pretty conservative, but maybe we ought to go talk to them. And so we did, and we were received enthusiastically there."

"The trail we were on had nothing to do with Essex," McConnell recounts. "But about the time we cut TI off, our purchasing manager said, you know, we should have Essex come in, because they've got something similar."

The two companies might have teamed up sooner if Fosnough had approached Amana's engineering staff. Instead, he entered through Amana's purchasing department because it was his company's familiar point of contact: salespeople from Essex schmoozed with purchasing agents from Amana to place the relay maker's old-line electro-mechanical parts. Still, when Foerstner and McConnell summoned Fosnough back to Iowa to present his microchip mock-up, the two sides met as kindred innovators. As far as Amana was concerned, it was enough that Fosnough was already committed to the concept of an electronic oven controller. Working together, the two sides could hustle out a finished product. Although Foerstner and McConnell had started their search as naive noninitiates, their diligent wanderings through Silicon Valley and their sojourn in Dallas had taught them much. "We already knew what we wanted, and there were things that we had learned that they didn't know," says McConnell.

Essex set about modifying its model to suit Amana's specifications. Fosnough jettisoned the general-purpose Intel 4004 microprocessor he had placed inside his prototype. It was too expensive. To make money on the deal, Essex needed to spend less than $25 on each control box its factory would turn out. That included every expense: the cost of the chip, the buttons, the display window, wires, supplemental circuit parts, the metal frame, and also the manufacturing costs to put all the pieces together. But if it stuck with the Intel microprocessor, Essex would blow the whole $25 and more just on the 4004. On the other hand, Fosnough couldn't find a suitable microprocessor to replace it. Copycat computers-on-a-chip were just beginning to seep out of the semiconductor industry. Therefore electronic equipment manufacturers—which Essex was about to become—were stuck between practices.

New concept microprocessors were still pricey. A custom-designed logic chip could be had for less, as long as you purchased a large enough quantity to spread out and absorb its development cost. Thus, while it remained the cheaper alternative, some equipment companies clung to the habit of commissioning a custom IC for each application. Accordingly, Fosnough ordered a custom chip from General Instrument Corporation. The controller logic required a lot of transistors, and as a pioneer in metal-oxide semiconductors, General had been making dense MOS microchips longer than most every other semco out there. To Fosnough, the company seemed most comfortable with MOS processing. Even so, "we had to go through a couple of iterations to get something that worked right," he says. "It was like pulling teeth."

Essex completed the control box engineering in about one year. The finished LSI chip integrated more than 3,000 circuit parts on a quarter-inch square. It operated a defrost cycle in which the controller switched on power for twenty seconds, then shut it down for forty. During a slow-cook cycle it switched on the magnetron for twenty seconds and then switched it off for twenty seconds. The oven could be programmed to defrost and cook in a single continuous sequence. Instead of using push-buttons for entering cooking modes and times, the appliance control featured a flat-glass touch panel that relied on the body's capacitance—its built-in electrical charge—to make the connections that sent settings to the computer chip. When the oven wasn't sintering foods, it showed the time of day in red stick numbers—the first appliance to harry homeowners that way.

Internally, Amana called the new microelectronically controlled oven its RR–6, for Radarange 6, signifying that this was the sixth revision of the original version introduced in 1967. But to consumers it was marketed as the Touchmatic. When Amana unveiled it at a meeting of wholesale distributors in January 1975, the appliance pros sat mesmerized in the auditorium. An article in the July 1975 issue of the trade magazine *Appliance Manufacturer* labeled it "Amana's Oven with a Brain." Touchmatic sold for $590, $100 more than the standard twist-dial version. Homeowners got their first crack at the oven in the summer of 1975, when Touchmatics began to appear in stores. Its instant popularity caught Amana unprepared.

"The combination of the bright digital display and this magic touch panel was awesome to people," says McConnell. "From the moment we introduced it, the reaction was almost indescribable. It was the hottest thing I ever went through. We couldn't make enough of the things for a year."

Still, Amana made them fast enough to double the number of ovens it sold that year to about 200,000. Its revenue increased by about $50 million. Amana rocketed past Litton to become the undisputed top seller among microwave makers.

It didn't maintain that position through too many years. In fact, already by the end of Touchmatic's first twelve months, competing oven makers began bringing out magic models of their own (although Texas Instruments never made it successfully to market). Amana fought to maintain its sales leadership for a while, facing the competition by plunging into revisions and improvements, especially measures to reduce manufacturing costs so it could lower its oven's price. The costly controller was one of the first targets. Thus Essex found itself searching for a less expensive alternative to the custom LSI microcircuit from General Instrument just when programmable, general-purpose microprocessors became suddenly abundant.

When Essex had begun engineering its first version of the controller in 1973, Intel's pioneering 4004 had been the only microprocessor Fosnough could lay his hands on. But the avalanche of new microprocessors had begun undiscernibly even by then. At the end of 1972 Rockwell had started selling a microprocessor called the PPS–4. In 1973 and 1974, Fairchild, National, Signetics, Toshiba, AMI, and other semcos brought out new versions of multipurpose computing chips. In 1974, Texas Instruments unveiled its TMS–1000, the first in a string of micros that TI promoted as low-cost controllers for such products as toys and games. By the middle of 1974, nineteen microprocessors were either already available or said to be coming. One year later, that number was forty. By 1976, fifty-four microprocessors were in contention. "It was clearly a time of wide-ranging experimentation," characterized Ted Hoff and Bob Noyce in a later magazine article.

Accordingly, Essex ran trials using Rockwell's PPS–4, which turned out to be too difficult to program. It fiddled with Intel's 8048, a micro that incorporated the memory that held programming side by side with the logic circuitry on a single chip. The assembly worked faster because the logic banks didn't need to send out laboriously to an entirely separate read-only memory chip to retrieve instructions. Essex tried out microprocessors it could purchase for only a dollar apiece. Just one year after the first ever computerized appliance made its head-turning debut, Essex enjoyed more microprocessor options than it could even consider. Microelectronic reasoning had just intersected with appliances, the new order had just met the old, and already the chipsters were subverting themselves with cheaper, faster, better microprocessors that assured that Amana's trail would be closely followed.

☰ 12 ☰

Call Forwarding

VERSATILE, PROGRAMMABLE, multifunctional microprocessors could not satisfy every need for microcircuitry. They worked very well for straightforward command and control, such as managing cooking times and oven ray intensity. But special-purpose microchips still remained essential for other particular and demanding duties. When walk-and-talk cellular telephones were created in a high-intensity, ninety-day crash project at Motorola in 1973, they relied on a single-purpose IC that could synthesize radio frequencies. That was the only job the chip could perform, but without it, cellular—the way it's construed today—could not have emerged.

The cell system that Motorola cobbled together in such a breathless rush in 1973 relied upon other critical parts as well. It took a lot of organizational muscle, with critical, coordinated contributions coming from people in all sorts of ranks and roles. Such as John Mitchell, an executive with the engineering expertise, the foresight, and the clout to point an entire corporate division to the task. And Marty Cooper, another engineer-turned-executive, who worked far enough on technology's advance to envision a whole new device from scattered pieces being developed here and there. Or Rudy Krolop, an insightful, excitable industrial designer who sidestepped the dictates of the corporate bureaucracy when it interfered with a job he found ineluctably compelling.

Still, the group could have never even attempted the whole heroic effort without the capabilities of a particular chip that began its life back in 1968, when Don Linder was still a newly minted engineer. At his workbench in a Motorola communications lab, Linder started poking around with integrated circuits, trying to create the frequency-synthesizing device that, if it worked, would trounce a secure and serenely profitable little enterprise inside the company. At the time, Motorola reacted the way you'd expect any powerful and protective megacorp to react. It tried to stop Linder's investigations.

That could have been easy because Donald Linder's work threatened Motorolees of a higher rank. Linder was an engineer inside a group called Applied Research, which developed new ideas for the company's communication division. The dispute amounted to an intracompany tussle, a kind of now-versus-later turf fight that pitted the considerable muscle of a successful business position against the anticipation of catastrophic change.

"It was a disruptive technology," says Linder of his early IC experimentation. "It was going to put some of our people out of business. Not everybody welcomes progress with open arms, because there is always something that you have to give up."

Still, the research prevailed. Linder might have heard the sniping of the corporate rivals he threatened, but his bosses screened him from any sort of undermining action. At Motorola, established interests could not impede the forward run of research. The company retained a kind of schizoneurotic understanding of how advancing technology could sabotage it as readily as advanced technology sustained it.

"We said for years that in five to seven years you'd better throw away what you've got. It's gotta be replaced and you'd better be the guy who replaces it," attests John Mitchell, the Motorola careerist who was one of the managers insulating Linder's early investigations. "If you think you can perpetuate something's life because it's such a beautiful what-have-you, you're going to get a shocking surprise someday. So we always worked at the next generation."

Executive commitment to the future was a distinguishing characteristic of Motorola. It was one manifestation of a culture of change inbred at the company's founding. Brothers Paul and Joseph Galvin started Motorola in Chicago in 1929 (it was called the Galvin Manufacturing Corporation until 1947), making products called battery eliminators. As electrification spread during the period between the two great wars and as homes wired into the grid, battery eliminators let people keep using old radios that had been made to run on storage batteries. The eliminators converted them to run on house current instead. But battery eliminators faced elimination themselves as electrification grew widespread and more people bought radios they could plug straight into their walls. Therefore, as early as 1929, recognizing the ephemera built into technical necessities, the Galvins added home radios as an additional product line. Their company grew into an electronics industry dynasty by similarly turning whenever technology cranked another cycle. By the end of the 1960s, Motorola divisions made transistors and microchips; consumer products, including TVs, radios, and hi-fis; electronic parts for cars; and military gear.

In two-way radios, the communication division kept current by following what Martin Cooper called *the religion*: truths, laws, and unalterable dictums. "One example of the religion is *smaller and lighter*," he illustrates. "Whenever you looked at a new generation, it had to be smaller, had to be lighter. Because a portable radio or a pager was not functional unless it was easy to carry around."

Cooper joined Motorola as a research engineer in 1954. He headed development teams that built the first high-capacity paging systems. His crews created personal police radios that helped get cops out of cruisers and onto the sidewalks. In 1970, Cooper became a vice president, serving as general manager of the systems division, which was part of the newly elevated communication sector. As such, he joined with Mitchell and other execs to make regular pilgrimages to Phoenix, home of Motorola's microchip division. They went several times each year for chip tutorials from the company's semiconductor sages.

"One of the Communication Sector's distinctive competencies was our relationship with our semiconductor group," says Cooper. "We leaned on them to do silicon-gate CMOS [complementary metal-oxide semiconductor], because we needed low battery drain to do portables. [CMOS chips sip very little electricity.] And they, of course, would lean on us to generate sales volume, because the only way that they could make money was by selling a lot of these things. So there was a symbiosis between the two divisions." For the radio makers, better technology from their colleagues in Phoenix enabled them to adhere to their religious tenets. "With integrated circuits," says Cooper, "you ended up with much lower cost, higher reliability, and functions you could not even think about doing without using integrated circuits."

Linder's work with ICs in the systems division—which began in 1968, a bit before Marty Cooper became its chief—produced a special-purpose microchip called a frequency synthesizer. It replaced the banks of small, carefully shaved crystals that were otherwise used to tune two-way radios to specific channels. Motorola aimed to build small walk-and-talk radios with more channels because the more channels a radio had, the more useful it became in big, urban radio networks—especially in radio-telephone networks, where subscribers could engage in private conversations by patching into the regular landline phone system. If a person wanted to make a call but one channel was busy, a multichannel radio could skip to the next and the next and the next until it found an open channel. Of course, with more channels available on a radio, the greater its chance of finding an open one. With more channels available for conversations, a radio service could support more people.

But using the premicro crystal tuning method, a radio needed a separate crystalline vibrator for every channel it supported. Because they were so difficult to manufacture, the crystals were expensive. That made multichannel radios more expensive, especially models with a whole lot of channels that required a whole lot of separate crystals.

But even if the crystals had been cheaper, they still wouldn't have worked for the types of two-way radios Motorola was angling to build by the late 1960s. That's why Linder's bosses made sure his work moved forward no matter how strenuously the crystal makers protested. The company specialized in small, lightweight portables that a person could tote along clipped to a belt or dropped into a briefcase. For the sorts of megachannel radios that Motorola envisioned, you'd never find room inside a handheld to pack in separate crystals to cover each channel. The designers of moveable wireless faced an apparent dilemma: either restrict the number of available channels, or install two-way radios in automobiles alone, where you could use the trunk to carry all the gear. Linder's frequency synthesizer helped solve the problem by significantly reducing the amount of space that megachannel two-way radios required. It replaced the crystalline tuners with a single silicon circuit that used semiconductor logic to set a two-way to open channels. (Early renditions of the frequency synthesizer used multiple chips until integration densities increased enough to accommodate all the functions on a single chip.)

The innovation would soon become urgently essential for Motorola. In 1972, its multichannel radios would have to transmute into megachannel radios overnight in order to get cellular telephones through their contentious birthing pains.

In the beginning, it didn't look like a mad dash to demonstrate portable cellular would ever be necessary. Cellular's birthing began as a predictably monotonous proceeding on July 17, 1968, when the Federal Communications Commission (FCC) asked for comments on expanding what it called "common carrier high-capacity mobile radio operations." As the government referee that parcels out the airwaves—the radio-magnetic spectrum—the FCC juggled the interests of television and radio broadcasters, police and fire dispatchers, pagers, airline pilots, two-way talkers on radios and wireless telephones, business data satellite exchangers, scientific researchers beaming telemetry to spacecraft, military cryptologists, and every other organization that wanted to send radio signals. The commission most often moved with the deliberate lethargy of a weighty bureaucracy. Its actions came only at the end of protracted, disjointed studies, hearings, and deliberations, from which the FCC eventually issued Opinion and Order memoranda and Report and Order memoranda.

In 1968, the FCC sought to expand mobile radio mostly because more people wanted car phones. Those weren't simple two-way radios that could connect only with other radios. Rather, they were roving phones that dialed in over the air waves to connect to the regular wire-line telephone network, permitting private conversations with anyone who owned a phone. The problem was, the air waves—the spectrum—that was allotted to radio-phone systems was too narrow. It didn't contain enough channels to accommodate all the people who wanted to equip their cars for calling. Therefore the companies that operated the systems were turning away subscribers. In metropolitan New York, for example, the mobile system supported only 543 customers, with a waiting list more than six times as large. As a remedy, the FCC planned to take away some of the underused spectrum that was assigned to UHF television and allocate it to two-way services instead. The questions confronting the FCC were what services, run by whom.

American Telephone and Telegraph, AT&T, first proposed a cellular setup. The arrangement would use the scarce air-wave spectrum more efficiently by dividing a region into cells so that channels could be reused from cell to cell. With the inadequate radio-telephone systems then in use, an occupied channel was tied up across an entire city. But because cellular chopped a region into a matrix of adjoining cells, a channel occupied in one cell could be used simultaneously by a different caller just several cells over—separated by enough distance so that their radio waves wouldn't interfere with each other. Because channels could be used and reused simultaneously across a service area, cellular could accommodate more callers.

But to make the arrangement work, phones had to support an awful lot of channels. In one cell, the radio phone would call on a set of channels that was entirely different from the channels it had to use in the neighboring cell, which were different from the channels in the cell next to that one, and so on. The radio wouldn't start to reuse channels until it reached more distant cells, providing enough separation to avoid signal interference. A setup that provided, say, fifty channels in each cell—providing fifty simultaneous calls per cell—might require a phone that could cover one thousand different channels. They'd be grouped into twenty blocks, of fifty distinct channels per block, to be used in twenty neighboring and nearby cells.

What's more, economics demanded a system that could accommodate many subscribers in order to pay for the infrastructure cellular required. With antennas in each cell, a central base station for each region, all sorts of call-management and processing equipment at every site, and networking gear to knit all the sites into a coherent and united system—so a call that began in one cell could be handed off to another as the caller crossed boundaries, for example—cellular operators would have to cover sizable expenses. Therefore their systems would need a lot of subscribers, a lot of paying customers, to cover the expense of building and running the networks. To get a lot of customers, they needed a lot of channels.

AT&T specified car phones rather than portables out of practical necessity, relying on cars to trundle all the weighty electronics it figured its phones would need. Its technocrats calculated that communication would require big radios with juiced-up transmitters to beat the transmission difficulties in the high-end spectrum. It also wanted to run the cellular systems solo as the only licensed operator across the United States. At the time, that request wasn't too fanciful. AT&T—known unaffectionately as Ma Bell—provided most of the car phone service in the United States. In fact, at the time, AT&T was the coast-to-coast telephone monopoly that provided most telephone service of any kind. (It was eventually broken up by a federal court order in 1984, segmenting national phone service into independent, regional Bell operating companies.) AT&T bought some equipment from Motorola. In fact, it used Motorola's IMTS, the Improved Mobile Telephone Service, for its precellular car-calling systems in cities all over. But for the most part, AT&T relied on its own Bell Labs for invention, and it manufactured much of its own equipment. Therefore the brass at Motorola figured that a coast-to-coast car phone system run by AT&T would cut Motorola out of a lot of equipment deals.

Early in the FCC proceedings, Motorola wasn't too concerned about that possibility. AT&T wanted to operate its car cells high up in radio-wave spectrum, in the 900-megahertz range. Motorola argued that 900 megahertz wasn't suitable for communication. Radio waves propagated poorly in that area of the spectrum. Instead, Motorola lobbied the FCC for a lower frequency allocation, around 450 megahertz. Radio signals behaved better in the lower range. Communication would be easier.

Still, the company conducted research, ran tests, and began developing gear for both the 450- and the 900-megahertz bands. It would sell what equipment it could up in the higher frequency. But Motorola poured most of its efforts into developing equipment for the lower frequency it expected the FCC to open up for radio-telephone talk.

Near the end of 1972, the company flinched when it learned that the FCC was preparing to issue rulings that ran counter to Motorola's interests. "We panicked," says Mitchell. "Up until that time, we had said that AT&T can be up there in that crummy, 900-megacycles spectrum. We want 450. But we didn't get it. So we said, ho boy, now we really got a problem."

Mitchell had been an engineer before he was an administrator. Born to Irish immigrants, he studied the trade on Chicago's south side at the Illinois Institute of Technology, paying his way with summer earnings he made as lifeguard captain at Chicago's Oak Street beach. When that money ran out, he joined the Navy's Reserve Officer Training Corps for its tuition aid. After graduation, Mitchell spent three years as an officer aboard a destroyer, where he learned to lead by recognizing and cultivating a person's individual abilities. Back in the civilian workforce, he started as an engineer in Motorola's communication business on September 28, 1953, soldering at a lab bench like every beginning engineer at Motorola, learning about communication equipment through hands-on encounters.

Mitchell ended up managing corporate affairs, rising to the office of president in 1980 and vice chairman in 1988, placing him second in command inside the top-floor suite of the tower, Motorola's headquarters building that rises like a lone domino on the suburbanized prairie of Schaumburg, outside of Chicago. But back in 1972, when AT&T was making off with cellular phones, Mitchell was assistant general manager of the communication sector, the number-two guy. His principal duty was to drive the division's technical initiatives.

He felt two strong objections to the FCC's direction. First, it was setting up AT&T as a monopoly provider of the new mobile phone service. Motorola wanted competitive services, which would create more customers for its radio-phone equipment. Secondly, the FCC was preparing to license only mobile services, not portable systems that could move with people in and out of cars, indoors and out, even up elevators with people.

"I said, whoa, John, you've had this vision that you inherited when you got to Motorola of talkin' to people on the move. You don't talk to cars. You talk to people."

Mitchell brought together the division's top lieutenants and its technical trust at a conference-room table. "I said to our guys, what can we do to put together a portable and leapfrog their proposal?"

They could do plenty. From its habit of innovating, Motorola had already created a lot of radio-phone pieces that were far more advanced and capable than all the Ph.D.s at AT&T thought possible. With the micrologic advances it had cajoled out of its semiconductor sibling, the separate chip-making Motorola division down in Phoenix, the company had pushed miniaturization far enough to permit handheld cellular. It thought. All those pieces had yet to be assembled.

"We said, the only way we can sell this is to do something dramatic to get their attention," explains Mitchell. Therefore Motorola reserved a small auditorium in Washington's Watergate office building. It would take the room for one week in March 1973, to show off to the FCC and anyone else with influence the portable cellular system it could build today.

That gave the communication group ninety days to create the thing, by pulling together disparate developments scattered throughout its labs. The work was done off-budget, as a bootleg program, because it had come up too quickly to write into an accounting ledger.

The job fell to Marty Cooper's systems division, the standing experts in radio phones at Motorola. Don Linder did the actual lab work. He was a section manager then, with regular authority over about a dozen research engineers and technicians. But for the ninety-day sprint, many more white-coats were mustered. Linder's boss, Chuck Lynk, the manager of applied research, cut the interference for him, wielding his rank where work was needed from outside development sections. In all, the team swelled to about three dozen people. Linder drew up their orders in the form of technical drawings illustrating the product and all its parts. As the pieces came in, he wired them together, tested the unit, and then sent back parts for modifications. The program came off like three consecutive months of exam week all-nighters, racing to convince officialdom to change course because self-contained phones were possible.

The choreography involved several microelectronic bits, including Linder's own frequency synthesizer. Another was the system management chip, an insect-size telephone control center that was necessary to keep each individual phone in sync with the large multi-phone network it tied into. For example, the chip worked the logic that enabled a handheld to recognize its own phone number and therefore to respond to calls dialed to it. In Motorola's IMTS radio-telephones, the corresponding circuitry filled a metal diptych the size of Volume K of *Encyclopaedia Britannica*. The Phoenix semiconductor foundry finished reducing that book to chip size when Linder's crash development was in full swing. He had to take it on faith that the micros would work. "They made the portable unit possible," he says, "but the first samples of this logic circuit were coming available in January of 1973. We started the project without even having those samples in our hands. But it was a direct replacement for something that we already had ten years experience with, so all that we needed was to be sure it would work."

He pulled together non-semicon parts as well, such as a specially designed dipole antenna that compensated for the poor radio-wave propagation in the 900-megahertz zone. He had to parse electrical needs carefully because the phone had to run on a battery, the bane of portability because batteries run down so rapidly. He had to fit in a microphone at a mouthpiece and a speaker at an earpiece. Most importantly, he had to sculpt and squeeze all the agglomerated components, electronic and nonelectronic alike, into a case that was compact, convenient, and compelling enough to make even communication pros take notice.

Designing the portable's enclosure was particularly prickly. The product had no precedent. Nothing like a carry-around phone existed. Its case would have to be a kind of crossbreed between a walkie-talkie radio and a princess phone with a built-in dial. At the same time, it would have to exhibit a techno-chic aspect that would make a person want to grab it and press the number pad. The design job landed abruptly in the lap of Rudy Krolop, the accidental aesthete who ran the industrial design studio for Motorola's communication pros.

Both Krolop and the studio were anomalies. Before Motorola tumbled into cellular, it made mostly on-the-job radios for cops and Forest Service smoke jumpers. They were gritty, workaday affairs that hardly seemed to require much aesthetic fine-tuning. But Krolop had demonstrated the importance of form to the division when he was an on-the-rise designer in the company's consumer products division in the late 1950s. The communication operation borrowed him to help stylize its Handie-Talkie portable radio. Krolop's radio, nicknamed "the brick" for its sturdy aspect, showed that good design also played well in he-man markets. By the early 1970s, Krolop employed nine designers in his communication sector studio.

Krolop himself had stumbled into the field accidentally. At St. Ignatius High School in Chicago he was training informally to become a comic until a schoolmate, Bob Newhart, out-joked him. So after graduation Krolop joined the Marine Corps. From the Marines, he enrolled in college to study accounting. "I hated every minute of it," he recalls.

Therefore he felt grateful when the Marines called him back in 1950 to fight in the Korean War. "I said, *Now when I get out I'm gonna know what I want to do.* But that didn't help either. I got out of the Marine Corps in about '52 and I still didn't know. I went back into accounting."

Of course, accounting seemed no better to Krolop after the war. He was packing up to leave the University of Illinois at Champaign to take a foreman's job in a can factory. But his roommate stopped him with the question, *Why don't you just get out of accounting and study something else?* But what? Finding that something else was the cause of Krolop's agony. So the roommate rummaged in his desk for the Illinois course catalog. He had never looked at the book himself. When he opened it the spine shot out a crack. "Believe me," says Krolop, "I can hear it to this day." The catalog fell open to a page listing classes in industrial design. The two young men peered down in naive perplexity. Recalls Krolop: "he said, *How about, you know, industrial design? You're always sketchin' something.* I said, *What's industrial design?*"

Krolop started at Motorola in 1956, at the age of 26.

He was sixteen years into his tenure when the cell phone assignment arrived breathlessly in the last days on 1972. "I was sitting in my office one day and my phone rings and Marty Cooper calls me. Marty and I were friends. Every Monday morning he'd come into my office with another great idea. So he called me up and he said, *What are ya doin'?* I said, *Just sittin' here waitin' for you to call.* He says, *Come on to my office.*"

There, Cooper outlined the project. He ran through the contents Krolop's shell would need to enwrap. He laid out the functions the package would have to perform, the ear piece, the mouth piece, the number pad for dialing. He discussed the urgency and importance of the project. "So we talked for about a half an hour, and he says, *You want to do it?* I say, *Okay.* He says, *There's a problem though.* He says, *We only got six weeks to do it in.* I say, *Marty, you're jerkin' me.* He says, *No.* He says, *Are you gonna do it?* I say, *Okay.*"

Linder and the rest of the team had already been at work assembling the phone's innards. Now they needed the box, the shell, the outer form those innards would occupy. Krolop put his entire studio to the task, pulling them from work on an upcoming line of two-way portables, from a new mobile system, from a radio control center for the Chicago police. A few of his staff were graphic artists who made signs and labels for Motorola. They had never shaped a physical product before. Krolop wanted their phone ideas too. He told everyone to make sketches. But the sketches didn't go far enough. He told all nine designers to make a model instead. Make it any damn way. Just make it right away.

Three days later they played show-and-tell. Cooper sprang for cocktails and dinner at Lancers Restaurant, a haunt cater-corner from the office at Algonquin and Meecham. In a private dining room, each contestant got up in turn to pitch his creation. One showed a pocket-size rectangle that slid open like a match box, elongating to expose its mouthpiece. Cooper and Krolop loved it, but they'd never have time to build it. They chose a design by Ken Larson. It picked up the nickname "the shoe phone" because its bottom jutted out like the toe of a lady's old-style, lace-up shoe. The extended base positioned the microphone nearer a speaker's lips.

It was a solid, sturdy, easy-to-manufacture box made distinctive by the eccentric flair at its base. Its number pad was on its face, so as you held it to dial a number, you pressed comfortably into your palm. It lifted up gracefully to your ear without any change of grip. Its ergonomics were pat, intuitive. It looked like a phone. You could figure out how to use it on sight.

"The image was very important," says Krolop, "because we wanted everybody to embrace this thing. It was something brand new, and they had to say, *Yes, this is good, this is what I want*. They had to picture themselves using and living with this thing, and carrying it around, with the image of them holding this thing up and making a phone call. The sense of power and pride and all had to be staggering."

The engineers found the program staggering for the hours and the efforts it demanded. They adopted the wry, snide, bickering demeanor of men on military maneuvers or otherwise united in duress. They snickered the term *shoe phone* to connote the spoofy, hidden phone in the shoe of Maxwell Smart, the mock Bond from the 1960s secret-agent television series *Get Smart*. Linder assumed the informal title MFIC, mother fucker in charge. At the end of three months, with two phones completed in time for the Washington gala, the builders felt dissatisfied with their creations. Engineers like to make things that work, and while the first shoe phones worked well enough to sway the Federal Communications Commission, they never could have performed in an actual, for-keeps cellular system operating across hundreds of channels. The early logic chip only supported about twenty. "Regardless of how impressed people were with it, we knew in our hearts that we could have done better if we were given more time," Linder laments.

Motorola also proposed some modifications in the cell setup to accommodate portable communicators. AT&T had originally specified large cells because its phones could use larger antennas stuck on car roofs, and its trunk-load of electronics could beam out powerful signals without draining a tiny battery. But Motorola's lower-power portable phones would require more concentrated signals that could penetrate buildings. Therefore, Motorola restyled the cellular concept, calling for smaller cells arranged in a honeycomb pattern to assure adequate signal strength. And it wrote in a provision to cut a phone's transmission power when a talker rode an elevator to the top of a building. Otherwise a lone phone might act like a tower antenna and send its signal far enough to scramble up distant cells.

Motorola called its all-in-one handset the DynaTAC 1—the TAC, meaning Total Area Coverage, the trade name for Motorola two-way systems. Cooper, Mitchell, and a cadre of Motorolees took the system to Washington at the end of March 1973 to wow FCC commissioners, their staff, and some influential congressional representatives. They set up in New York a month later, mostly to splash the invention to the media and thereby win wider attention. A photo of Mitchell chatting on

DynaTAC 1 appeared in the Soviet Union's *Pravda* newspaper. *Collier's Encyclopedia* carried a similar shot in its annual summary volume for 1973. The FCC didn't grant all of Motorola's wishes. Instead of allowing full-bore competition, it provided for duopoly services in the metropolitan regions. Still, that was better than giving AT&T every slice of the pie. And, most important, the systems would be portable.

A decade passed before cellular services appeared commercially, beginning in 1983. First came test systems, installed in Chicago, Baltimore, and elsewhere in the mid-1970s to establish the specifications and operating requirements that went into the commercial services to come. Manufacturers, wireless operators, and regulators had to work out such problems as how to meld mobile and portable technologies into one seamless service. Beyond such technical refinements, a large measure of delay came from the usual bureaucratic impediments, compounded by the corporate maneuverings of communication companies jockeying to win licenses to operate cell services.

The first generation of cellular telephones sold by Motorola in the mid-1980s, using single-chip frequency synthesizers, communicated over 666 channels. Some current models can cover several thousand. One microchip provides the capability.

Common Computing

MICROCHIPS MADE POSSIBLE such new tech tools as cell phones, shirt-pocket calculators, and kitchen wares controlled by adaptations of the same micro-logic that managed Apollo moon shots. In their turn, those unprecedented products gave a goose to greater chip development by providing eager and abundant outlets for more chips and more capable chips that were smaller, faster, and cheaper. Self-nurturing like the yin and the yang, the good living provided by chips produced even better chips, which provided yet better living, which called forth still better chips, and so on.

But computers, the premier electronic implements, worked outside of that cycle for a long time. Integrated circuits certainly improved computers. But the big, brainy, so-called thinking machines had reached their pinnacle independently. At least they seemed to be at their height to the people who made them. The attitude was inherited from scientists in the thrall of their own achievements. Howard Aiken was such a person. In 1943 Aiken had built a pioneering computer called the Mark I. It was fifty-one feet long and eight feet high, and therefore it was too large to fit inside a suburban ranch house, never mind on a desk. Mark I was preelectronic. It used electro-mechanical relays that passed along current by clapping together their two metal contacts. When the Mark I clacked through a calculation, its thousands of relays closing and opening and closing and opening in neuro-synthetic cadence made so much racket that two people standing near it couldn't converse. They had to shout back and forth to each other.

Howard Aiken is most remembered for the misobservation he sniffed in 1947 to discourage the formation of a pioneering computer business when it was still only contemplated by J. Presber Eckert and John Mauchly, the University of Pennsylvania duo who had made the world's first fully electronic model, the ENIAC, in 1945. Reacting to Eckert and Mauchly's plan to start a company that would sell such machines, Aiken said there would never be more than a handful of problems that would require a computer to solve. Therefore, he said, all the world would never need more than a handful of computers.

As the commercial computer trade rose in opposition to Aikin's desires, the machines inevitably improved with each striding improvement in microchips. At their heart they became nothing more than dense arrangements of transistors. Therefore as silicon alchemists packed their chips with more transistors arranged in ever more clever configurations, the computer pros pasted them into machines that grew faster, smaller, more powerful, and less expensive. But the steady advance did little to make computers popular. They remained aloof and elite, reserved for a privileged class, like bone china and silver flatware.

Popularly approachable computers arose out of a whole new set of precepts that the scientist An Wang acquired through his strivings to become a business icon. Wang discovered that the challenge confronting computers was not to find problems to solve. The challenge ahead for computers was to get them out among people. It was to grow populous by becoming somewhat smaller than tract housing. Wang learned that even ordinary people could find work for computers if computers were made so that ordinary people could work them.

He uncovered that principle gradually and unexpectedly, tumbling toward mass computing simply as a means to keep his company alive and to make it prosper. The adaptations An Wang made to make his business successful sped the transformation of computers from enshrined oracles, aloof and mysterious, to knock-around assistants for Everyman. Wang changed the way the whole surviving computer industry approached the sacred machine by turning computers into accommodating, everyday implements before anyone else even thought to try.

Born in China, Wang came to America in 1945 after surviving the depredations of Japan's occupation during World War II. He was twenty-five years old. He had already earned an electrical engineering degree from Chiao Tung University in Shanghai, and he had learned practical electronics by designing radios from scavenged parts for the Chinese army during the war. In the States he enrolled at Harvard. After sixteen months of study, he earned a doctorate in physics in 1947.

By that time Mao's communists had seized control of his native country. Dr. Wang wasn't about to be yoked to anyone's ideology. "I . . . knew myself well enough," he wrote in his 1986 autobiography, *Lessons*, "to know that I could not thrive under a totalitarian Communist system. I had long been independent, and I wanted to continue to make my own decisions about my life." Therefore he resolved to remain in the United States.

The dispossessed Chinese immigrant was merely looking for work when he found computing in 1948. At the time the field was a research activity, not a business. Wang signed on as a research fellow at the Harvard Computation Laboratory mostly because the job was convenient. He knew nothing about computers, but the lab sat on the Harvard campus, close to where he already lived. Wang went to work under the supercilious Howard Aiken, who ran the computation lab for the university.

As a first assignment, Aiken told Wang to find a way to store information inside a computer, something that wasn't possible at the time. The young physicist chewed on ideas only through June 1948 before he invented magnetic memory cores. Those were the small, doughnut-shaped metal rings that, after Wang's innovation, were wired together like medieval coats of mail and attached to the big computers of the era. They kept track of the separate ones and zeros that together constituted the words that told computers what to do. This development of large-scale memory made computers programmable: They could store their own instructions as rewritable software. Therefore you could change the function of a computer simply by feeding in a new, different arrangement of ones and zeros that represented a different set of instructions. Before that, a computer that was set up to, say, tabulate census data could do little else. As big as it was, the machine wasn't flexible enough to turn around and investigate, say, seismic echoes in order to guess where oil may hide underground. Before Wang invented memory cores, the only way to give a computer a new job was to open it up and rearrange its circuits.

The invention provided a first product for Wang Laboratories. In June 1951, at age thirty-one, the doctor set up his business as a one-man operation in Boston, underwritten by his life savings of about six hundred dollars. The venture started like a horse bet, with just a fistful of cash backing one man who had only hopefulness and rigid will to combat a very thorough absence of experience. His company resided in one barren room, yet Wang chose a plural for its title because he had a hunch the business would grow. *Laboratories* sounded bigger.

At the time, electronics still meant mostly vacuum tubes. But soon Fairchild, Intel, Motorola, National, Raytheon, Texas Instruments, and all the other semcos would appear and start their scramble to find mass markets for silicon microchips. They provided resources Wang used to sustain and expand his laboratories. To survive, Wang Labs had to learn as it grew, maturing like an organism that bends and twists to suit its environment. Adaptation was the company's overriding business strategy: forget all the management-theory humbug, just keep moving. "I have come to see that the key to long-term survival for a company is adaptability," An Wang wrote in *Lessons*. "One can sense change even if one doesn't know where it will ultimately lead."

From its founding in 1951, the company worked through six distinct product types—creating them, absorbing their lessons, dropping them, and moving on—before it finally hit full stride in the mid-1970s. Wang himself performed a lot of the technical derring-do. But most importantly, he set the stage by establishing an ambitious and hyperactive company that remained agile enough to learn how to sell computers by making them useful and by making them easily usable—computer makers today awkwardly call the quality *user-friendly*.

Wang Labs was an extension of its founder, a corporate expression of his tireless striving, self-encouraged toward greatness no matter how small the steps that led it there. His workers would learn to refer to him as *the doctor* or as *Dr. Wang*, and they would approach him feeling a combination of awe and jittering fright. The man himself was small, compact, fastidious, and fittingly dapper. You could glimpse his magisterial air in the February 1969 cover photo of *Product Engineering* magazine. Wang looked out from the page as he showed off one of his new creations, a computer-in-hiding called the LOCI. Two fingers cradled his ever-present cigar while his hand rested atop the prized machine as if it was the blue-ribbon hound in a dog show. His expression asked ironically, did you expect anything less?

In the beginning, in addition to selling memory cores for computers, little Wang Labs also tried to peddle bits of equipment. The doctor designed electronic instruments and shopped them around to likely buyers. When he found one, he built the device himself, making implements like digital counters that could measure the speed of a spinning shaft, or automatically record blood counts, or track the nuclear decay rate of radioactive materials. He made these first machines for the environment he knew best, the scientific laboratory. As he worked, Dr. Wang also absorbed their business lesson: to make a sale, find specific tasks that electronics performs better than the prevailing method.

From that experience Wang learned to make electronic controllers for manufacturing equipment, especially big, metal-cutting lathes and grinders that moved their cutting heads with intricate care in order to gouge out precise shapes and patterns. The control boxes became a standard Wang product. From those the company parlayed into semiautomatic, electronic typesetting machines for newspapers. They replaced the antique, geared contraptions that set type as slugs of hot metal that couldn't be changed without remelting an entire line of type and starting over.

That was in the mid-1960s. By that time integrated circuits had appeared, and electronic miniaturization was starting to stride beyond space gadgets and top-secret army blasters. Wang had grown into a bustling concern of about thirty-five people. Its first million-dollar year came in 1964 on the strength of the typesetter. Wang took in about $30,000 for each machine it made, and it made about seventy of them over the life of the product.

But for Wang the product's life ran only about three years, ending abruptly in 1965. The labs only *made* the typesetting machines. It didn't promote and sell them. That job fell to its partner, a separate company called Compugraphic. In 1965, Compugraphic confided that it would also start making the machine on its own. Instantly the product that accounted for two-thirds of Wang's business was gone. What could the company do but adapt?

In fact, the adaptation was already underway, with a replacement product growing out of the doctor's tireless technical fidgeting. Dr. Wang was still the lab's chief scientist and chief engineer—in effect if not in title—even as he handled all of its management decisions. That was the only way he could ever run a company. Even when he sold public stock to raise cash in 1967, he structured the offering so that shareholders wouldn't have any say in how he ran the store. His ego extended so deeply into the organization that his self-esteem equaled the stature of Wang Inc., and he wore the company's rising fortune with the same aplomb with which he donned his dapper bow tie. Even after Wang Labs grew very large, its founder maintained an active and intimate command over its technical and its business operations—until illness forced him away.

Accordingly, the fast success of the typesetting machine hadn't slaked the doctor's enthusiasm to find new uses for electronics. Wang was ready with a new product, in a whole new field, before the typesetting machine quite vanished. Based on a method Dr. Wang had worked out for simplifying mathematical calculations, in 1965 the labs introduced its logarithmic calculating instrument, a machine that became better known by its acronym, LOCI. Its clever circuitry—devised by the doctor during his ordinary, incessant ritual of thoughts and fidgets—gave the product a distinct technical advantage, enabling it to perform advanced math better than any other machine of a similar size.

It was a calculator, but it was a whole separate species from the midget machines that would begin to appear in the early 1970s, spawning like reptiles from the Cal Tech hand calculator that Jerry Merryman made at TI the same year Wang came out with LOCI. Cal Tech and its first-generation offspring were simple, four-function, add-subtract-multiply-divide calculators. Similarly, before LOCI, mechanical and electro-mechanical adding machines handled only addition and subtraction. LOCI was a much more powerful number fudger. It was a small-scale computer at heart, but it was set up to gnash through the complicated number problems performed all the time by scientists and engineers. Although it was compact for its day, the machine still filled a fair corner of a desk. A low, flat extension at the front of the squat metal box held number keys and other buttons marked with strange ciphers and used to enter problems. A bar across LOCI's face flashed solutions as lighted numbers inside Nixie tubes. The calculator was imposing to operate, but scientists, engineers, and mathematicians couldn't buy a better way to perform complicated math. Lawrence Livermore Laboratories at Berkeley bought a LOCI. So did other big research centers. By 1966, Wang was selling ten per month, at about $6,500 each.

Wang Labs at the time remained wholly attuned to technology, the area its founder understood comfortably. It hired independent agents to sell the wares it made. The only nontechnical workers on its permanent payroll were secretaries and a lone bookkeeper, Martin Miller. Fiddling with a LOCI in spare moments, Miller realized that the machine could make his accounting job a whole lot easier if only LOCI itself was easier to use. His discovery came as a revelation to the industrious doctor. Wang reworked the machine to create a second calculator, this one demystified somewhat so nonscientists could use it.

Starting in 1966, Wang Labs marketed its model 300 as an office machine fit for nontechnical professionals. Importantly, it was programmable: You could feed it instructions that would make it perform specific types of calculations that aided specific professions. Therefore Wang could sell more model 300s by providing software programs aimed at professionals with special math problems to solve. The larger the profession, the better. Doctors would pay $1,700 for a gawkish, table-top box that could calculate critical chemical-therapy doses quickly and accurately, as long as they didn't have to be computer mystics to run the things. For civil engineers, a specially programmed 300 determined the loads that bridges could bear. Car dealers used it to work out loan payments on the spot so that sales negotiations wouldn't drag out for two days as amortization rates were figured by head and hand. Dr. Wang absorbed another business lesson: When making computers that perform specific jobs, you'll sell a lot more if those jobs benefit large populations.

In 1967, on the strength of its calculators, Wang Labs pulled in nearly $7 million in sales. The thirty-five people employed in 1964 had multiplied by more than ten, to more than four hundred.

Thus encouraged, the company brought out a more capable desktop calculator, the model 700, in 1969. It contained only low-density integrated circuits, the only kinds commonly available then. Like its predecessors, the 700 was programmable. Also like its predecessors, it was really a small-scale computer going incognito. The disguise was deliberate. At the time, when you called a thing a computer, you invoked the lofty gods of pre-microelectronics. As the doctor observed in his autobiography, "it is a lot easier to sell a calculator—even an expensive one— than it is to sell a computer. For one thing, we could sell a calculator directly to the user, and we were good at that. In contrast, in the late 1960s and early 1970s, the decision to buy a computer would involve top management at most corporations . . . . There would be committees and meetings with the company's data processing people and a great deal of deliberation . . . . The same was true when selling to the government: use the word *computer* during a sales call, and all of a sudden, you would be awash with questions about specifications, requirements, and red tape."

You would also be selling against IBM, the titan of the business. When mainframes ruled, the term *computer* meant IBM. The actor Walter Mathau plied it to all the world when he played a harried business executive in the 1971 film *Plaza Suite*. Upset when he finds an error in a financial report, he doesn't ask, *Why didn't the computer catch this*? Instead he asks, *Why didn't the IBM catch it*? A handful of competitors also made mainframes, but next to IBM they were glibly called the seven dwarfs—RCA, GE, NCR, Honeywell, Burroughs, Control Data, and Sperry, although it was never clear which company represented Dopey, and which Sleepy, Sneezy, Grumpy, Bashful, Happy, or Doc.

Wang stayed successful by staying out of their company. The 700 sold more popularly than its predecessors. In 1970 Wang moved $27 million worth of its three math machines. The enterprise employed 1,400 people.

But at this pinnacle, the doctor decided to leap out of the business. Serenely confident, characteristically astute, he sensed change again. The IC-inspired calculator wars were beginning. Electronic portables—led by the Sharp QT–8B and the Canon Pocketronic—hadn't even appeared yet. But already, even among desktop machines, electronics' miniaturization was making it easier for other companies to make capable calculators. Competition from other manufacturers had already eroded the price of Wang's most basic model, the 300, by more than half, knocking it down to about $600. Ever vigilant, Dr. Wang foresaw the coming of LSI microchips that would reduce all the functions of his machines to a single speck of silicon. "When that happened," he observed, "the calculator business would belong to those who made large scale integrated circuits—and that would not be us." The time had come once again to adapt.

Staying true to pattern, Dr. Wang had already espied a promising next direction. He'd seen fissures in the edifice of Delphic computing. The doors to the temple were opening, and he decided to step inside by finally making a computer that would bear the name.

Even as late as 1970, mostly just very large organizations operated computers because most computers were still mainframes. The closest most offices came to a computer of any sort—at least to a computer that dared to call itself one—was through an intermediary company called a service bureau. It was a computing specialist: A service bureau operated a mainframe and did nothing else. It sold computing time to companies that couldn't afford the expense or even just the bother of owning their own oracle.

In 1968 Wang itself had bought a service bureau in order to acquire its expertise in computing. The outfit, Philip Hankins Incorporated, or PHI, operated a brawny IBM 360 mainframe in Watertown, Massachusetts, about twenty minutes from Wang's new home in Tewksbury. It was said to be the most powerful data-processing station in all of New England. The department store chain Filene's, for one, paid Hankins to process its weekly payroll, letting the fulming 360 steam through its workers' weekly time specs, with all their many variants of pay rates and hours worked, vacation time, sick days, commissions, and terminations. The arrangement was called time-sharing: You bought time on the computer, sharing it with all the other companies that also bought processing time from the service bureau. Computing was so expensive and so difficult that most companies just couldn't get any closer than that.

The gap in the bricks that Dr. Wang first perceived came from the PDP–8 minicomputer, created by Digital Equipment Corporation in the late 1960s. Digital was Wang's neighbor, situated in the Massachusetts mill town of Maynard. Kenneth Olsen, descended stubbornly from Swedish ancestors, an alumnus not of Harvard but of its neighbor, MIT, had started Digital just five years after An Wang had set up his own hopeful little enterprise. Digital had made electronic components until its pioneering PDP swept it to stardom. The PDP–8 represented a new class of information-handling device called a minicomputer. The concept was still fresh when a PDP–8 installed at Intel inspired Ted Hoff to design the first chip-born computer, the model 4004 microprocessor.

For sheer power and might, the mainframe still ruled. But minicomputers possessed some friendlier attributes that made them more widely appealing and accessible. A mini was a smaller, less imposing machine that sold in greater numbers than mainframes simply because it shed the mystique. A mini-computer's logic circuits were organized to work more efficiently, so they didn't need to follow as many instructions as a mainframe followed to get to the end of a task. Shortened instructions translated to smaller, more manageable programs. Therefore minis didn't need the racks and racks of memory cores that mainframes used. (At the time, small silicon memory chips were still just in the making from Intel.) One minicomputer could sit in the space of a tidy file cabinet instead of in the garage-sized room a business still needed to park a mainframe.

What's more, the programs were written using new, simplified computer languages that were easier to comprehend than the dense coding that earlier machines required. That opened the programming trade to a larger group of people. Therefore ordinary companies could hire somewhat ordinary people to operate minicomputers. And a mini was less expensive, capitalizing on the economy and the manufacturing efficiency available from integrated circuits—fewer internal components made for easier, lower-cost assembly.

Smaller, cheaper, more manageable and accommodating, a minicomputer just didn't demand all the special ministrations that a mainframe required. Computer operators could shed the white robes. They could silence their secret mutterings and incantations. They remained specialized experts. Computing was still too difficult to become breezily popular. But minis promised to spread into the sort of large, expansive market Wang coveted. They also played to the doctor's pride: me, a computer maker.

But when he started development of Wang Labs' first minicomputer in 1970, the doctor didn't forget the lessons his business had taught him. He had learned from the Compugraphic double-cross to maintain diversified product lines—make and sell a few good things, in case one goes away. And he understood solidly that computers that solved specific problems sold best. And Wang was inquisitive and restless enough by nature to move in multiple directions anyway. Therefore, alongside his ardent desire to make a minicomputer of his own, the doctor embarked on a simultaneous second direction. To help fill the void of its vanishing calculators, Wang Labs also set out to make word processors. In 1970 they were an emerging class of special-purpose computer. When the company applied its principle of accommodating ordinary people, it created a word processor so successful that it showed everyone around how computers should be built. It showed the whole world how to popularize computing.

☰ 14 ☰

New Language

THE THOUGHT TO MAKE a special-use computer specifically to manage words grew upward from one of Wang Labs' appointed idea people. Manufacturing companies employ people to stare out at the horizon. They're called new product planners, and their job is to spot distant opportunities. They try to find undiscovered places to sell their company's goods, often by adapting those goods to some urgent new use. They propose changes here and improvements there in order to suit a product to some human need that has gone hitherto unmet, or maybe just poorly met. At Wang Laboratories in the late 1960s, the new product planner who first spotted word processing was a man named Ed Lesnick.

Lesnick may forever remain unsung. He was only a catalyst. The actual metamorphosis of automatic typing into computers for the masses was accomplished by Harold Koplow, an itinerant mathematician who was alternately regarded as a hero and a miscreant at Wang Laboratories. Still, popular computing owes Ed Lesnick a debt for pointing An Wang toward word processing when the doctor cast about for calculator replacements in 1970. Lesnick had developed a passion for the concept, and he conveyed to his boss how perfectly computers that made words would work within the Wang strategy. They performed a specific job, and that job would entice a whole lot of people to buy the product.

In his autobiography the doctor recounted how "I read a study noting that while the average factory worker is supported by about fifteen thousand dollars' worth of tools and machinery that improve his productivity, virtually the only equipment supporting an office worker is a four-hundred-dollar electric typewriter plus pencils and paper. Computers . . . were not a presence in the lives of ordinary office workers. This said to me that the office was untracked territory when it came to the question of using technology to improve productivity. Moreover, there were more office workers than factory workers."

But none of those office workers and maybe just a few of the corporate overlords who bought equipment for those office workers had ever heard of Wang. The company was unknown outside of the circumscribed power-calculations crowd. Wang was entering word processing as a stranger, a new kid in an unfamiliar neighborhood.

What's more, Wang Labs wouldn't have the streets to itself. Lesnick didn't invent the idea of managing words with a computer. He found the concept already afloat. Lesnick first saw it working at Philip Hankins Inc., the computing service bureau that Wang Labs had purchased in 1968. One of the programs PHI fed into its IBM mainframe told the computer how to set up pages automatically in time with a typist who stroked in ABCs, punctuation marks, and all the other symbols that any ordinary secretary or other page-maker banged onto sheets of business bond thousands of times a day. Instead of processing numbers, a computer's most common function, the mainframe processed words, becoming the world's most powerful typewriter.

At the time that was not an ordinary or obvious use for digital thinkers. A computer at its core performs mathematics alone. To manipulate words, it had to give a numerical representation to each letter that each rapid, careless keystroke indicated, converting each instantly to some odd, binary number string of zeros and ones. It could go to work on those, assembling letters into words and words into sentences and sentences into pages according to programmed instructions that reduced every action, fundamentally, to a mathematical operation performed on the binaries.

Through mathematical operations it could be programmed to account for the fact that the keys indicating dot-space-space signified a sentence's end, which might be the same sentence end that another typist indicated as dot-space, which in both cases had to be presented differently when it landed at the end of a line than did simply space, although it could be handled the same as question-mark-space-space or exclamation-mark-space-space. The computer also needed mathematical operations that somehow enabled it to properly present the keystrokes $14.92 when they came up at the end of a line. The approach was the same that later computers—even today's personal computers that are physically so much smaller than the PHI IBM—used to process music and pictures and the like. They break each entity into imperceptibly small pieces and assign to all the pieces binary representations that can be manipulated breathlessly by the millions of transistors in an integrated circuit, then reassembled to present the song or picture or what have you. Mere word handling required a lesser amount of processing, but late in the 1960s the problem was still complex enough to challenge even a mainframe's might.

By the time Dr. Wang embraced the idea, a few companies were already out with office-scale attempts at word computers. The primary one came from IBM, which sold a machine called its Magnetic Tape Selectric Typewriter, or MTST. Therefore not only was Wang arriving new, unknown, and untried; it was also moving in beside some toughs who had already made claims to the territory.

At least their early page-makers weren't yet very advanced. At the start of the 1970s, the machines called word processors were mostly just electric typewriters crossbred with computer printers and given some memory. They could keep track of the words a secretary typed, but he or she couldn't see the words because the contraptions had no screens. To review a line, the secretary had to wait for the typewriter-cum-printer to bang it back. Even to find the line, the secretary had to endure awkward and elaborate search procedures. The market still awaited a compelling approach to word processing.

But at first Wang didn't have any better ideas. The company's quick rise in calculators had occurred because its founder's method for electronically manipulating numbers worked better than any other. With word processing, the best Wang Labs could do was ape the prevailing approach. It reworked the computer inside of its model 700 calculator, wiring it to manage words instead of numbers. The company bought Selectrics from IBM to double as the typewriter and the bang-it-back printer attached to the computer. The Wang 1200 word processing system went on sale in 1971. The company made only 3,000 of the things. They didn't work. The Selectrics supplied by IBM were seconds. They typed back crooked lines. But beside that, the machines just didn't offer any sizable advantage over competing attempts to automate typing. To break out of obscurity, Wang needed a product that wasn't just as good as the others. It had to be far better.

That decisive stride came from Harold Koplow, a wayward software engineer who was actually a pharmacist just working as a software engineer. It came almost as an afterthought of destiny. Koplow was the most unusual of computer programmers. He undertook the remaking of Wang's word processor under a strange circumstance: in a state of rebellion and facing imminent departure from the company he ended up rescuing instead. A whole stunning confluence of unlikelihoods provoked Harold Koplow to create office automation at Wang in 1975 in a creative stroke that also made computers mass-consumable by making them close to effortless to use.

As much as Dr. An Wang set the stage for such developments—by establishing a hyperactive company that strove to sell computers by making them useful and easily usable—it took bright, quirky Koplow to apply those principles in the extreme, designing a word processing computer that coddled people rather than frightened them. In some ways the two men were similar. Both could be stubbornly insistent and even imperious. Both inclined more toward movement than to brooding contemplation: You can't think your way to success, but if you keep your feet moving, sooner or later you'll walk into it.

But whereas the doctor affected a state of subtle majesty, Koplow was impetuous. He was brash. His risible spirit could flash with ire when provoked, but mostly he was mirthful, convivial, and youthfully playful. His big grin concealed nothing. It reserved nothing. Koplow rolled through life with a sense of amusement so detached he could laugh down bandits waving a gun, which he did a few years before he joined Wang. A carload of them had cased the Boston pharmacy where he worked weekends. One Saturday they watched him lock up and stroll toward home with a small brown bag in his hand. They cruised beside him and demanded the loot. Koplow laughed. The desperadoes waggled a gun barrel. Koplow shrugged and gave up the bag. The outlaws squealed away with what their victim describes as the cold goods: Popsicles he'd planned to share with his wife.

Koplow had attended pharmacy school because his father was a pharmacist and because he couldn't enroll at the elite MIT because tuition was too expensive. But when he started mixing medicines in 1962, at age 22, he discovered that he disliked the practice as much as he had disliked the course work. By the time the hold-up occurred in 1963, he was only a part-time druggist, working to finance a recreational diversion into math and physics. He ran through the course catalog at Boston University before he formally enrolled as a graduate student at Tufts University in 1964, eager to preserve a draft deferment. He earned a master's degree in physics in 1968, a year that physicists stood in unemployment lines.

So Koplow became a teacher, coaching adolescents in math and science at the junior high school he had once attended. He liked the work well enough to think he might settle into teaching as a permanent vocation. Yet he continued scanning classifieds. He noticed some outfit called Wang Laboratories in Tewksbury advertising for recent math and physics grads. Apply Department NC.

Department NC stood for Department Ned Chang, which was really just Ned Chang, Wang Laboratories' one-person programming team—although Ned himself wasn't really up on programming. Desperate, Department Chang hired Koplow the day of his interview in October 1968. Koplow was twenty-eight years old. At last he'd found work that befitted his mathematical agility.

His first job was to write a batch of software instructions for model 300 calculators, to expand their appeal to more professions. Both the doctor and Department Ned Chang expected the assignment to consume about a year. Koplow finished in a few months. Then he rattled around the office, shouting for a new challenge.

In a short time, pharmacist-physicist-teacher-software engineer Harold Koplow grew nearly indispensable at Wang. It wasn't just that he could assemble codes of ones and zeros in some kind of coherent order. Koplow's coherent orders were also shorter and more efficient than other people's. A computer following fewer instructions and more orderly instructions finishes a task more quickly. Faster computers sell better.

Koplow headed the team that developed Wang's next desktop calculator, the model 700. Then he led the conversion of the 700 from a math machine to a word computer, creating the disastrous Wang 1200 word processor of 1971.

But that wasn't the failure that scuttled Koplow's rise, set up his banishment, and thereby established the conditions under which he revolutionized computing. Wang remained fast-moving and flexible enough to tolerate false starts like the 1200. Rather, Koplow fell when Dr. Wang fingered him for detonating the company's marketing program.

Harold Koplow became Wang Laboratories vice president of marketing purely through patronage. With the general business recession of 1974 sinking Wang sales, Koplow agitated to have Chuan Chu—who had joined Wang from Honeywell, one of the dwarfs—placed in charge of marketing and sales. "He seemed like a good guy, and I liked him, and so I rallied all the troops around to get him into that job," recalls Koplow. Chu returned the compliment by seeing that Koplow moved in under him, as marketing VP.

Suddenly Koplow was in an executive level, people-person job. But he felt unfluttered. He'd been in just as deep when he joined Department NC barely five years earlier. At that time everything he knew about computers came from an afternoon at Tufts, when he had sat through an extracurricular class that gave just a peek at an IBM-era Delphic oracle. Now, in 1974, Koplow crashed through a business school text book for training. For all his inexperience, he thought he was doing well in marketing. Sales continued to slide, but he blamed the continuing recession for that. Therefore he felt stunned when the doctor demoted him early in 1975. No longer the star, Koplow was exiled to long-range planning.

Long-range planning functioned apart from the product planning department where Ed Lesnick labored. Lesnick looked for looming opportunities, such as the word processor he championed. By contrast, long-range planning probed more distant pie-in-the-sky possibilities—although in fact, like every other corporate cubby hole at Wang, the department served whatever purpose the doctor assigned it. At Wang long-range planning was a minimum security half-way house, the place detainees idled before leaving the company. "Dr. Wang just didn't like firing people," Koplow explains. "Anyone who had ever been LRPed before me had been gone in six months or so. I thought I was history."

The situation was almost surreal. Koplow shared his cell with Dave Moros, a friend and colleague who had come to Wang when it acquired Philip Hankins Inc. Moros had been banished to long-range planning for transgressions of his own, but he made a good cellmate for Koplow. He was just as outspoken, just as irascible, just as independent.

Together in Department LRP, the pair could remain comfortably, irresponsibly idle. Sure, the boss had issued an assignment. Dr. Wang had told them to design a new word machine. But that was only busy work. This was the half-way house, after all. They were short-timers. In a few months at most they'd be gone. What did they care what the doctor wanted? How did they know if he even really wanted it? "I don't think Dr. Wang's real intention was for us to come up with a word processor design," Koplow reflects. "He was just giving us something to do while he straightened out his company."

The two men dismissed any idea of undertaking a technical design. Mere busy work didn't deserve that much effort. Instead, at the suggestion of Moros, they started writing a user's manual for a secretary's imaginary dream machine. It was just a lark. Ordinarily a user's manual was compiled as a last-second afterthought, hastily assembled after a new product was designed and built. They were almost always inadequate. For Koplow and Moros the work was breezy. It flaunted their rebellious irresponsibility deliciously. The pair worked on the guide only in the morning. Moros went home around noon.

Koplow went out on job interviews. If he didn't have an interview, he wandered the halls at Wang, gabbing with people. He felt comfortably at ease. He had never set out to join the computer guild anyway. He had wanted to be a pharmacist. Or maybe a physicist. Or maybe a teacher. Koplow was accustomed to transitions.

At least Ed Lesnick, still stumping for word computing at Wang, took the assignment seriously. He set up field trips for Koplow and Moros, sending them out to test drive the inadequate systems other companies peddled. The pair saw auto-typists from AES, Redactron, Vydek, and Xerox. They saw some models that experimented with display screens. The two men brought back a few ideas worth borrowing. But most of all they learned what to avoid in word processing. They also developed a strong conviction that they could do better.

Gradually their mornings' endeavor grew more serious. Together they imagined a machine so effortlessly accommodating that it would make even their user's manual nearly unnecessary. Give someone from the typing pool less than an hour's instruction, they figured, and then she should be able to find her own way on the keyboard. They stuck on a video screen the size of a portable TV that could display about half a typed page at a time. More than just that, the screen gave the computer a means to talk to the typist. Koplow and Moros devised instructions and suggestions to flash onto the tube, sometimes when a secretary asked for help, sometimes automatically, when a wrong key was pressed erroneously. They created insertion buttons and deletion buttons, and they wrote out instructions in straightforward sequences that any secretary could follow by intuition alone. They worked out all the essential page-handling operations and presented them in lists a secretary could read on-screen so that she could pick a task to perform from a menu and then let the machine set it up.

Forget the oracles' arcane computer commands. They knew as surely as they knew Wang's guiding principle—that the way to sell computers was to make them effortless for untrained people—that secretaries weren't about to join any tech-adoring coven. Let them simply glide more glibly through their day's load of letters, reports, memos, and maybe an occasional dull memoir. Let them turn out every page free of any embarrassing corrections conspicuously retyped over an eraser's smudge. That would bring office workers running to buy the machines.

Each time Koplow ventured out for a job interview, he returned more eagerly to his confinement at Wang. He felt unimpressed by IBM. He felt unimpressed by Exxon. He felt unimpressed by Monroe. He felt unimpressed by Xerox. He felt unimpressed by computer and electronics companies of every stripe. Many were ready to put him to work on their sizzling new this and their latest mega that. Some invited him to join projects that were designing word computers. Some of them invited him to join efforts to make general-purpose computers. All of them thought that their upcoming products were destined to smash barriers, break records, reorder the universe. Koplow thought every one of them was daft.

"When I saw what everybody else was doing and what they wanted me to do, I thought, that's really hokey. I thought, the stuff I'm designing, this user's manual, is much better than anything that they have. I got more interested in the machine. And so we finished the user's manual."

The book amounted to what product planners call a machine's functional requirements: the jobs it must perform. Make a word processor do all these things, and you'll have one dandy word processor. As they approached the end of summer 1975, six months into their banishment and already late for their final departure, both Moros and Koplow felt confident of their achievement. Says Koplow, "we fully expected Dr. Wang to like it. We were not prepared for other people in the company to pan it, which they did. But Dr. Wang ignored them."

Following past practices, the doctor directed that the Koplow/Moros letter-maker be built by adapting another Wang product. This time they'd use the VS, a minicomputer that the doctor had put into development earlier that year. It would serve as a central hub, processing words for a gang of workers who typed contentedly at terminals that plugged into the VS like the arms of an octopus. That was how minis were commonly used, as computing stations for groups of workers, such as bank tellers, check-out clerks, purchasing agents, or inventory pickers. It was another approach to time-sharing, with a team of people sharing the brain power of one computer as they engaged in a practical workday task.

But a few weeks later, the doctor backpedaled. The VS was moving too slowly through development. He didn't want to hold up the word processor to wait for it. He knew tech business too well to dawdle unnecessarily over any good concept. On September 28, 1975, when Koplow and Moros gathered in his office for another of their periodic meetings to plan the wordmaker, the doctor asked if they had any better ideas about building a computer that could realize their dream machine user's manual.

Well, as a matter of fact, Koplow had been thinking about that very question. He had never much liked the idea of using the VS as a central word processor anyway. He had seen some time-sharing minis during his many excursions to computer havens outside of Wang. He had watched them juggle tasks, trying awkwardly to manage the separate chores of printing, of filing away briefs or memos or stray bits of unfinished text, of accepting the fast-clacking keystrokes of professional typists working several at a time from separate keyboards. The demands overloaded the computers. "You had to worry about someone else bogging down the machine, so that your program would take forever to execute," he had learned.

"Why couldn't someone have their own, dedicated computer and not have to share it with other users," Koplow reasoned. He argued that such personal-use computers could be powered by microprocessors, those new, ready-made computers on a chip pioneered by Intel's model 4004 just four years earlier. By this time, Intel's more capable model 8080 computing chip had been out for less than a year, battling imitators from, it seemed, just about every other foundry in the semiconductor business. Koplow felt intrigued by the possibilities the micros promised. The works inside a personally sized computer built around a microprocessor would be smaller because all the logic circuitry would reside on just one chip. It would be easier to manufacture because the microprocessor would replace the complicated logic circuit that otherwise would be assembled out of separate parts. Best of all, microprocessors would be cheaper. At the time, says Koplow, they weren't magnificently cheaper than separately assembled logic boards. But they offered economy enough to support the approach.

The idea wasn't wholly original. During his recent odysseys, Koplow had uncovered a few attempts at one-person word computers. Some were powered by general-purpose microprocessors, the same as he proposed. But even when they supported just one clacking typist, they failed for the same reason that the time-sharing gang systems failed: The computing chips were overburdened. They were asked to do too much.

"I knew that one microprocessor couldn't handle all the tasks associated with doing filing and printing and capturing key strokes," he explains. "Other companies tried, but they had a hell of a time writing a little operating system for these little devices to do these three tasks. Printing, filing, capturing key strokes and displaying them on the screen was a lot of work for these little Intel 8080s and Motorola 6800s. They were slow."

Therefore Koplow suggested a divide-and-conquer configuration. He reasoned that ready-made microprocessors might handle all the jobs quite handily if he distributed micros among the separate tasks. Rather than asking a secretary to share one, he would put a complete, micro-built computer on the desk to handle her typing alone—assuming that a microprocessor was capable of even that. Hastily he wrote a program to test the speed of Intel's 8080 with its 5,000 industrious transistors. It needed speed enough to place keystrokes into a memory buffer within 30 milliseconds—30 thousandths of a second—in time to take the next fervid stroke and the next one and the next one after that while the microprocessor, in the meantime, assembled the sequence of letters into a tidy page and, simultaneously, worked out the conversions needed to post each one on a cathode-ray tube instantly so that the typist felt like his or her fingers were physically attached to the merrily moving, phosphorous blip sweeping dutifully across the green screen just inches atop his or her hands, leaving words in its glowing swath.

Intel passed the exam. Its 8080 could keep up with a fleet-fingered typist. That was enough. Koplow figured that for filing, according to his spread-the-wealth approach, he'd connect one computer to another separate computer. Powered by its own microprocessor, it would store notes and letters and everything wordy and fetch them dutifully when called for from a personal desktop typer. A bunch of people could share one, the same way they shared the four-drawer file cabinet. And when a typist wanted to render one of the filed pages onto actual paper, a key on that typist's private console would tell the file-cabinet computer to send it to a printer that was also wired into the network. The printer would have its own microprocessor, too, to control paper feed and character selection and all those special concerns.

In less than a year, as the summer of 1976 just started, Wang Laboratories brought out its Word Processing System—a title that seems prosaic only in hindsight. It was called the WPS. Its typing station, the personal computer part, was an all-in-one console not much wider than a weighty electric typewriter, with a keyboard built into the housing that also held the screen. The free-standing file cabinet, about half the size of a desk, could juggle the work of three secretaries and support a couple of printers. Or, in a higher priced version, a more capacious file cabinet equipped with platter-sized magnetic memory disks could support fourteen stations. Each station contained its own Intel 8080.

When the WPS was first demonstrated at an office equipment expo in New York on June 21, 1976, "people saw text editing done on a screen, and they thought it was magic," wrote Dr. Wang in *Lessons*. The first naive noninitiates who drummed on Wang keys apologized to the screen when it told them they erred. Most had never seen floppy disks before. Some cut open the disks' protective sleeves, thinking the thin black plastic was only decorative packaging. One customer called Koplow about a particular page she couldn't get her WPS to set up for her. He told her to send him a copy of the file so he could take a look. She mailed him a photocopy of her diskette.

"The key to the Wang Word Processor," attests Koplow, "was to make it easy for a mere mortal to run what in essence was a computer, but what to the user looked like nothing more than a typewriter with a new, intuitive interface." With a Wang, the computer stayed in the background while it took over the drudgery, indenting new paragraphs, tabulating neat vertical columns, ending lines crisply near the right margin, deleting errors, inserting second thoughts, and moving around words and whole blocks of words.

Thus began office automation: the substitution of computers to perform all the brainless necessities that drag at the tail of corporate administration. In Iowa, Steven Gustafson had employed two secretaries full-time when he was corporate attorney at Amana in the pre-Wang 1970s. Twenty-five years later, as he prepared to retire from the bar, he scarcely filled one-tenth the working hours of one. That spring tide in efficiency began in 1976 when Wang Laboratories first made computers mass-consumable by making them close to effortless to use.

As the first word processor worthy of the name, the Wang also introduced people to the idea of personal computing. Offices built around a Word Processing System worked remarkably like offices today. Individual workers used personal-size, individual computers. But at the same time, each private machine was knit into a network containing other private machines, with a file server in the center to service them all. What changed with time was scope and function. As the individual computers grew more affordable and more functional, they grew more plentiful. They grew more affordable largely because their two primary components, logic and memory chips, grew cheap. They grew more functional as those two parts simultaneously acquired greater speed, power, capacity, and capability. Microprocessors progressed very quickly past the point where anyone had to wonder if they could keep up with a top-grade typist.

In fact, in 1978, a little more than a year after Wang introduced its WPS, Koplow stuck a better logic chip inside new models. He replaced the Intel 8080 with the Z–80 microprocessor from Zilog because the Zilog cost less, but it did more. It was a product of the competitive tumult that wrung ever faster, cheaper, smaller circuits out of fractious ambitions. Intel defectors Federico Faggin and Masatoshi Shima started Zilog in 1974 when they became eager to make their own run at silicon stardom. Faggin was the circuit designer hired by Intel early in 1970 to manifest Ted Hoff's original, 4004 microprocessor. Shima was one of visiting Busicom engineers who had arrived in June 1969 to oversee development of the calculator chips that Hoff had turned into the 4004. Shima had stayed, joining Intel and directing design of the 8080 chip in 1974. Bob Noyce would later call him the world's most influential microprocessor designer. That's very high praise. But in the large scheme of events, Shima and Faggin and even Bob Noyce himself were only a few of the many strivers who advanced their art by responding to the enticements of corporate ownership.

Likewise, Wang Labs wasn't the only organization to permute computing toward popular acceptance. With microprocessors, any person could make a computer if he or she had enough patience and determination, plus some basic skills in circuitry, an electronics parts catalog, and a soldering stick. The impossibly difficult components, the logic engine and the memory, suddenly could be bought ready-made. Hobbyists and other electro-enthusiasts were already in thrall of the idea that they could own their own private computer when Koplow started putting personal machines to work in offices in the mid-1970s. Mail-order computer kits from the likes of Altair and Osborn are commonly considered the predecessors of today's ubiquitous personal computer.

The accepted genealogy is frequently recited: A coupon ad for the Altair 8800 appeared in the January 1975 edition of *Popular Electronics*; the Apple I arrived in 1976; Radio Shack and Commodore topped Apple with more manageable machines; IBM introduced its personal computer in 1981, called the PC in an appropriation of the entire category's title for IBM's particular brand. But those presumed progenitors of popular computing did not feint toward popularity. They were not accommodating or accessible. They were still fit only for specialists and slavering enthusiasts. They wore the designation "personal" not because they were chummy companions but simply because they were sized for one person rather than for dozens. They did not begin computing's migration toward universal acceptance. They merely grew into the principle that Wang first firmly established: The way to sell a lot of computers was to make them suitable for a lot of people.

For a while the success of Wang Laboratories proved the fact. By 1978, it was shipping nearly 800 WPS typing stations every month, a sales rate that brought in $198 million that year, or twice what the company had made in 1976. Sales doubled again in 1980 and again in 1982. That year the company made number eleven on the list of computer giants compiled by *Datamation* magazine, an industry trade journal. Before, Wang hadn't even broken into the top fifty. Koplow was a vice president again, directing the further development of word processing and expanding toward ever more capable office automation.

But he left Wang Laboratories in 1982 over fall outs with An Wang's elder son, Fred Wang, whom the doctor was grooming to take over the company. Koplow moved into and out of a few ventures before he went back to school in 1999, enrolling to earn a Ph.D. in mathematics just for fun at the University of Florida in Gainesville.

The company ran on momentum for a few years after Koplow's departure. At the height of its success in the middle of the 1980s, Wang Labs sold close to $3 billion of its computers per year. Then, as if to prove the point about adaptation, Wang Labs sank with stunning swiftness the moment it stopped moving. Koplow was gone. Moros was gone. Other key innovators were leaving just as the company was at its pinnacle. Soon, Wang's premier office machines were eclipsed by personal computers that were more multifunctional: With software to program them, they performed word processing in addition to loads of other tasks. The labs had no new products to answer the challenge. Instead it merely attached itself to the PC development, bringing out an IBM-like product of its own. But the company was no longer initiating technology turns, only following them. It disappeared soon after its founder died in 1990.

≡ 15 ≡

Building Muscles

FOR FEATS OF CEREBRAL PURITY like word processing or any other kind of computing that occurred indoors, microchips advanced their influence simply by repeating the chip-makers' mantra: *smaller, faster, cheaper*. Electrons that moved more rapidly among smaller, more densely packed transistors boosted brain power, engorging electronic equipment with undreamed of abilities that grew even more capable while, paradoxically, they also grew less expensive. Personal computers, pagers, and bar-room video games metamorphosed to wallet-size computers, feather-light cell phones, three-dimensional fantasy blasters, and the Internet, all because the chips that powered them grew mighty and then still mightier.

But the impact of processing power alone was blunted when it ventured outside the sheltered lab, office, family room, movie theater, or fun arcade. If chips were going to expand their influence inside hulking, hard-working machines, they had to do more than just think. They also had to perform physical labor, which meant they had to move things. That required the combination of different types of transistors on one IC. To pass along enough electrical current, say, to energize a motor, vibrate a stereo speaker, or activate a relay, a circuit required brutish power transistors—large by micro-world standards, they were specially built to work as high-energy switches. But they would share the same miniature real estate with delicate, low-energy logic transistors arranged as computer circuits to tell the power transistors when to turn on and when to turn off. Both power-passing transistors and logic circuitry had advanced as separate achievements of the semiconductor arts. Their combination in a single smart-power chip did not loom as just another inevitable consequence of Moore's Law.

Much of the bedrock allure of making microchips was that you formed so many transistors at once, on one bit of silicon, by performing relatively few processing steps. But different transistor types required entirely different process recipes. Therefore combining them on a single chip would require somehow shuffling up and combining their manufacturing processes, mixing and overlapping and resequencing all those separate baths and maskings and bake-oven diffusions and vapor evaporations and all the rest.

Still, some burghers of the silicon establishment liked the concept enough to send researchers probing for ways to make such chips. By 1986 about ten semicon houses were investigating some form or other of a combination smart-power micro. That same year, two institutions combined to ramrod the development. Motorola brought a pinnacle of microchip experience and achievement to the partnership. Its mate, Delco Electronics, occupied only the second tier of the semiconductor hierarchy. But it was a semco nonetheless, and therefore the marriage was somewhat unusual, uniting two companies that might otherwise compete. Yet each company possessed special abilities that the other required for the undertaking. Therefore, together, the pair set out to create a smart-power microchip that General Motors—the world's largest automaker and Delco's corporate parent—wanted urgently to control its cars' antilock brakes. Antilocks were the automotive break-through du jour, and GM was gaining in a contentious race against the whole global auto industry to claim the lead in developing the favored feature.

Above the daunting technical obstacles, the project's biggest challenge turned out to be the excess vanity that Motorola brought to the task. The semiconductor industry as a whole—especially leaders like Motorola that had survived the commercial reorderings that came with each new technology turn—had witnessed so many victories by 1986 that it was easy to read former successes as assurances of future ones.

"I don't think anybody down there realized just how difficult a job this was going to turn out to be," recounts John Shreve, the engineering manager who headed Delco's smart-power development team. "They felt like, hey, we're going to knock this thing out and get on with life and do a whole bunch of other parts just like it. I can remember talking to one of my counterparts down there when we first got started. He said, 'we'll whip this thing out in nothin' flat.' Well, I just didn't buy that. That didn't make any sense to me at all."

Thus even in the face of technical problems that at times appeared insurmountable, Shreve's greater management challenge became organizational: To bust the barriers obstructing smart power, he had to restore some of the requisite humility that the more accomplished player had lost. Second-string Delco had to adopt an underdog, against-the-odds determination that could rescue the project from the insouciant swagger of its partner.

It contributed technical prowess too. Delco's junior partner status derived from its business position, not from inabilities. It wasn't a semiconductor house as much as it was an application house, using chip technology in the equipment it built for automobiles. Therefore it limited silicon development to products most useful in cars. But its researchers evinced the same eager enthusiasm that had drawn every other zealot into the field.

Shreve was a typical case. He'd been smitten by semiconductors even as a kid in mid-century Missouri, acquiring a fascination for transistors first and then, when they appeared, for ICs. While earning an electrical engineering degree at the University of Missouri, Columbia, in the early 1970s, he devoured the few courses the school offered in IC technology. As a fresh new grad in 1974, he turned down an offer to go to Dallas because Texas Instruments wanted to put him to work in product testing. Shreve wanted to design semiconductors. He joined Delco instead for the chance to lay out microcircuits for car radios. A few years later he transferred to Delco's IC design center. From there he took on engineering management of smart-power research in mid-1985 before Delco hooked up with Motorola.

Fastidious and precise, thoughtful, organized, and industrious, leading by his example and with a reassuring consistency, Shreve presided over the nearly ten Delco researchers engaged in the smart-power project. Together they felt an elevated sense of responsibility. They recognized that their assignment amounted to a crucial next step for car electronics in particular and for microelectronics in general.

"We were in the infancy of automotive electronics," explains Larry Hach, another alumnus of the smart-power program. "From everything we were seeing in the '80s, automotive electronics was the place to be. We were just a couple years into powertrain controllers. We were just on the verge of anti-lock brakes. We wanted to be a player. We were going to be a player and we saw a big future. This development was required, so we had to go after it. It was a necessity."

But at the same time, Delco recognized that it was biting off a big hunk of unfamiliar technology. The smart-power development it envisioned would represent a major achievement for any chip house, even ones with more experience and credentials than this car company division. Delco's institutional skills were adaptive more than creative: It parlayed semiconductor inventions made elsewhere into electronic components for automobiles.

Delco had begun its life as the electronics arm of General Motors in 1936, making nothing more auspicious than car radios. In 1954 it joined the semiconductor business, making germanium transistors to replace some of the vacuum tubes in its roving music machines. Not only were the new models smaller—a big deal when the box has to ride inside a dashboard—but the transistorized car radios also consumed less power. That was an even bigger deal because Delco's radios had to run on a car's twelve-volt battery-based electrical system. In 1957 Delco jettisoned tubes entirely, introducing the first all-transistor auto radio, a special model stuck in the expansive Cadillac Brougham, one of the era's smooth-sailing highway super-tankers. Delco began developing integrated circuits in 1962, the same year it completed a new semiconductor plant in its home town of Kokomo, Indiana—another prairie town where industrious denizens had developed a knack for making things. Five years later, in 1967, it started using its ICs in automotive voltage regulators. By 1974 it was fiddling with microcircuitry to control early, experimental versions of both air bags and antilock brakes. In 1978 Delco brought out engine control computers.

By the mid-1980s, the people who made motor vehicles had learned the value of microcircuits from the salvation they had brought. Semiconductors had given cars a second life late in the 1970s, at a time when an awful lot of thought-filled adversaries predicted exactly the opposite. The critics claimed that cars had grown too populous, fouling the air and consuming too much of their sustaining fuel. Chastened, the mobile culture had awaited collapse from the weight of its own success.

But the collapse never came, largely because computerized engine controllers made cars clean and efficient.

With automobility thus secured, car companies grew giddy in the 1980s as they glimpsed new possibilities from microelectronics. They envisioned such safety systems as air bags and antilock brakes and such security features as keyless remote-control door locks. They foresaw such performance enhancers as intelligent shock absorbers, computerized gear shifting, four-wheel steering, and sure-footed traction control. They anticipated such alluring comforts as hands-free mobile telephones, voice-controlled air conditioning, and digital music systems, plus a whole lot of other wish-list features—satellite-guided navigation, radar-scanning speed control, rain-sensitive windshield wipers, infrared night vision, antiglare mirrors, tires that inflate themselves, and video entertainment consoles for the kids in the back seat.

But a car simply didn't have room for all the separate control circuits that such features would require, each packaged in its attendant black box that would have to be fastened somewhere in the cabin or under the hood. Besides, individual micros and power transistors and other supporting parts would become too expensive if engineers added as many as they imagined. They would also make a car more complicated to assemble, which would pile on more onerous expense. And on top of all that, the bundles of wires they would add to an auto would create an unmanageable tangle. One prototype model that Buick put together at the time had so many wires running to the driver's side armrest that the door wouldn't close. Its hinges bound up on the fat dendrite of copper.

Greater micro-integration was essential if car designers were ever going to fit so many aspirations inside any single automobile. They needed IC controllers that could do more than one job at a time. That was the role envisioned for smart power. It aimed to simplify electronic machine control, consolidating more electronic activities within fewer parts, by providing chips that could perform multiple functions.

Semiconductor companies on their own weren't quite prepared to make this new kind of combination chip. Sure, they felt incentive enough to try. Until the onslaught of mass-consumable computers and so many other electronic gadgets in the 1990s, cars represented the largest single market for microcircuits. Motorists in the United States alone bought about ten million new vehicles every year. That meant that if you could find some irresistible way to use micro-control inside every complicated flivver, you might sell as many as ten million chips as a first-year's reward.

The problem was that those flivvers were just so impossibly complicated. Car circuits required special built-in provisions to operate reliably under the weird conditions encountered aboard autos. They had to be tough, to withstand abuse, and to endure circumstances that would detonate any ordinary circuit. But for all the special measures they required, the ICs also had to be made on the cheap because cheap was the most car companies would pay for them. Economy was a long-standing custom in Detroit, Seoul, Stuttgart, Tokyo, Wolfsburg, and all the other car capitals. The wheeling consumers they courted didn't have bottomless pockets like space agencies, defense ministries, and big corporate computer departments. All told, ordinary semiconductor suppliers found the automotive environment alien, inhospitable, and outright spooky.

But Delco's corps of semiconductor savants understood the extraordinary needs of car-borne computers as only auto insiders could understand them. They straddled the two realms, working as both tough-minded car-biz suppliers and inquisitive semiconductor researchers. Fitting electronics inside automobiles was their professional specialty.

By the time smart-power development rolled around in 1985, the radio maker had fully transformed itself into a savvy electronic specialist with a back door to tech-hungry automobilia. Shreve and all his colleagues in Delco's semiconductor group weren't about to let anyone else steal the fun and glory to come from putting intelligence inside the world's most popular machines.

But Delco's chip fabrication experience was limited mostly to making the older, Oreo-cookie-style, bipolar microchips. It also made a lot of individual power transistors. It had a much shorter history making CMOS chips, the highly integrated complementary metal-oxide semiconductors that made up most computing circuits.

That's why it set up the partnership to create smart-power chips. James Himelick, a Ph.D. who worked in Delco's advanced development department, chose Motorola after investigating smart-power research initiatives at about ten semiconductor companies in early 1986. He visited National. He visited Texas Instruments. He visited the Japanese chip-maker Hitachi. Of them all, Motorola's semiconductor operation down in Phoenix seemed to have the best ideas for accomplishing the daunting combination of dissimilar transistors. In fact, at the time Motorola already produced an early take on smart power. General Motors was building the chip into its Cadillac Allante, a showy status car that was still undergoing engineering and design. The IC was much too expensive for a popularly priced auto, and it lacked all the capabilities of a full-blown smart-power approach. Still, it stepped in the right direction, elevating Motorola above the pack of other hopefuls.

For Motorola's incentive, joining the partnership gave it an exclusive entry point into the coveted automobile business. As a product partner with Delco, it ipso facto became a preferred supplier to GM.

John Shreve assembled his team for the first joint smart-power project meeting on July 23–25, 1986, in Kokomo. Developers and program managers from Delco and Motorola agreed to reconvene quarterly to assess progress, to wrangle over problems, and to keep their two teams in sync. The agreement stipulated that separate project teams at the two companies would work in parallel. They'd coordinate their chip designs, coordinate the processes they developed for making the chips, then run the processes in parallel so that a combination circuit made by Motorola would look the same as one made by Delco. That way they could be used interchangeably in automobiles.

The program aimed to integrate not just power transistors and logic transistors but also to add a third type to the smart-power combination. A section of bipolar transistors would work as signal processors, tuned to accept the continuous stream of sensor readings that told a chip's adjoining logic circuit about conditions aboard the auto. The readings arrived as raw electrical impulses, and the bipolars would convert them to a digital format that the logic circuit could comprehend.

Of the three types, the tiny CMOS logic transistors were by far the most delicate. The electricity that passed through the large power transistor would scramble any adjacent logic circuitry if it bled too close. Therefore much of the challenge of making smart power was to find a way to shield and isolate the chip's logic section. That was to be Motorola's greatest contribution: It had worked out an isolation technique it called etch-refill.

But when time came to transfer the concept from planning to actual prototype production, Motorola couldn't get enough working chips to come out at the end of its fabrication line. Its yields were too low. Therefore processing costs ran two to three times higher than expectations.

At the same time, organizational problems at Motorola were making the technical ones impossible even to approach, much less to solve. The company couldn't keep people on the project. Competing semcos raided its Phoenix staff greedily, hiring away engineers in order to acquire some of Motorola's expertise in the same combination chips it sought to invent with Delco. Piracy was the penalty the industry took from rivals who acquired a technical lead in any promising new direction. The practice worked as a corollary to the common temptation people felt to defect from a semco to start their own. Even if they didn't want to run their own show, talented researchers could often find another aggressive semiconductor company willing to pay more for their expertise.

But that explanation didn't help relations with Delco. "One of the things that angered me the most was that we went through people at Motorola almost like water," Shreve recounts. "We never had a stable workforce down there, while it was always the same basic group of people here." Technical progress would stutter with each staff change as newcomers in Phoenix acquainted themselves with the project's complexities. "We had design issues that were extraordinarily difficult," Shreve emphasizes. "We had many meetings with Motorola, and I really raised hell with them, because they were constantly running different people through the program and we weren't getting anywhere with them."

The problems became too difficult to ignore one year into the research, when Motorola brought out its first prototype smart-power chips in June 1987. Delco followed in August. The samples didn't work.

"They were awful, ugly," says Shreve. The problems were so widespread he couldn't even figure where to start to make corrections. "It was just a mess. And I was thinking, God, how are we ever going to get this thing straightened out?"

The situation forced Motorola to get serious. The smart-power project wasn't a what-if, wouldn't-it-be-nice, pie-in-the-sky research experiment. A customer was waiting, and it was a customer that Motorola didn't want to disappoint.

"Everything in the automotive industry is time-driven," Shreve explains. General Motors had already scheduled the device into one of its 1991 vehicles. Engineers were already designing that car to accommodate a particular antilock braking system, and other engineers were designing that system around the smart-power chip that had just come off the pilot line unfit to use for anything more than paving gravel.

"We had a committed program with production schedules to meet and deliveries to make," says Shreve. "We had to deliver this thing. We needed to make this thing work. We just didn't know how we were gonna get there quite yet. But we didn't feel like we were incapable of doing it. We had never developed anything before that we had to just completely throw in the towel and say we can't make this work." This group of developers wasn't about to be the first.

Spurred by Shreve's haranguing and by the stark evidence of the scrambled prototypes, Motorola took two measures to juice its half of the program. The first was organizational: It relocated its smart-power research team. Originally, the group had labored as an attachment to Motorola's power-transistor section at 52nd Street in Phoenix. That had doomed it to neglect from managers who had no inherent interest in IC development. The guys at 52nd made transistors, and to them the smart-power program amounted to little more than a costly distraction. The engineering and development it required sopped up resources that the business chiefs would rather commit to their own projects, and it wasn't yet returning a dime to their bottom line.

Therefore Motorola moved the development team out of power transistors and placed it inside what Motorola called its Bipolar Analog IC Division in Tempe, Arizona. That was an appropriate home. The managers at Tempe knew ICs. They recognized the value of smart power, and they anticipated that it could become a lucrative new product. Therefore the move stabilized the program and brought it the priority attention it required.

Next, Motorola abandoned the etch-refill isolation method that was causing it pains—the same etch-refill method that had bought it the partnership in the first place. The technique involved etching out a tub on the surface of chip-to-be. The tub was then refilled with silicon of a different formulation than the surrounding area, creating a distinct zone inside the tub. The logic circuit would then be built within the refilled tub to separate it from the high-energy power transistors placed around it. Conceptually, the approach looked solid. But Motorola had trouble polishing the wafer surface flat so it could perform more processing steps after refilling the tubs. Too often it polished away too much of the fill inside the tubs. It couldn't get the thickness right.

It proposed a different technique entirely, called double-buried layer. The method started by creating specks of silicon impurities on the foundation that would become a chip. Next it covered the whole foundation with another layer of silicon, burying the specks. Then it deposited another set of specks on the new top layer of silicon, right above the original ones. When the layered silicon was baked long and hot, the top specks and the bottom specks diffused, or spread, until they joined and penetrated the two layers top to bottom. Thus they created vertical towers of specially formulated silicon that provided the structures for power transistors—ones that would be well insulated from other transistor circuits eventually cooked onto the finished chip.

Paradoxically, in Kokomo, Delco had an easier time with the original, etch-refill process. Therefore it stayed with the technique for a while, while Motorola pursued double-buried layer. But eventually Delco also switched to the replacement method. After all, the original program aim had been to keep the two teams in sync. Besides, double-buried layer turned out to be the cheaper approach. Etch-refill, the concept that had encouraged shanghai raids on Motorola, died after it was cut from the smart-power program.

With the program thus stabilized and redirected in Phoenix, two years of problem-solving still remained. "Some of the most difficult problems stemmed from the fact that the part didn't stand up to certain automotive fault conditions," says Shreve. They were those pesky, special circumstances that occurred only aboard autos. One of the most befuddling concerned a condition called "loss of reverse battery." The circuit had to be rigged so that the chip would survive if, beating one-in-a-hundred-thousand odds, some idiot mechanic hooked up a car's battery backward. It was bad enough that the error would send current flowing the wrong way through the microchip—that condition was simply called "reverse battery." Loss of reverse battery occurred when the mechanic realized his or her error and hastily yanked off the crossed battery connections. As it collapsed, the backward flowing current would tear up the chip. "This turned out to be a very difficult problem to solve," Shreve notes, "because when you lose the battery connections, there is no place for the stored energy (inside the chip) to go until a current path—usually destructive—is found." As a remedy, the circuit designers strategically placed current-limiting components on the chip to keep the exiting, reversed-battery current from rising destructively high.

It was the sort of provision only a mobile IC would require. Therefore it took the nuanced experience and the dogged insistence of an auto initiate like Delco to work such measures into microchips that also popped off the manufacturing line at the peanuts-per-part prices that mass automobility demanded. As much as Motorola contributed to the partnership in its breadth and depth of semiconductor savvy, it gained in the car-culture insights that rubbed off from Delco, and not just the technical ones. Delco also contributed enough insecurity and no-white-flags determination to counterbalance the glib confidence that might have buckled when the technical problems didn't yield as easily as Motorola had expected.

Both sides reaped rewards. Motorola started producing smart-power ICs first, supplying the chips that controlled the antilocks on the 1991 Pontiac Grand Am, which went on sale late in 1990. Delco followed close behind, starting production in August 1990 for parts used in GM's 1992 cars.

EPILOGUE

Mutual Aid

THE ELECTRONIC REGENERATION of automobiles has progressed so relentlessly in the dozen years since the first smart-power chips appeared that cars are starting to resemble robots. Especially in the most advanced models, drivers serve as control-room operators. They enter commands through familiar mechanisms like the gas pedal and brake pedal, but those controls aren't connected to any automotive hardware anymore. Instead they are computer input devices. By stomping one pedal or mashing the other, motorists relay their intentions to the car's controlling computers. The computers—which are monolithic logic chips packaged in protective black boxes—decide how much fuel to dump into the engine to make the car accelerate while maintaining vital stability. Computers determine how much brake pressure to apply to stop it safely. The new SL500 that Mercedes-Benz introduced in 2002 features a fast-thinking system called Sensotronic Brake Control that can tell when a driver wants to stop the car fast, in an emergency maneuver, and when he or she just wants to roll to a gentle rest at an intersection or maybe in the driveway. Systems under development will even disconnect steering wheels from front ends. Small motors will point a car this way or that, responding to commands from a chip that reads a driver's steering inputs.

Of course, for a car like the Mercedes SL that sells for $85,000, buyers can absorb the expense of such exotic, first-generation features as brakes that feel for foot pressure. It takes a while for such aggressive advances to trickle into everyday automobiles. Most often they make it because car companies and the equipment makers that serve the car companies and the chip houses that supply the equipment makers all remain eager to penetrate the mass market. They make more money when they sell millions and millions of a thing. Therefore every party in the commercial chain participates in the relentless pursuit of economy, striving by every means available to make a product more and more affordable so that more and more people will buy it. They improve manufacturing methods, streamline production, find lower-cost components, revamp the product's design, simplify this or that function, consolidate fragmented pieces, and replace complicated mechanisms.

Producers endure the hardships of reengineering only if compelling motives encourage them. With integrated circuits, mass markets didn't arise as an accidental consequence of chips becoming cheap. Rather, ICs grew to be economical and abundantly useful enough to shape culture because their producers were enticed by the rewards of mass-market consumption.

In 1987, the year that Motorola's smart-power problems became woefully apparent, 137 million automobiles plied roads in the United States alone. U.S. motorists bought about 10 million new vehicles each year. For chip companies, cars *were* the mass market, and their allure kept Motorola in the game—with John Shreve haranguing loudly in its ear—when it couldn't master its own vaunted etch-refill process. The market's allure sent the semiconductor power humbly to entreat Delco, its lesser partner, to allow the entirely different double-buried layer approach, in thorough repudiation of Motorola's early hubris.

Similarly, Motorola's breakneck dash to develop portable cellular started as a desire to make radio-telephone service available to a large audience. Wang got into word processors when the doctor recognized that armies of secretaries would be well served by some computer automation. Amana applied micro-logic control to its oven merely to attract consumers who might be tempted by other brands.

And those are only a few prominent examples. Many developments and innovations relied on microchips to make products more suitable and appealing to run-of-the-mill consumers in all their vast numbers. Microchip makers accommodated them by supplying progressively more compact, powerful, and inexpensive integrated circuits that could make equipment even more capable and less costly—the way the bounding calculator companies egged metal-oxide semiconductors out of so many compliant chip concerns simply by providing a place to sell vast masses of the dense little circuits.

But consumer culture and the laissez-faire lifestyle motivated chip innovations by providing more than just a lot of buyers. The ordinary folk making up the mass market were willing to embrace change rather than to cling insecurely to inherited behaviors. The social and commercial hierarchies remained malleable and impermanent so that impertinent upstarts wielding better ideas could bludgeon their way into the established order. With individual initiative valued above any fawning reliance on government or other power elites for protection, no significant shields impeded competition. Competition goaded producers to try harder.

Such conditions still largely prevail, and therefore innovation continues apace, even after the chip biz has matured into an industrial colossus. In 2001, semiconductor companies collectively sold $139 billion of products around the world. That translated to 60 million integrated transistors—that is, individual transistors built into microchips—for every person on the planet. Given the ongoing gains in chip density, that figure was expected to grow to one billion transistors per person, made annually, by 2010. Despite its ascension in size and stature, the chip-making business hasn't yet been beset by stifling, sclerotic impediments to innovation and change.

New developments continue to crowd the news. In May 2002, just weeks apart, Intel unveiled two new chips intended to encroach into new territory for the dominant chip-maker. Its Itanium microprocessor aimed to carve a market for Intel in the sort of high-powered computers that serve up information instantly to the many travelers cruising the Internet. Intel also talked up an experimental, three-in-one chip that was similar in intent to the smart-power combination: integrate dissimilar circuit types to improve performance. Intel's three-in-one combined special flash memory for holding information, logic circuitry for control, and analog circuits to handle communication tasks. The company crowed that the integrated chip, when eventually released, would shrink cell phones to the size of lapel pins and computers to wrist watch scale.

At the same time, Texas Instruments announced it had joined with another chip house, Advanced Micro Devices, to effect a similar combination. The partners were uniting memory circuits, logic circuits, and digital signal processing—that's DSP, the all-important translation between digital codes and discernible sights and sounds.

Not to be outdone, in September 2001 Motorola revealed that it was about two years away from selling a new chip built from a combination of silicon and the semiconductor material gallium arsenide. It will make cell phones cheaper, the company boasted.

Then, in February 2002, IBM let loose a new IC it called the world's fastest. The chip combined silicon with germanium, the first transistor material used productively, to create a rapid-response micro meant to run in telecommunication's switches—the special-purpose processors that route and direct data along the Internet.

Such technical advances still bring all the customary opportunities for competitive gains. For example, experts expect an upcoming microprocessor called Opteron to give Intel's Itanium a good battle when it becomes available in early 2003. Opteron will power the same class of high-capacity professional computers that Itanium seeks to conquer. According to early indications, Opteron will outperform its big-name rival.

Opteron is the product of Advanced Micro Devices, a successful and enduring chip company that is still just one-sixth the size of Intel, a colossus that makes about $26 billion annually selling chips. Both Advanced Micro and Intel spilled out of Fairchild Semiconductor at about the same time. In 1969, a year after Gordon Moore and Bob Noyce cut out to create Intel, flamboyant Jerry Sanders led a second band of defectors from Fairchild, establishing Advanced Micro. It is still largely known in the negative: the company that is not Intel. Its Opteron chip isn't likely to knock off its big brother. But it will level the balance between the two companies some. It will certainly force Intel to do much better if it expects to make any money selling Itanium.

But Intel and Advanced Micro are peers as much as they are mismatched adversaries. Both are sizable—even with only one-sixth the sales of Intel, Advanced Micro still takes in more than $4 billion annually. Both have advanced very far from their fledgling insecurity, when a company confronts survival prospects less certain than a casino bet. Both have prospered through more than thirty years in an ever-changing, fiercely contentious field. Along with a bunch of others, some with corporate names that have grown comfortably familiar—including Hitachi, IBM, Motorola, and Texas Instruments—these companies are the IC establishment.

Still, they don't own all the good ideas. Ambitious new companies still spring up whenever chip dreamers spot developing opportunities that are unserved by the status quo. Lately that includes circuits tuned for data communication to support the sprawling information exchange known as the Internet. Mobile computing has emerged as another unmet need, helping people use that information as they travel around. In 1995, Transmeta Corporation formed in Santa Clara, California, to make microprocessors for portable computers. One year later, Cicada Semiconductor set up in Austin, Texas, making digital-signal processing ICs designed to speed up information exchange. Velio Communications, established in 1998 in Milpitas, California, develops chips for the telecommunications equipment that directs traffic on the Internet. Alchemy Semiconductor, a 1999 start-up in Austin, specializes in ICs that bundle logic and communication capabilities for use in portable information appliances.

Young as they are, those companies seem like stalwarts compared to tenuous LightTime. It was set up in far-off Oshkosh, Wisconsin, in February 2000 to develop the bold ideas of Dr. James Siepmann. A physician by training, Siepmann sidled into theoretical physics for its therapeutic value: He needed to engage his mind in order to fight off a severe depression that drove him out of medicine in 1998 when he was 38 years old. His musing brought him to conclusions that seemed to correct Albert Einstein's Special Theory of Relatively. When the official science circles spurned him, he set out to prove his ideas by building a device that uses them. The Light Clock he made in 2000 generates pulses at 10 billion ticks per second.

Such speed can be very important to people who use computer chips. A logic processor's rate of computation is determined by its clock speed, which is the interval at which impulses flick through the circuit—darting from transistor to transistor as the programming points the way. Very fast clock speeds are necessary for demanding tasks like digital video playback—of a ball game, perhaps. A chip must construct the moving pictures on the spot, in all their rich detail, by deciphering dense, long chains of computer data. Therefore Siepmann's LightTime is working on an IC-version of his Light Clock. It will make computer chips run something like five times faster than their current blinding rate, he says. What's more, the timing chip will be an opto-electronic IC. It will unite dominant electronic methods with photonics, the developing field of photon manipulation that is expected to outpace today's race of electrons.

Siepmann has as much on his side as every independent chip-thinker who preceded him and most likely every one who is to come. He remains staunchly committed to ideas, particularly his own. He won't compromise them. He approaches quandaries with a spirit of open inquiry—his concept of *purposeful ignorance* maintains that innovative concepts come from noninitiates who haven't been indoctrinated by the confining status quo. Siepmann doesn't like confinement. He doesn't like other people controlling and directing his energies. But he expects them to embrace his insights, and when they don't, well, he has courage enough to go solo, finding his own means to bring them to daylight.

Of course, none of those qualities makes his theories correct. None will assure that his products succeed. Jim Siepmann is just one member of the regenerative class of go-it-alone research entrepreneurs. Like each of the others, he may turn out to be a crank with nutty ideas, or he may one day be extolled as a visionary scientist and inventor who led his fellows to a higher peak of capability. Representation on this page won't make the difference. Neither will his proud, ardent wish to elevate his ideas. All the other inventors have that too. In the end, his concepts will rise or they will droop according to their contributions alone. The judges are impartial. They do not bend to the desires of just one man. We cannot hear his wishes anyway. They are lost amid the clatter and din made by so many eager seekers. As judges, we have so many choices. The open field for invention—with access unrestricted to any person with intelligence and the guts enough to give it a try—assures that a few of our choices will be superb: They will do the most for the great majority of independent people. As judges, we independent people will pick those.

NOTES

In most cases, each citation below lists the source of facts, information, and quotations contained in the entire paragraph that is cited. Exceptions are noted where they occur.

All interviews noted here were conducted by the author, unless otherwise indicated.

Chapter One: Thinking Small

page 4   So in May 1958 . . . (including some biographical material in the paragraph that follows); Jack Kilby, interviewed March 30, 2001, in Dallas. Biographical details are supported by the summary at www.TexasInstruments.com, accessed October 4, 2001.

page 5   Centralab operated more on the periphery . . . (including insights on the position of and conditions at Centralab, in the two paragraphs that follow); ibid.

page 7   burned through 2,000 tubes every month . . . ; this and other details regarding the ENIAC computer are found in Section VII, History, under the heading "Computer" in the *Encarta Encyclopedia* 2000.

page 10   "The Russians had big missiles . . . ; Kilby.

page 11   "It was pretty clear that semiconductors . . . (including information on Kilby's job search in the two paragraphs that follow); ibid.

page 12   Coincidentally, Kilby's letter . . . ; Willis Adcock, interviewed July 11, 2001, in Austin, Texas.

page 12   Willis Adcock was already a semiconductor celebrity . . . ; Adcock, and the article "Silicon Transistors: Impossible to Make" by George Rostky, available online at www.eetimes.com, accessed August 8, 2001.

page 13   The Semiconductor Products Division . . . ; Adcock.

page 13   . . . the Sherman facility supplied . . . ; ibid.

page 13   "They had a big machine . . . ; Kilby.

page 14   "I was allowed to define it," . . . ; ibid.

page 14   He had brought some ideas . . . (including TI's position regarding military research programs in the three paragraphs that follow); ibid.

page 16   To erase the congestion . . . (including Kilby's reasoning regarding the use of semiconductors in the two paragraphs that follow); ibid.

page 17　At this time, Texas Instruments . . . (including Kilby's observations on conditions in the lab at the time of his innovation); ibid.

page 18　He built up the idea . . . ; ibid.

page 19　The entry Jack Kilby penned . . . ; the wording of Kilby's notebook entry comes from the book *The Chip* by T. R. Reid, published in 1985 by Simon & Schuster.

page 19　Reaching that conclusion . . . (including factors that influenced Kilby's reasoning, in the paragraph that follows); Kilby.

page 20　What's more, Kilby's concept retained . . . ; Harvey Cragon, friend and colleague of Jack Kilby, interviewed March 30, 2001, in Dallas.

page 20　Kilby figured that such shrunk-down, . . . ; Kilby.

page 20　The most immediate challenge . . . (including details of the lab test in the paragraphs that follow); ibid.

Chapter Two: The Wild West

page 23　But Fairchild made silicon transistors . . . ; information regarding the founding principles of Fairchild Semiconductor and its early achievements comes from the commemorative booklet Fairchild Semiconductor, item MISC-581 of the Special Collections and University Archives, Stanford University Libraries, Stanford, California.

page 23　But the same shoddy quality . . . (including details of the conditions and motives behind Hoerni's early investigations at Fairchild); Jean Hoerni, interviewed in 1986 by George Rostky; item M-851 of the Special Collections and University Archives, Stanford University Libraries.

page 25　Shockley's vocation as physicist . . . (including biographical details of Shockley and the recollection of Frederick Seitz in the paragraphs that follow); *Biographical Memoirs*, the National Academy Press of the National Academies, available at www.nap.edu, accessed September 13, 2001. Biographical details regarding Shockley are also supported by Gordon Moore's article on William Shockley, "Time 100" in *Scientists and Thinkers*, available at www.time.com, accessed September 12, 2001.

page 28　Jean Hoerni was thirty-two years old . . . ; Hoerni. Supporting biographical details from Deborah Claymon, "Jean Hoerni, 1924–1997," available at www.redherring.com, accessed September 8, 2001; and from "Jean Hoerni Devised 'Planar Process,'" www.spectrum.ieee.org, accessed February 2, 2002.

page 29　Other laborers on the Ph.D. production line . . . ; biographical details regarding Robert Noyce—appearing both here and in subsequent chapters—are drawn from several sources. The primary ones are: Tom Wolfe, "The Tinkerings of Robert Noyce," *Esquire*, December 1983; the article "Robert Noyce (1927–1990)," from www.digitalcentury.com, accessed September 8, 2001; and the biographical profile "Robert Noyce," from www.ruku.com, accessed September 8, 2001.

page 29   Employee eighteen, Gordon Moore, . . . : Gordon Moore, interviewed in 1986 by George Rostky; item M-851 of the Special Collections and University Archives, Stanford University Libraries.

page 30   "Working for Shockley proved . . . ; Moore, "Time 100," *Scientists and Thinkers.*

page 30   The young organization fissured . . . ; Gordon Moore, interviewed April 19, 2001, in Santa Clara, California. Supporting information on the defection from Shockley Laboratory and the formation of Fairchild Semiconductor is from the article "The Role of Fairchild in Silicon Technology in the Early Days of 'Silicon Valley'" by Gordon Moore, *Proceedings of the IEEE,* January 1998.

page 31   They were the price of failure . . . ; information on Shockley and Shockley Laboratory from *Biographical Memoirs,* the National Academy Press of the National Academies.

page 32   Technoscenti who encountered him . . . ; numerous interviews and conversations conducted by the author confirm Shockley's standing.

page 33   Noyce finessed details . . . ; information on Noyce's role and the structure of the deal that set up Fairchild Semiconductor are drawn primarily from the booklet Fairchild Semiconductor, item MISC-581 of the Special Collections and University Archives, Stanford University Libraries, with support from the Noyce sources listed above.

page 33   But at the start . . . ; the letter from Hodgson to Noyce can be found in item MISC-581 of the Special Collections and University Archives, Stanford University Libraries.

page 34   "There were a lot of government contracts . . . ; Moore.

page 34   "We were really fairly naive . . . ; ibid.

page 35   Jean Hoerni headed the physics section . . . ; Hoerni to Rostky.

page 35   "When we were setting up . . . ; Moore.

page 35   "I became very interested . . . (including specific information on the circumstances and reasoning that led Hoerni to invent planar transistors, which continues to the conclusion of the chapter); Hoerni to Rostky.

Chapter Three: First Contact

page 40   But Fairchild made no immediate plans . . . ; Moore.

page 41   Robert Noyce got the job . . . ; ibid.

page 42   The patent procedure . . . ; information regarding Noyce and the planar patent is drawn from various sources, especially from the author's interview of Moore, from Moore's "The Role of Fairchild in Silicon Technology" article, and from the biographical references pertaining to Noyce that have already been cited. A thorough discussion of patent strategy and procedure is available in T. R. Reid's *The Chip*.

page 42   "Bob was a very creative guy . . . ; Moore.

page 42   Noyce was "quick to laugh . . . ; from interview notes recorded by Herbert S. Kleiman in 1965, item M-827 of the Special Collections and University Archives, Stanford University Libraries. Kleiman apparently did not audio record Noyce but rather recorded his notes, as well as his impressions, after a personal interview.

page 44   He considered Hoerni's invention *aesthetic* . . . ; ibid.

page 44   In January 1959, Noyce called together . . . ; Moore interview, and Moore's "The Role of Fairchild in Silicon Technology."

page 45   "So the elements of the idea . . . ; Robert Noyce, interviewed in 1986 by George Rostky; item M-851 of the Special Collections and University Archives, Stanford University Libraries.

page 46   Noyce may have heard whisperings . . . ; Moore.

page 46   Hoerni hinted that the basic concept . . . ; Hoerni to Rostky.

page 46   The patent office and, eventually, the courts . . . ; a thorough discussion of the patent dispute is available in T. R. Reid's *The Chip*.

page 47   Noyce said his idea to top a chip . . . ; Noyce to Rostky.

page 47   His idea for isolating the separate transistors . . . ; ibid.

page 48   Ideas were simply airborne. . . .; an explanation of Dummer's concept appears in the book *Semiconductor Integrated Circuit Processing Technology* by W. R. Runyan and K. E. Bean, published by Addison-Wesley in 1990.

page 48   "We were tremendously competitive . . . ; Charles Sporck, interviewed May 23, 2001, in Los Altos, California.

Chapter Four: Team Choices

page 50   As if to demonstrate the peril . . . ; information on Ewart Baldwin comes primarily from Moore, from Moore's article "The Role of Fairchild in Silicon Technology," and from "Business Week Reports on Semiconductors," a special report in *Business Week*, March 26, 1960.

page 52   At the moment no one could say . . . (including information in the following paragraphs about difficulties concerning the planar design); Hoerni to Rostky.

page 53   That year the hopeful firm sold . . . ; Fairchild's early revenue figures from Moore, and from "Business Week Reports on Semiconductors."

page 53   But no matter how noteworthy . . . ; "Business Week Reports on Semiconductors."

page 54   Similarly, Noyce did not debate or dither . . . ; Moore.

page 56   Similarly with ICs . . . ; Moore to Rostky.

page 56   Fairchild officially beat Texas Instruments . . . ; the timing of the introduction of the first integrated circuits is confirmed in Noyce to Kleiman, and in Jack Kilby, interviewed in 1986 by George Rostky; item M-851 of the Special Collections and University Archives, Stanford University Libraries.

page 56   By the time Fairchild brought out . . . ; information on Fairchild's business position from the booklet Fairchild Semiconductor.

page 57   Fairchild considered itself . . . ; Moore.

page 57   "After we got the first family of . . . ; ibid.

Chapter Five: Chipping Away

page 58   Texas Instruments had even started . . . ; *BusinessWeek*, March 26, 1960.

page 58   But they were crude devices . . . ; Kilby to Rostky.

page 59   Jack Kilby and his colleague . . . ; this episode, retold through the following paragraphs, is recounted by Harvey Cragon, interviewed March 30, 2001, in Dallas.

page 60   Meanwhile, at Fairchild . . . ; Moore.

page 61   Gordon Moore ran into . . . ; ibid.

page 61   What's more, to assure that . . . ; information on component testing from Cragon.

page 62   "We old designers that did . . . ; Rex Fritts, interviewed by telephone, June 21, 2001.

page 64   After a March 1960 exhibition . . . ; *Electronics*, April 8, 1960.

page 65   Not that the sale had been easy . . . ; information on TI's approach to the military and contract with the Air Force from Charles Phipps, a friend and former TI colleague of Jack Kilby, interviewed by Herbert S. Kleiman in 1965, item M-827 of the Special Collections and University Archives, Stanford University Libraries. Although most Kleiman audio recordings consist of notes and impressions recorded by Kleiman after the interviews, the collection includes a recording of an actual interview with Phipps.

page 65   "Their existence theorem . . . ; Kilby.

page 66   Alberts backed TI's solid-circuit concept . . . ; information on Alberts backing of TI despite its differences from the molecular electronics concept comes from Adcock. Specifics regarding the contract terms from Phipps.

page 67   Before the Cold War . . . ; Cragon.

page 68   The assignment to build the first . . . (including information on the structure of the computer and its tour); ibid.

page 70   The Air Force and Westinghouse used the term . . . ; for one example, see the article "Monolithic Computer" in *Electronics*, August 23, 1965.

page 71   Shortly after Cragon returned . . . ; Cragon.

page 71   In mid-1962, Texas Instruments began . . . ; "Minuteman Integrated Circuits—Study in Combined Operations" by R. C. Platzek and J. S. Kilby, *Proceedings of the IEEE*, December 1964.

page 71   Kilby calls such programs "stressful" . . . ; Kilby.

page 71   Beginning around 1963, both TI and Fairchild sold chips . . . ; Moore, Phipps.

page 72   Fairchild also supplied ICs . . . ; Moore.

page 72   NASA boasted that the lunar probe's . . . ; "Integrated-Circuit Makers Are Ready for the Big Buying Boom to Start," *Electronics*, January 11, 1965.

page 72   A Fairchild advertisement promised . . . ; ibid.

page 73   Nuclear-Chicago Corporation announced . . . ; *Electronics*, June 28, 1965.

page 73   Westinghouse Electric revealed . . . ; *Electronics*, October 4, 1965.

page 73   As the technology made such gains . . . ; "Integrated-Circuit Makers Are Ready for the Big Buying Boom to Start."

page 74   "He told them he would sell . . . ; Moore.

Chapter Six: Calculated Gains

page 77   "This was a period when TI . . . ; Kilby.

page 77   Haggerty had joined TI . . . ; biographical information on the life and career of Patrick Haggerty comes from various sources. The primary ones include the profile "Haggerty, Patrick Eugene" from the *Handbook of Texas Online*, www.lib.utexas.edu, accessed October 4, 2001, and the biographical summary at www.TexasInstruments.com, accessed October 4, 2001. Insight on his views and management principles come from *Management Philosophies and Practices of Texas Instruments Incorporated*, a compilation of presentations by Haggerty, published by Texas Instruments in 1965.

page 78   . . . a reprieve of the Regency transistor radio . . . ; information on the Regency radio and Haggerty's role comes primarily from Adcock, and from the press release "First Commercial Transistor Radio," released October 18, 1954, by Texas Instruments, available at www.TexasInstruments.com.

page 79   But the format . . . ; Adcock.

page 79   Some TI alumni claim . . . ; Adcock, Cragon, Kilby, and others.

page 81   In 1960 the Burroughs Corporation started selling . . . ; *Electronics*, January 1, 1960, and April 8, 1960.

page 81   In the December 1964 *Proceedings of the IEEE* . . . ; the paper is titled "Integrated Electronics, A Perspective." It is also available in *Management Philosophies and Practices of Texas Instruments*.

page 82   Moore makes clear that . . . ; Moore.

page 83   He spilled out his musings . . . ; Kilby.83

page 83   Kilby dismissed a couple . . . ; Kilby's reaction to Haggerty's ideas and his ruminations on calculator requirements are from Kilby.

page 85   "You'd be workin' at your desk . . . ; Jerry Merryman, interviewed March 31, 2001, in Dallas.

page 85   Therefore Merryman suspected . . . ; details of the October 20 meeting come from Merryman.

page 86   Kilby called the object . . . ; use of the term "sliderule computer" is recounted in the article "How the Computer Got into Your Pocket" by Mike May in the Spring 2000 edition of *American Heritage of Invention and Technology* magazine.

page 87   "Jerry was probably closer . . . ; Kilby.

page 87   But Kilby saw in Merryman . . . ; biographical information regarding Merryman from Merryman.

page 88   It was a complete engineering project . . . ; technical details regarding the calculator, as well as details on the development program running to the end of the chapter are from Merryman.

page 93   . . . a facsimile of Cal Tech went on sale . . . ; information on the cost and timing of the calculator introduction from www.vintagecalculators.com, accessed October 11, 2001.

Chapter Seven: Adding Contenders

page 95   Since then researchers had made them . . . ; some historical information on the development of field-effect transistors from www.pbs.org, accessed June 17, 2002.

page 95   "They could make a few, . . . ; Jay Lathrup, interviewed by telephone on October 24, 2001.

page 96   The biggest obstacle fell in 1962 . . . ; the account of Frank Wanlass' innovations is retold in *We Were Burning: Japanese Entrepreneurs and the Forging of the Electronic Age* by Bob Johnstone, published by Basic Books in 1999.

page 97   . . . the Silicon Valley start-up General Micro-electronics . . . ; information on the products and the business positions of both General Micro-electronics and General Instrument come from the article "The Expanding Market" by Jerome Eimbinder, *Electronics*, October 4, 1965.

page 97   Another big advantage . . . ; this discussion regarding the technical advantages of MOS microchips comes from the article "MOS Integrated Circuits Save Space and Money" by Donald E. Farina and Donald Trotter, *Electronics*, October 4, 1965.

page 99   The first MOS circuits sold mostly . . . ; "The Expanding Market."

page 100   By the mid-1960s, with Cal Tech . . . ; historical information on the arrival and progression of electronic calculators and portable calculators, continuing to the end of the chapter, comes primarily from Guy Ball, calculator historian and consultant, interviewed October 14, 2001, by telephone, and from summaries and articles available at www.vintagecalculators.com, accessed October 11, 2001.

Chapter Eight: Common Ground

page 105   In fact, by rights Ted Hoff . . . ; except where otherwise noted, background information and details related to the development of the microprocessor at Intel are told by Marican "Ted" Hoff Jr., interviewed March 21, 2001, in Los Altos, California.

page 107   After its fast rise to prominence, . . . ; this account of the motives that led to the founding of Intel provided primarily by Moore.

page 108   The new company's business plan . . . ; ibid.

page 109   The problem began with the fact . . . (including the design-cost analysis in the paragraph that follows); Hoff.

page 110   "The idea was, we were going to find . . . ; Moore.

page 111   Intel's founders staked the company . . . ; ibid.

page 111   In the meantime, to help support itself . . . ; Hoff.

page 112   The deal was like dancing . . . ; Moore.

page 117   "Our industry generally is driven . . . ; Leslie Vadasz, interviewed April 19, 2001, in Santa Clara, California.

page 118   To Gordon Moore, Hoff's innovation . . . ; Moore.

Chapter Nine: Great Debates

page 121   Datapoint had first lit . . . ; throughout the chapter, background information and details relating to the Datapoint terminal and the associations among Datapoint, Intel, and Texas Instruments come from two primary sources, Hoff, and the paper "A History of Microprocessor Development at Intel" by Robert N. Noyce and Marican E. Hoff Jr., published in *IEEE Micro* in February 1981.

page 122   To put the project on a crash course . . . ; throughout the chapter, information on Faggin's role is provided by Hoff, and by the paper "A History of Microprocessor Development at Intel."

page 123   Yet Intel hesitated . . . ; in this and the following chapters, details concerning resistance to the microprocessor concept come from Hoff. They are generally supported in "A History of Microprocessor Development at Intel."

page 125   "He couldn't say no . . . ; Sporck.

page 126   Intel's seams were stretching . . . ; this account of Intel's business position comes primarily from the prospectus issued by the company and its underwriter, C. E. Unterberg, Towbin Co., on October 13, 1971, to support its first public sale of capital stock.

page 127   Then, in May 1971, an opportunity arrived . . . ; Hoff, and "A History of Microprocessor Development at Intel."

page 127   It was more generalized . . . ; throughout the balance of the chapter, Gelbach's role is recounted by Hoff, with some details obtained from "A History of Microprocessor Development at Intel."

page 127   Before Gelbach had left Dallas . . . ; "A History of Microprocessor Development at Intel."

page 128   TI, in the meantime . . . ; Cragon.

page 129   The announcement in *Electronic News* . . . ; it is reproduced in "A History of Microprocessor Development at Intel."

page 129   For one, there was the meat packer . . . ; Vadasz.

page 129   Noyce wrote of a . . . ; "A History of Microprocessor Development at Intel."

page 129   Intel established education . . . ; ibid.

page 130   Successions of improved all-in-one processors . . . ; a summary of Intel's milestone microprocessors is available at www.intel.com, accessed February 19, 2002.

Chapter Ten: Changing Guards

page 135   Essex had been at the relay trade . . . ; this discussion of Essex's business position and its strategy concerning electronics comes from William Hopkins, former Essex vice president of marketing, interviewed by telephone on August 7, 2001.

page 136   The company hired Bob Fosnough . . . ; the incidents retold through the balance of the chapter come from the recollections of Robert Fosnough, interviewed by telephone on November 16, 2001.

Chapter Eleven: Computers for Cooks

page 140   Amana Refrigeration had introduced . . . ; the relative market positions of Amana and Litton are from Dan McConnell, a former Litton vice president, interviewed by telephone on December 27, 2001.

page 140   Yet over at Essex . . . ; Fosnough.

page 142   Beginning in 1966, Richard Foerstner . . . ; Richard Foerstner, interviewed June 15, 2001, in Davenport, Iowa.

page 142   Dan McConnell was an electrical engineer . . . ; McConnell.

page 142   Their motives to computerize cookers . . . (including the paragraphs that follow); McConnell.

page 143   Sales by innovation was . . . ; throughout the chapter, insight and information on Amana's corporate culture and the character of its founder, George Foerstner, comes from Richard Foerstner; McConnell; and Steven Gustafson, former Amana General Counsel, interviewed by telephone on August 21, 2001. Information on the founding and history of Amana primarily comes from www.cr.nps.gov, accessed November 20, 2001, and from www.amana.com, accessed February 22, 2002.

page 145   Still, micro-capabilities had grown . . . ; Foerstner.

page 147   "What we wanted was . . . ; Fritts.

page 147   "The trail was fairly long . . . ; the discussion of Amana's search for a semiconductor partner, including its dealings with Texas Instruments, comes from McConnell.

page 150   After the rebuff from Litton . . . ; Fosnough.

page 150   The two companies might have . . . ; McConnell.

page 150   Essex set about modifying its model . . . ; Fosnough.

page 151   The finished LSI chip . . . ; technical and operating information regarding the oven can be found in the article "Amana's Oven with a Brain," published in the trade magazine *Appliance Manufacturer* in July 1975.

page 152   "The combination of . . . ; McConnell.

page 152   Still, Amana made them fast enough . . . ; sales figures and market position information are from McConnell.

page 153   When Essex had begun . . . (including the discussion of microprocessor trials in the paragraph that follows); Fosnough.

Chapter Twelve: Call Forwarding

page 155   Still, the group could . . . ; information and insight regarding corporate infighting comes from Donald Linder, interviewed by telephone on September 20, 2001.

page 155   "We said for years . . . ; John Mitchell, interviewed May 3, 2001, in Schaumburg, Illinois.

page 156   Executive commitment to the future . . . ; historical information on Motorola that appears throughout the chapter is found primarily in *Motorola: A Journey Through Time and Technology*, a commemorative booklet published by the Motorola Museum of Electronics, Schaumburg, Illinois, in 1994.

page 156   In two-way radios, the communication division . . . (including interactions with the semiconductor makers described in the following two paragraphs); Martin Cooper, interviewed by telephone on September 21, 2001.

page 157   Linder's work with ICs . . . ; the full discussion on the function of a frequency synthesizer and tuning crystals come from Linder.

page 158   In the beginning, it didn't look . . . ; a summary of the regulatory proceedings involved in the creation of cellular telephony is available in "Cellular Telephone Regulation" by Mark R. Hamilton, in *Telecommunications Policy and Regulation, 1990, The Year Ahead*, volume one, published by the Practicing Law Institute in 1990.

page 161   AT&T specified car phones . . . ; Mitchell.

page 161   Early in the FCC proceedings . . . ; ibid.

page 162   Near the end of 1972, the company flinched . . . (including the description of Motorola's specific objections and the explanation of its response in the paragraphs that follow); ibid.

page 163   The job fell to . . . ; descriptions of the technical aspects of the development program, appearing through the balance of the chapter, are from Linder.

page 165   Designing the portable's enclosure . . . ; information on the development of the phone's case, appearing through the balance of the chapter, are from Rudy Krolop, interviewed by telephone, September 18, 2001.

page 165   Both Krolop and the studio . . . ; all biographical information regarding Krolop, ibid.

page 168   Motorola also proposed . . . ; Mitchell.

Chapter Thirteen: Common Computing

page 171   Reacting to Eckert and Mauchly's plan . . . ; insight and some detail into Howard Aiken's background, including this misapprehension about the role of computers, are in the autobiography of An Wang, *Lessons*, with Eugene Linden, published in 1986 by Addison-Wesley.

page 172   Born in China . . . ; biographical background and details regarding An Wang, ibid.

page 173   The invention provided a first product . . . ; most background information and details on the formation, growth, and general approach of Wang Laboratories, ibid.

Chapter Fourteen: New Language

page 183   The thought to make a special-use computer . . . ; credit to Ed Lesnick comes from Harold Koplow, interviewed by telephone on December 13, 2001.

page 184   In his autobiography . . . ; *Lessons*.

page 184   Lesnick didn't invent the idea . . . ; ibid.

page 186   It reworked the computer inside of . . . ; Koplow.

page 186   That decisive stride came from . . . ; throughout the chapter, including the account of his rise, fall, and rise at Wang Laboratories, ibid.

page 189   Now, in 1974, Koplow crashed through . . . ; this detail is recounted in the book *Riding the Runaway Horse: The Rise and Decline of Wang Laboratories* by Charles C. Kenney published by Little, Brown & Company in 1992.

page 189   For all his inexperience, he thought . . . ; Koplow.

page 189   Long-range planning functioned apart . . . ; the full account of the development of the Wang Word Processing System, ibid.

page 196   When the WPS was first demonstrated . . . ; *Lessons.*

page 196   The first naive noninitiates . . . ; Koplow.

page 196   In Iowa, Steven Gustafson had employed . . . ; Gustafson.

page 197   In fact, in 1978 . . . ; Koplow.

page 197   Bob Noyce would later call him . . . ; "A History of Microprocessor Development at Intel."

page 198   By 1978, it was shipping nearly 800 . . . ; information on the sales rates of the WPS from *Lessons,* and from Wang Laboratories annual reports for the years 1978, 1980, and 1981.

page 198   Koplow was a vice president again . . . ; Koplow.

page 199   The company ran on momentum . . . ; a full account of the company's demise can be found in *Riding the Runaway Horse.* The idea that Wang Labs declined because it stopped innovating when it lost its key innovators comes from Koplow.

Chapter Fifteen: Building Muscles

page 202   "I don't think anybody down there . . . ; John Shreve, interviewed by telephone on March 8, 2001.

page 202   I can remember talking to . . . ; Shreve, interviewed April 27, 2001, in Kokomo, Indiana.

page 203   Shreve was a typical case . . .; all biographical information relating to Shreve, ibid.

page 203   "We were in the infancy . . . ; Larry Hach, interviewed April 27, 2001, in Kokomo, Indiana.

page 203   But at the same time, Delco recognized . . . ; James Himelick, interviewed April 27, 2001, in Kokomo, Indiana.

page 204   Delco had begun its life . . . ; historical information regarding Delco is found at www.delcoelect.com, accessed April 27, 2001.

page 205   But a car simply didn't have room . . . ; this summary of the challenges confronting automotive electronics, including the information in the three paragraphs that follow, comes primarily from Himelick, and from Shreve.

page 207   Shreve and all his colleagues . . . ; this sentiment was widely expressed by Shreve and others during various interviews.

page 207   But Delco's chip fabrication experience . . . ; Himelick.

page 207   That's why it set up the partnership . . . ; ibid.

page 207   John Shreve assembled his team . . . ; the starting dates come from Shreve, in an e-mail response to questions from the author, received on December 17, 2001.

page 208   But when time came to transfer . . . ; the explanation of the difficulties encountered in making the etch-refill ICs comes from Himelick, in an e-mail response to questions from the author, received from Himelick on December 19, 2001.

page 208   At the same time, organizational problems . . . ; Hach.

page 209   But that explanation didn't help . . . ; insight into the relationship between the companies, the technical problems they encountered, and the urgency they felt, related through five paragraphs, are from Shreve.

page 210   The first was organizational: it relocated . . . ; Hach.

page 210   Next, Motorola abandoned the etch-refill . . . ; the discussion of the problems and remedy to etch-refill in the ensuing paragraphs comes from Himelick.

page 211   With the program thus stabilized . . . ; Shreve.

page 212   Both sides reaped rewards . . . ; the production dates are noted in Shreve's e-mail of December 17.

Epilogue: Mutual Aid

page 215   Such conditions still largely prevail . . . ; production statistics and forecasts are available at the website of the Semiconductor Industry Association, www.semichips.org, accessed May 21, 2002.

page 215   Its Itanium microprocessor . . . ; see *The Wall Street Journal*, May 29, 2001, page A1.

page 216   Intel also talked up an experimental . . . ; see *The Wall Street Journal*, May 17, 2001, page B8.

page 216   At the same time, Texas Instruments . . . ; ibid.

page 216   Not to be outdone . . . ; see *The Wall Street Journal*, September 9, 2001, page B6.

page 216   Then, in February 2002, IBM . . . ; see *The Wall Street Journal*, February 25, 2002, page B6.

page 216   Opteron is the product of Advanced Micro . . . ; historical information regarding Advanced Micro Devices is available at www.amd.com, accessed May 16, 2002.

page 217   Young as they are, those companies . . . ; information concerning the company LightTime and its products, as well as biographical details pertaining to James Siepmann, come primarily from Siepmann, in an e-mail response to questions from the author, received from Siepmann on June 2, 2002.

INDEX